GILBERT

AF709332

Legal Ethics

THOMAS D. MORGAN
Oppenheim Professor Emeritus
The George Washington University Law School

Ninth Edition

GILBERT

444 Cedar Street, Suite 700
St. Paul, MN 55101
1-877-888-1330

Printed in the United States of America

ISBN: 978-1-63460-709-4

Acknowledgments

The author thanks the American Bar Association Center for Professional Responsibility for permission to reprint excerpts of the Model Rules of Professional Conduct or other copyrighted material from the Center.

Summary of Contents

Capsule Summary

Capsule Summary

I. RESERVING THE PRACTICE OF LAW TO LAWYERS

A. BASIC PRINCIPLES

Laypersons may represent themselves *in propria persona*, but only lawyers may represent persons other than themselves.

B. ACTIVITIES THAT CONSTITUTE THE "PRACTICE OF LAW"

"Practice of law" is not defined by the ABA Model Rules. Courts generally apply one of two tests: (a) the ***history and custom*** test, which relies on whether the activity ***traditionally*** has been handled by lawyers; or (b) the test which determines whether there is a ***need for professional judgment***.

1. Judicial Determinations in Specific Areas

Appearing in a judicial proceeding, drafting documents that ***affect substantial legal rights*** or obligations (but ***not merely filling in blanks*** on standard forms), tax planning, giving legal advice (but ***not*** a layperson's ***publication of a book containing general advice*** and forms), and prisoner legal assistance by lay prisoners have all been held to be the "practice of law." However, the Supreme Court has struck down regulations designed to prevent lay prisoner assistance where the state has not provided ***reasonable alternative forms*** of legal aid for prisoners.

C. SPECIFIC CLASSES OF PERSONS PROHIBITED FROM PRACTICING LAW

Many states' laws expressly prohibit the practice of law by certain classes of persons:

1. **Judges and Court Officers**
2. **Law Students and Law Clerks**—However, some states make exceptions for student training programs under a lawyer's supervision.
3. **Corporations**—Generally, a corporation may not represent itself or furnish representation through its employees who are licensed attorneys. (Exceptions exist for professional law corporations and nonprofit group legal services providers.)

D. EFFORTS TO PROHIBIT PRACTICE OF LAW BY NONLAWYERS

Sanctions against nonlawyer practitioners include injunctions, criminal prosecution, or denial of the right to fees.

E. OBLIGATIONS OF LAWYERS IN PREVENTING UNAUTHORIZED PRACTICE

The ABA Model Rules require lawyers to assist in preventing the unauthorized practice of the law by nonlawyers. A lawyer ***may not***: (i) ***aid a nonlawyer in the practice of law***, (ii) ***share fees with a nonlawyer***, or (iii) ***enter a partnership with a nonlawyer*** if ***any*** partnership activity involves the practice of law.

II. REGULATING THE RIGHT TO PRACTICE LAW

A. SOURCES OF REGULATION

1. State Regulation

The practice of law affects the public interest and is thus subject to regulation by the states.

a. **Inherent Judicial Power**

Unlike other professions, ultimate regulatory power often rests with the courts rather than the legislature. The regulation takes the form of Rules of Professional Conduct adopted by each jurisdiction's highest judicial authority.

b. **Regulation by State Legislature**

Many state legislatures, however, also have power to enact statutes regulating some conduct of members of the legal profession.

c. **"Integrated" Bar**

Many states ***require*** practicing lawyers to join the state bar association and become subject to its rules.

d. **Regulation by Multiple States**

Lawyers are subject to regulation by ***each*** state in which they are ***admitted*** to practice, regardless of where they actually practice, and ***also*** in any state in which the lawyer lawfully practices temporarily.

e. **No Preclusion of Federal Regulation**

State regulation does not preclude additional federal regulation of lawyers where the lawyers' activities are within the scope of applicable federal law.

2. **American Bar Association as Source of Model Regulation**

Many standards for the practice of law are proposed by the organized bar, particularly the American Bar Association ("ABA").

a. **ABA Model Code of Professional Responsibility (1969)**

The first ABA standards, the Canons of Professional Ethics (1908), were replaced by the ABA Model Code, consisting of aspirational Ethical Considerations and mandatory Disciplinary Rules.

b. **Model Rules of Professional Conduct (1983)**

In response to criticism of the Model Code, the ABA approved the ***Model Rules***, a set of standards in a "Restatement-type" format. The ABA Model Rules are expressed in "black letter" rules, followed by sometimes extensive Comments.

c. **Revision of Model Rules (2002–2003)**

Extensive changes in the substance of many of the Model Rules were made as recommended by the ABA Ethics 2000 Commission. References in this summary to principles of the Model Rules will be made to the relevant Model Rules as revised in 2002–2003 and thereafter.

d. **Widespread impact of ABA Model Rules**

The 1983 Model Rules have been adopted in some form by all states but California. As of 2017, even California is considering new rules with content close to that of the ABA Model Rules.

e. **Interpretation the Model Rules and Other Law Governing Lawyers**

Judicial opinions are influential sources for clarifying the meaning of the Model Rules. Other sources include ***advisory opinions*** from the ABA ("ABA Opn.") and state bar associations. In 2000, the American Law Institute published the Restatement (Third): The Law Governing Lawyers, a comprehensive set of principles based on rules and case law from all over the country. Many citations in this Summary are to provisions of that Restatement.

f. Testing the Model Rules on the Multistate Professional Responsibility Exam ("MPRE")

The MPRE tests the current version of the Model Rules and other legal principles governing lawyers, whether or not they have been adopted in the state in which the applicant is seeking admission. Principles stated in this Summary are based on these national authorities, which you will need to know for the MPRE, but once you enter practice, you will be governed by the Rules of Professional Conduct as adopted by the state supreme courts where you practice.

B. STATE COURT REGULATION OF GENERAL ADMISSION TO PRACTICE LAW

Each state establishes its own standards for admission. These standards must have a ***rational connection*** to the applicant's ***fitness or capacity*** to practice law. U.S. citizenship is ***not*** a constitutionally acceptable requirement for admission, nor is limiting bar admission to a state's own residents.

1. Intellectual Capacity

Most states require graduation from an ABA-accredited law school. Nearly all states require passage of a bar examination.

2. Determination of "Good Moral Character"

States have a valid interest in high moral standards, including mental and emotional stability, of persons admitted.

a. Investigative Procedure

An applicant usually fills out a detailed questionnaire, lists references, and submits fingerprints and photographs for identification, after which a committee of examiners investigates moral character. If questions arise regarding fitness to practice, a ***hearing*** is set. The burden of proof is on the applicant, but she is entitled to ***procedural due process*** and ***appellate review***.

b. Conduct Relevant to Determination of "Good Moral Character"

Any past conduct reflecting upon honesty and integrity is relevant.

(1) Conviction of Crime

Crimes involving an intent to defraud or intentional dishonesty for personal gain may be enough to show lack of good moral character because integrity and an ability put another's interest first are important qualities of a good lawyer.

(2) Crimes Not Necessarily Establishing Lack of Character

Crimes such as adolescent misbehavior and some acts of nonviolent civil disobedience are usually not enough by themselves to disqualify an applicant.

(3) Effect of Concealment

Concealment or a false statement by the applicant is ***itself*** evidence of lack of character sufficient to deny admission, even if not discovered until after admission to practice.

(4) Rehabilitation

An applicant can still gain admission if she can demonstrate sufficient remorse and rehabilitation.

3. Duty of Lawyers Not to Aid Admission of the Unqualified

Many states require applicants to submit letters of reference from lawyers. Lawyers are subject to discipline if they knowingly make a false statement of material fact in such letters or fail to correct a misapprehension known to have arisen.

4. Admission on a Faster Track by Reciprocity

Each state determines the conditions for admission to its bar, but practicalities have led to lawyers wanting to practice in states in which they have not been previously admitted. Although requirements vary from state to state, many states admit such lawyers by ***reciprocity***, without a bar examination. Most of these states limit such admissions to lawyers from ***other states that allow reciprocity,*** *i.e., admit each other's lawyers in this way*. Most states require a lawyer from a non-reciprocity state to pass a written examination. The distinction has been approved against Equal Protection challenge.

5. Unauthorized Practice of Law

If a lawyer practices in a jurisdiction in which he is unauthorized, he may be guilty of the unauthorized practice of law.

6. Temporary Multi-Jurisdictional Practice

Model Rule 5.5 allows lawyers to "provide legal services on a temporary basis" in jurisdictions in which they are unlicensed under four circumstances.

a. Association with Local Lawyer

Temporary practice is allowed if the lawyer associates with a locally admitted lawyer who actively participates in the matter.

b. Litigated Matter

Temporary practice is usually allowed if the lawyer obtains permission to appear in the sister state's courts in connection with a ***particular*** case (admission ***pro hac vice***). Such permission is normally granted as a matter of ***comity***.

c. Arbitration or Other Alternative Dispute Resolution Proceeding

A lawyer can provide services reasonably related to an alternative dispute resolution proceeding that is reasonably related to his practice in a state where he is admitted if the forum does not require pro hac vice admission for those services.

d. Lawyer's Usual Practice

A lawyer may provide services that arise out of or are reasonably related to the lawyer's practice in her jurisdiction of admission.

7. Prohibition of Permanent Practice

The granting of authority to temporarily practice in a jurisdiction does not permit the lawyer to continue to practice in that jurisdiction, nor may she ***hold herself out*** to the public as having authority to practice there.

a. Corporate Counsel Exception

An in-house lawyer for a corporation, government agency, or other organization may usually work for his sole client in states in which he is not licensed.

b. State Regulation of Those Engaged Exclusively in "Federal" Practice

If federal legislation provides for admission to and regulation of an area of practice, it ***preempts*** state regulation of that practice. Where ***no*** federal regulation exists, the rule is unclear. However, some authority supports the view that states may not bar out-of-state lawyers from practicing federal law in the jurisdiction.

C. ENGAGING IN FEDERAL COURT AND INTERNATIONAL PRACTICE

1. Admission to Practice in the Federal System

Each federal court at ***each level*** independently grants admission pursuant to its own rules. Most simply require state bar admission plus a separate application. However, a few courts now require that applicants complete certain relevant courses (*e.g.*, federal civil and criminal procedure).

2. Practice of International Law

A foreign lawyer engaged in international practice has no right to practice in a particular U.S. jurisdiction or forum. However, several states now specially license foreign lawyers as "***legal consultants***" to give advice regarding the law of the countries where they are admitted to practice.

III. THE CONTRACT BETWEEN CLIENT AND LAWYER

A. INTRODUCTION

The client-lawyer relationship is best understood as a contract between them. Terms are implied by custom and professional rules, but many may be varied by agreement.

1. Lawyer as Agent

As an agent of his client, a lawyer is subject to the standards of a fiduciary and the rest of the law of agency (*e.g.*, she may not be hired to perform illegal acts).

2. Lawyer as Fiduciary

Fiduciary standards require a lawyer to put the interests of the client ahead of the lawyer's own. Part of those standards mean that changes in the contract between lawyer and client will be construed against the lawyer and scrutinized for fairness.

B. FORMATION OF THE LAWYER-CLIENT RELATIONSHIP—LAWYERS' DUTIES REGARDING ACCEPTING EMPLOYMENT

1. When a Lawyer-Client Relationship Is Formed

A lawyer-client relationship is formed by ***consent***, when a prospective client ***reasonably believes*** a lawyer has agreed to represent her, ***or*** by ***court appointment***.

2. No Obligation to Accept Every Case

Unlike English barristers, American lawyers need not take every matter presented to them. But since 2016, the ABA has prohibited lawyers from knowingly discriminating in any aspect of their law practices, and that principle may be extended to decisions as to which cases the lawyer decides to take.

3. Duties to a Prospective Client

Though the lawyer-client relationship is not formed until the parties both agree, a lawyer owes some duties to a prospective client who consults the lawyer about obtaining legal assistance. These include the duty to ***protect confidential information***, which also ***prohibits*** the lawyer from representing any client with ***interests materially adverse*** to those of the prospective client if the lawyer has acquired ***significantly harmful*** information. The lawyer also has a duty to ***protect a prospective client's property*** and to give ***competent legal advice*** if the lawyer gives any advice at all.

4. Duty to Reject Certain Cases

The ABA Code and Model Rules identify at least seven situations where the lawyer ***must refuse*** employment; *i.e.*, where:

a. A ***disciplinary standard or other law would be violated***;

b. The lawyer's ***physical or mental condition is impaired***;

c. The lawyer is ***unable to act competently***;

d. The lawyer's ***personal feelings interfere*** (as opposed to community pressure);

e. The client is ***already represented***;

f. The client's ***motive is harassment or malicious injury***; or

g. The client's ***legal position is unsupportable***.

5. Agreeing on Scope and Objectives of Representation

A lawyer should act in a way reasonably calculated to advance the client's legal objectives. However, the scope and objectives of the representation may be defined and limited by agreement (*e.g.*, limitation of representation to particular subjects or limitation of remedies to be pursued). Any limitation must be reasonable and the client must give informed consent.

C. SPHERES OF AUTHORITY OF LAWYER AND CLIENT

1. In General

The ***client***, with some exceptions, must be allowed to make ultimate decisions on the purposes of the representation and issues going to the merits of its resolution.

2. Matters Within Client's Authority

Decisions on matters that substantially affect the client's rights must be made by the client. In civil cases, these include the ***settlement or compromise of an action*** (but the client may ratify an unauthorized settlement) and the ***dismissal or abandonment of a case***.

a. Criminal Cases

The client in a criminal case, after receiving the lawyer's advice, must make decisions regarding important matters such as ***what plea to enter***, ***waiver of jury trial***, ***whether to testify***, and **whether to appeal**.

3. Matters Within Lawyer's Authority

The "means" are usually within the lawyer's authority, except for issues affecting cost and impact on third parties. The lawyer's authority generally extends to matters ***required by law***, most ***procedural*** matters, and ***judicial admissions***.

4. Special Problem—Decision-Making by Clients with "Diminished Capacity"

The lawyer should try to maintain a ***normal relationship*** with such clients, including ***consulting with them about major decisions***. If this is impossible, the lawyer may seek appointment of a guardian. Similar principles may apply to representation of ***minors.***

D. FORMAL DUTIES THAT LAWYERS OWE TO CLIENTS

1. Duty of Competence

This duty includes: (i) ***ability*** to perform required services; and (ii) ***care*** in performing those services.

a. **Ability to Represent Client**

Lawyers should not attempt to handle legal matters they know or ***should know*** they are not competent to handle, without implementing a plan to become qualified or associating a lawyer who is competent. A lawyer ***may act*** in ***emergency*** matters, but should ***limit*** his action to what is reasonably required to get past the emergency.

b. **Care in Representing the Client**

A lawyer must exhibit adequate preparation and thoroughness appropriate to the complexity of each matter.

c. **Remedies for Breach of Duty**

(1) **Malpractice Liability**

The most common remedy for incompetent representation is a malpractice suit.

(2) **Setting Aside a Criminal Conviction**

A criminal conviction may be set aside where errors of counsel deprived the accused of the constitutional right to ***effective assistance of counsel*** that caused ***actual prejudice***. Few convictions are set aside on this basis.

(3) **Setting Aside a Civil Default Judgment**

Generally, courts are reluctant to set aside civil judgments. The client (as principal) is usually charged with the errors of his lawyer-agent, but the court may set aside default judgments if there is a ***reasonable excuse*** for the lawyer's error.

2. **Duty of Diligence**

The Model Rules require a lawyer to act with ***reasonable diligence and promptness***. A lawyer may not unnecessarily delay resolution of a matter.

3. **Duty of Zealous Representation**

Zealous representation is defined by the Model Rules as the duties of competence and diligence. Traditionally, zeal in ***litigation*** matters has meant that the lawyer must act as an ***advocate*** and rcsolve any ***doubts in favor of the client***.

4. **Duty of Communication**

The Model Rules require a lawyer to explain a matter so that the client can make an informed decision. This requires a lawyer to: (i) keep the client ***informed about the status*** of a matter; (ii) comply promptly with ***reasonable requests for information***; (iii) reasonably consult with the client ***about the means*** to be used; (iv) promptly inform the client about ***circumstances requiring informed consent***; and (v) be certain the client understands any ***relevant limitations on the lawyer's conduct*** imposed by the rules of conduct.

5. **Duty of Confidentiality**

See infra, Chapter III.

6. **Duty of Loyalty**

See infra, Chapter IV.

7. **Duties with Regard to Client Property**

A lawyer must keep the funds and property of clients ***safe*** and ***entirely separate*** from the lawyer's own assets.

a. Separate Bank Accounts

Funds belonging to clients must be deposited in ***separately identified*** bank accounts ("trust accounts"). Generally a lawyer may not deposit personal funds in the trust accounts (commingling), which must be in the state of the lawyer's office, absent client consent to the contrary.

(1) Expenses Advanced by Client

The Model Rules require that client advances for ***costs or expenses also*** be deposited in the trust account.

b. Withdrawals from Joint Funds

A lawyer who receives money belonging in part to the client and in part to the lawyer must deposit the ***entire*** sum in the client's trust account. If the lawyer's share is fixed and ***undisputed***, it must be withdrawn ***as soon as possible***. ***Disputed funds*** may ***not*** be withdrawn until the controversy is resolved. Furthermore, the lawyer cannot disburse funds potentially belonging to a ***third party*** except as authorized by the client or court order.

c. Client's Property (Other than Funds)

The lawyer must label and identify securities and other property and deposit such property at once in a ***safe deposit box*** or other ***secure storage facility***. Today, this requirement has special implications for handling client electronic material in a way that protects against third-party hacking.

E. THE OBLIGATION OF CLIENT TO LAWYER—FEES FOR LEGAL SERVICES

1. Timing and Content of Fee Agreement

With a client not regularly represented by the lawyer, the client must be informed of the basis or rate of the fee ***before or within a reasonable time*** after agreeing to the representation.

a. Required Subjects

The client must be told of the ***fee amount*** or the ***basis*** for its calculation, the ***scope*** of the work, and ***likely costs*** to the client. The agreement should be (but except in a contingent fee case, is not required to be) in writing.

2. Requirement that Fees Be No More than Reasonable

Courts may refuse to enforce fee agreements that are "unreasonable," "clearly excessive," or "unconscionable," and such agreements may also subject the lawyer to discipline.

a. "Reasonableness"

The fee's reasonableness depends upon ***all relevant circumstances***, including factors such as the ***time and labor*** required, the ***novelty and difficulty*** of the issues, the required ***skill***, ***customary fees*** charged in the area, the ***amount involved,*** the ***result obtained***, and the ***experience, reputation, and ability*** of the lawyer.

b. Fee Arbitration

Several states provide arbitration review for dissatisfied clients, usually on a voluntary basis. However, proposals are being made to make them mandatory, and a comment to the Model Rules urges lawyers to submit to arbitration.

3. Special Problems of Contingent Fee Agreements

a. Propriety of Contingent Fee Agreements

Contingent fees are permitted, subject to regulation designed to prevent abuses.

(1) Specific Requirements

In addition to the requirements for regular fee agreements, the Model Rules require that a contingent fee agreement must:

(a) Be in a writing ***signed by the client*** (note the distinction from other fees);

(b) State how the fee is to be determined, including provision for settlement, trial, or appeal;

(c) Identify expenses and the method for their deduction; and

(d) Be followed up with a written statement accounting for disposition of the recovery.

(2) Maximum Limits

Court rules in a few states fix maximum percentages that a lawyer may charge under contingent fee contracts. Most states require ***court approval*** for contingency contracts on behalf of ***minors***.

b. Where Contingent Fees Prohibited

The Model Rules prohibit contingent fees in ***domestic relations*** cases (*e.g.,* divorce, alimony, property settlement, or support). However, some courts ***permit*** such fees in ***post-divorce*** proceedings (*e.g.,* past due alimony). Contingent fees are also ***prohibited*** in ***criminal cases and for the securing of favorable legislation***.

4. Recovery in Quantum Meruit

If a contingent fee arrangement is void for public policy reasons, courts usually permit the lawyer to recover the ***reasonable value*** of his services ("quantum meruit"). In the ***absence of a fee contract***, the lawyer is also often entitled to quantum meruit.

5. Minimum Fee Schedules

Fee schedules established by bar associations ***violate the antitrust laws***. Fees are now established exclusively by private contract, by court order, or by controlling legislation.

6. Legislative Regulation of Fees

Congress and some state legislatures have set ***maximum*** fees for some types of services (*e.g.*, workers' compensation claims, representation of indigent criminal defendants). Because of a sometimes harsh effect on a lawyer's fee in certain cases, some statutes provide that the ceiling applies only to a lawyer's "ordinary" services, allowing ***additional*** reasonable fees for "extraordinary" services.

7. Setting Fees in Class Actions, Derivative Suits, and Certain Civil Rights Actions

Courts usually apply the ***"lodestar" approach***, using an hourly rate as a basis and adjusting it based on complexity, amount recovered, uncertainty of result, etc. However, the ***common fund method*** (*i.e.*, awarding the lawyer a percentage of the recovery) is often used when a lawyer recovers a substantial sum for the plaintiff or a class.

a. Negotiating Fees as Part of Settlement

The Supreme Court has held that if a defendant offers a generous settlement but insists that the plaintiff's lawyer take less than a reasonable fee, the lawyer may have a duty to accept the settlement. Thus, many lawyers now negotiate fee arrangements with the class in advance, not limited by what the court or settlement provides.

8. Protecting Lawyer's Right to Compensation

a. Lawyer's Duties in Collecting Fees

Lawyers should be "zealous" in efforts to ***avoid controversies*** with clients over fees. Lawyers must be careful to avoid overreaching in using self-help remedies and should not sue a client unless necessary to prevent fraud or gross imposition by the client or if the client refuses to pay a fee claim asserted in good faith.

b. Retaining (Possessory) Lien

In many states, lawyers have a possessory lien on all property, documents, and funds belonging to the client that come into the lawyer's possession by reason of employment. Ordinarily, a lawyer need not turn over documents prepared by him and not yet paid for. However, a retaining lien on ***files needed*** by the client is ***void***.

c. Charging (Nonpossessory) Lien

In many states, lawyers also have a "charging lien" that gives the lawyer the right to have ***any fund or recovery*** she obtains for her client serve as security for her fees and disbursements in that matter. The charging lien has the advantages of application to funds not in the lawyer's possession and a right to ***affirmative enforcement***.

(1) Limitations

The charging lien is limited to fees and costs incurred in that particular action, not for other fees owed by the same client.

(2) Time Lien Attaches

Most states permit assertion of a charging lien only upon judgment or settlement. However, provided the lawyer gives ***notice*** to the defendant and the lien attaches to the cause of action, a client may ***not*** defeat it by settling ***directly*** with the defendant.

F. TERMINATING THE LAWYER-CLIENT RELATIONSHIP

Either the lawyer or client may seek to terminate the relationship before completion of the matter.

1. Withdrawal by Lawyer

A lawyer may not simply terminate the lawyer-client relationship at will. Withdrawal may be made only on the basis of one of the grounds recognized in Model Rule 1.16.

a. Duty to Withdraw

A lawyer ***is required*** to withdraw under the following circumstances:

(1) The employment ***violates professional conduct rules***;

(2) The lawyer is physically or mentally ***unable to continue*** the employment;

(3) The client's purpose is ***harassment or malicious prosecution***; or

(4) The lawyer has been ***discharged*** by the client.

b. Permissive Withdrawal

Where withdrawal is not required, the lawyer has a general duty to continue the employment to its natural conclusion, but the lawyer is ***permitted*** to withdraw under certain circumstances, such as:

(1) There is ***no material adverse effect on the client***, even if the client objects;

(2) The client ***involves the lawyer in illegal conduct***;

(3) The client makes ***repugnant demands***;

(4) The client ***fails to fulfill obligations*** to the lawyer (*e.g.*, refuses to pay fee);

(5) The client ***has made the relationship unreasonably difficult*** (*e.g.*, noncooperation);

(6) The client ***freely and knowingly consents***; and

(7) ***Other good cause*** for withdrawal exists.

c. General Obligations of Lawyer in Withdrawing

There is a duty to ***safeguard rights and interests*** of clients. The lawyer must:

(1) Obtain ***court permission*** in ***litigation*** matters;

(2) Give adequate ***notice*** to the client so other counsel can be retained;

(3) ***Refund*** unearned fees; and

(4) ***Promptly return*** all papers and property to which the client is entitled.

2. Discharge by Client

The right of a client to terminate the lawyer-client relationship is ***virtually unconditional***. The lawyer may be fired ***at any time, with or without cause***. Provisions purporting to make the lawyer's employment ***irrevocable*** are ***void***.

a. Continuing Fiduciary Duty of Lawyer

Even discharge without cause does ***not*** relieve the lawyer of all fiduciary duties.

b. Liability of Client to Lawyer Under Fee Contract

The client may remain ***contractually liable*** to the lawyer (for fees, etc.) if the discharge is ***without cause***. Recovery would most often be in quantum meruit.

c. Liability of Third Parties for Inducing Discharge

The lawyer may have an action for ***interference with contractual relations*** against third persons who induce discharge without cause.

IV. DUTY TO PROTECT CONFIDENTIAL INFORMATION OF THE CLIENT

A. INTRODUCTION

1. Three Basic Legal Doctrines

Both the evidentiary ***attorney-client privilege*** and ***work product doctrine, as well as*** an ethical ***duty of confidentiality***, protect the confidential information of clients.

2. Period During Which Duty and Privileges Apply

Both the duty and the privilege ***extend beyond*** the lawyer's actual employment.

a. Before Employment

Confidential information disclosed to a lawyer in discussions ***preliminary*** to actual employment is protected, under ***both*** the attorney-client privilege and the confidentiality obligation, and sometimes the work product doctrine.

b. After Employment Ceases

The duty to preserve confidential information ***continues after*** the lawyer is no longer employed by the client.

c. **After Client's Death**

The attorney-client privilege continues after a client's death, although some courts allow privileged information to establish the intended beneficiaries under a client's will.

3. **Permitted Disclosures Within Law Firm**

Unless the client specifies otherwise, a lawyer may properly discuss the client's affairs with partners, associates, secretaries, etc. The lawyer may also give information to ***outside personnel*** (accountants, etc.) for legitimate purposes if the client does not object. However, the lawyer must exercise reasonable care to prevent employees and associates from disclosing confidential information.

B. ATTORNEY-CLIENT PRIVILEGE

The ***legal*** privilege of nondisclosure governs the extent to which a lawyer may be compelled to disclose in ***court*** proceedings what the client has revealed in confidence.

1. **Scope of the Privilege**

The four basic elements needed for the privilege to apply are: (i) there must have been a ***communication***; (ii) between someone who was or wanted to be a client to an ***attorney acting as such at the time***; (iii) the communications must be made ***in confidence***; and (iv) the communications must be made for the ***purpose of obtaining legal advice***.

a. **Revealing Incriminating Physical Evidence**

The privilege applies only to ***"communications"***; it does ***not*** protect incriminating documents or physical evidence turned over to the lawyer.

b. **"In Confidence" Requirement**

If the communication takes place in less than confidential circumstances, the privilege may be lost. Subsequent disclosure by the client may ***waive*** the privilege. However, an unsuspected ***eavesdropper*** can be prohibited from testifying about the communication.

2. **Special Cases to Which Privilege Applies**

a. **Corporate or Government Client**

The confidential communication privilege extends to corporate and government clients when made to both in-house and independent lawyers. Note that, although the privilege does not cover non-legal advice (*e.g.*, business advice), the privilege is ***not*** lost when nonlegal and legal advice (a mixed communication) are contained in the same communication.

(1) **Personal Confidences of Corporate or Government Officials**

Generally, a corporate or government lawyer is ***not*** the lawyer for individuals connected to the entity. While the entity may assert the privilege with respect to communications from such persons, the entity may release the information to enforcement authorities or others who may use it against the individuals.

b. **Information Shared by Clients with Common Interest**

If two or more clients have a common interest in a matter, they and their lawyers may share information without losing the privilege. However, the privilege is ***not*** applicable in subsequent litigation between/among the clients.

3. Exceptions to the Attorney-Client Privilege

a. Consent by Client

When the client consents to disclosure, the lawyer may disclose privileged information and the privilege is lost for it thereafter.

b. Disclosure of Future Crime or Fraud

The attorney-client privilege ***does not cover*** a communication in which the client seeks to further the planning or commission of a ***future*** crime or fraud that the client later commits. The privilege ***does protect*** revelations of ***past*** crimes or frauds.

c. Disclosure for Lawyer Self-Protection

A lawyer may reveal sufficient information to defend himself against charges of ***negligence or misconduct***, and to ***collect fees*** owed the lawyer.

4. Responsibilities of Lawyer in Asserting the Attorney-Client Privilege

a. Duty to Assert Privilege

A lawyer has a duty "to advise the client of the attorney-client privilege and timely to assert the privilege unless it is waived by the client."

b. Wrongful Order to Disclose

When a court wrongfully orders a lawyer to disclose privileged information, some courts hold that the lawyer ***must refuse*** to disclose ***at all costs*** (*e.g.*, jailed on contempt charge). The ABA Model Rules provide that the lawyer ***may disclose*** when required by court order. The ***preferred approach*** would be for the lawyer to assert all ***nonfrivolous claims for confidentiality***, and then, if the client so directs, allow himself to be held in contempt until the matter is reviewed on appeal. But the Model Rules do not require the lawyer to put himself in contempt in this way.

5. Waiver by Disclosure or Failure to Object

Failure to assert the attorney-client privilege, or voluntary disclosure of the privileged information, waives the privilege ***forever***. Importantly, waiver with respect to one item may waive ***all*** items dealing with the ***same subject matter***.

a. Inadvertent Disclosure

In discovery, if a lawyer inadvertently turns over privileged information along with required material, courts often deem the privilege not waived if the lawyer has taken reasonable measures to prevent such an occurrence and immediately seeks to reclaim the material.

C. WORK PRODUCT DOCTRINE

1. What Qualifies as Work Product

The work product doctrine is a creature of the civil discovery process. It protects against compelled disclosure any:

a. ***tangible material*** (or its intangible equivalent in unwritten or oral form),

b. ***not itself part of the underlying facts*** of the case, and

c. ***prepared by a lawyer for litigation*** then in progress or reasonably anticipated.

2. **Differences Between the Attorney-Client Privilege and the Work Product Doctrine**

a. **Work Product Not Limited to Communications Between Client and Lawyer**

The issue is whether information was collected or a document was prepared in anticipation of litigation. A lawyer's memorandum describing news reports about the case would be work product, for example, but it would not be privileged.

b. **Privilege Protection is Absolute; Work Product Protection is Conditional**

A court may never order disclosure of attorney-client privileged information but it may order turnover of work product material if the opposing party has a substantial need for the material and is unable to get it without undue hardship, e.g., the witness whose statement was taken by the plaintiff is now deceased.

3. **Differences Between Treatment of Ordinary and Opinion Work Product**

a. **Ordinary Work Product Is Material That Meets the Criteria Just Described**

b. **Opinion Work Product Consists of the Lawyer's Mental Impressions**

A court will only require disclosure of a document recording a lawyer's plans or judgments about a case when "extraordinary circumstances" require disclosure. That disclosure standard is almost never met but it means that, unlike privileged material, protect of even opinion work product is not absolute.

D. PROFESSIONAL DUTY OF CONFIDENTIALITY

Besides the attorney-client privilege and work product doctrine, lawyers have a ***professional duty*** not to reveal a much larger body of confidential client information.

1. **Professional Duty Broader than Privilege**

Under the ***Model Rules***, a lawyer may ***not*** reveal ***any*** information ***relating to the representation***. That is so much material that the law permits or requires a lawyer to disclose it in situations where the law prohibits disclosure of privileged information.

2. **Differences Between Privileged and Confidential Material**

a. **Identity of Client**

Generally, the name of a client is ***not*** a "communication," for example, and hence is not privileged. However, the fact that the client consulted a lawyer is related to the representation and thus confidential.

b. **Fee Arrangement with Client**

Although fee arrangements are not protected by the attorney-client privilege, they are confidential, and a lawyer is ***not*** ethically free to disclose them without client consent.

c. **Presence of Strangers**

The duty of confidentiality applies to information learned from, or in the presence of, third parties.

d. **When Lawyer May Reveal—Implied Authority**

Sometimes, confidential information must be disclosed if the lawyer is to represent the client at all. When the court asks the lawyer who she is there to represent, for example, she may disclose the client's name.

e. Physical Evidence

Neither the privilege nor the duty requires or permits the lawyer to take possession of or help secrete fruits or instrumentalities of a ***crime***. If the lawyer takes possession, he ***must*** give the physical evidence to the police, even if it incriminates the client, although the lawyer may keep it long enough to do necessary tests.

3. Use of Information for Lawyer's Benefit

The Model Rules prohibit use of the information only if it would be ***detrimental*** to the client, but agency law will likely require the lawyer to turn over any financial gain from the disclosure to the client.

4. Exceptions to Duty of Confidentiality

Exceptions to the attorney-client privilege (client informed consent, lawyer self-defense) apply to the duty of confidentiality. In addition:

a. Affirmative Revelation of Future Crime or Fraud

The Model Rules permit disclosure of any ***act, whether or not a crime***, that threatens persons with ***reasonably certain death or substantial bodily harm***.

b. Financial Harm

The Model Rules permits revelation of client information to prevent, mitigate, or rectify ***substantial*** financial harm ***reasonably certain*** to occur because of a client's past or future crime or fraud ***using the lawyer's services***.

c. Securing Legal Advice About Ethics Compliance

A lawyer may disclose information relating to the representation to get legal advice about what ethics rules require her to do in a problematic situation.

d. Compliance with Law or Court Order

A ***court may compel*** the lawyer's disclosure of relevant, unprivileged information. The whole discovery process is premised on such disclosure, for example.

e. Detecting and Resolving Conflicts of Interests in Change of Employment

A lawyer changing employment may disclose ***unprivileged*** confidential information to the potential new employer to detect and resolve any conflicts of interest, but only if doing so will not prejudice the client.

V. DUTY OF UNIMPAIRED LOYALTY—CONFLICTS OF INTEREST

A. INTRODUCTION

The Model Rules prohibit a lawyer from representing one client in a manner ***directly adverse*** to another client or under circumstances that ***materially limit*** representation because of other responsibilities or interests. However, a lawyer may represent a client in spite of a conflict if: (i) ***the conflict is consentable***; ***and*** (ii) the client gives ***informed consent, confirmed in writing***.

B. CONCURRENT REPRESENTATION OF CLIENTS WITH CONFLICTING INTERESTS

1. General Standards

Concurrent conflicts of interest arise when a lawyer represents one client ***directly adverse*** to another of the lawyer's clients, ***even in unrelated cases***, or when the lawyer's representation of one client is ***materially limited by obligations to another client***.

2. **Lawyer's Obligation in Such Situations**

   a. **Nonconsentable Conflicts**

      A client may not waive his lawyer's representation (i) of an opposing party in the ***same litigation***, (ii) where a reasonable lawyer would not be able to render ***competent and diligent representation*** to each client, and (iii) where the representation is ***prohibited by law***.

   b. **Informed Client Consent**

      In most cases, however, a lawyer may proceed in spite of a conflict, but only after obtaining each client's ***informed consent, confirmed in writing***.

3. **Application of Standards—Litigation Matters**

   a. **Criminal Proceedings**

      Each accused is ***constitutionally*** entitled to assistance of his own counsel. It is the ***duty of the court*** to appoint separate counsel whenever differing interests arise.

   b. **Personal Injury Litigation**

      Several persons injured in the same mishap may have potentially differing interests, which could make multiple representation improper, absent informed consent.

   c. **Other Civil Matters**

      Conflicts of interests among clients may exist in matters such as divorce, where differing interests are present (*e.g.,* property division, child support). Bankruptcies and receiverships also usually involve diverse interests, which often make multiple representation improper.

   d. **Representing Opposing Clients in Unrelated Matters**

      Absent consent, a lawyer employed by a client to provide legal services in a lawsuit may ***not*** simultaneously agree to represent another party in a different lawsuit against that same client. No actual effect on lawyer judgment need exist since a lawyer must avoid even the ***appearance of divided loyalty***.

   e. **Lump Sum Settlement for Several Clients**

      Each client must consent to the aggregate settlement after being advised of the existence and nature of ***all claims*** involved in the proposed settlement, and the ***participation*** of each person in the settlement. The same requirements apply to ***multiple criminal defendants*** considering guilty or nolo contendere pleas. Note that unnamed members of a ***class action*** are usually ***not*** regarded as clients for this purpose.

4. **Application of Standards to Common Nonlitigation Matters**

   In ***real estate transactions, borrower-lender situations***, and comparable other matters, a lawyer may not represent both parties without full disclosure of potential conflicts and the parties' informed consent, confirmed in writing. But sometimes the conflict will be so great in such cases as to make the conflict nonconsentable.

5. **Special Problems of Corporate Counsel**

   Lawyers employed by a corporation serve the ***entity*** rather than its constituent parts. The Model Rules allow the lawyer to represent both the corporation and individuals when no conflict is involved, but the Model Rules also impose responsibilities when the lawyer discovers wrongdoing on the part of a corporate officer or employee.

6. Special Rule for Legal Aid Work

A 2002 Model Rule amendment permits a lawyer to give pro bono ***short-term, limited services*** without determining whether she has a conflict of interest, unless she has actual knowledge of a conflict. Moreover, work done at the legal aid clinic will not disqualify other members of a lawyer's firm from representing a client in a matter adverse to the short-term legal aid client.

B. PERSONAL INTERESTS THAT MAY AFFECT LAWYER'S JUDGMENT

A lawyer must not allow a personal interest to detract from loyalty to the client.

1. Financial Interest Adverse to Client

A lawyer may not knowingly acquire any property or financial interest that is adverse to the client unless the client expressly consents.

2. Prohibition on Acquiring Interest in Subject Matter of Employment

A lawyer is prohibited from purchasing or otherwise acquiring any interest in the claim or property that is the subject matter of the litigation, except to secure fees and costs. Client consent ***cannot*** waive this prohibition.

3. Publication Rights Concerning Subject Matter of Employment

Prior to the conclusion of ***all*** aspects of the case, a lawyer may not acquire publication rights from the client as to the subject matter of the employment.

4. Business or Financial Transactions with Client

Lawyers entering business deals with clients must overcome a presumption of ***overreaching*** or undue influence. The Model Rules specifically require that the terms must be ***fair and reasonable***, in ***understandable*** form, and given to the client ***in writing***. Also, the client must be advised ***in writing*** to get ***independent counsel***, and the client's ***consent*** must be ***in a writing signed by the client***.

5. Gifts or Bequests to Lawyer

A lawyer may not solicit a substantial gift or bequest from a client. An ***instrument*** giving the lawyer a substantial gift must be prepared by another lawyer unless the gift is from a close relative.

6. Sexual Relationship with Client

A lawyer may not have a sexual relationship with a client, or official of an organizational client who deals with the lawyer, unless the relationship predated the representation.

D. INTERESTS OF THIRD PERSONS AFFECTING THE LAWYER-CLIENT RELATIONSHIP

A lawyer's duty is to the client, not any third person whose interests would impair the lawyer's independent judgment and loyalty. Thus, a lawyer may ***not accept compensation*** from a third person for services to the client without the ***client's informed consent*** and ***protection of the client's confidential information.*** Nor may a lawyer accept employment by non-client laypersons who would have the ***right to direct or control*** her professional judgment in representing clients.

1. Representing Liability Insurer and Insured

Despite potential conflicts, it is proper and quite common for a lawyer selected by the insurance company to represent both the company's interest and the policyholder's because both want a finding of no liability. However, the lawyer still has a duty to avoid conflicting interests and impaired loyalty that do arise (*e.g.*, disputed policy coverage issues).

2. **Juvenile Court Proceedings**

The lawyer is an ***advocate*** for the ***juvenile client***, and responsibilities are owed to the child, even if the child's parents are paying the fee.

3. **Service on Board of Legal Services Organization**

A lawyer accepting a Board position owes duties to those whom the organization serves and to her own clients. She must not participate in decisions as to which conflicts arise between those interests and must notify the Board when her private clients will benefit from decisions being made by the Legal Services Organization.

E. CONFLICT BETWEEN INTERESTS OF CURRENT AND FORMER CLIENTS

A lawyer has a ***continuing duty*** to protect the former client's confidential information but a more limited duty of loyalty to such clients.

1. **Prohibition on Representation in Same Matter**

A lawyer may ***not*** successively represent opposing parties in the ***same*** litigation.

2. **Prohibition on Representation in Substantially Related Matters**

A lawyer may not take a position materially adverse to a former client in a matter that is ***substantially related*** to the prior matter. The critical issue for determining a substantial relationship is whether confidential information of the former client would "materially advance" the position of the lawyer's current client.

3. **Consent of Affected Clients Can Waive Conflict**

A lawyer wishing to proceed to represent the current client in the face of a former client conflict must get informed consent, confirmed in writing, from ***both*** the former client and the current client.

F. IMPUTED DISQUALIFICATION OF AFFILIATED LAWYERS

The prohibition on representing clients because of a conflict of interest extends to persons affiliated with the lawyer in a "firm."

1. **Private Law Firms**

The most common application is to partners, associates, and other lawyers in a private law firm, including those working at the firm's offices in ***different cities***.

a. **When Disqualified Person Has Left Firm**

If the person with a conflict ***leaves the firm*** and takes the former client with her, leaving no records and no person with confidential information about the matter in the firm, the firm is no longer prohibited from representation. The converse is also true. When a person ***leaves a disqualified law firm*** without having obtained any disqualifying information, the lawyer may work on the matter at the new firm.

2. **Other Practice Organizations**

The disqualification rule also covers corporate legal offices. Where there is no common economic interest, however, *e.g.*, ***lawyers sharing office space, government legal offices***, the prohibition is less likely to be applied if each lawyer's confidential information is adequately protected.

3. Lawyers Related as Spouses, Parent and Child, or Siblings

Firms for which related persons work are not automatically barred from representing opposing interests, but the two related lawyers may not themselves represent directly adverse clients (absent informed consent).

4. Screening as a Remedy

For many years, a law firm ***could not screen*** a disqualified lawyer who joined the law firm and thus continue representation against a former client of that lawyer, subject to exceptions such as former government lawyers or former judges. Now, screening can allow the representation to continue if (a) the screening is timely, (b) the screened lawyer gets no part of the fee in the case, and (c) written notice is provided to the former client at reasonable intervals indicating how the screen is working.

G. LIMITATIONS ON REPRESENTATION BY PRESENT AND FORMER GOVERNMENT LAWYERS

1. Model Rules

a. Personal and Substantial Involvement

A former government lawyer may not represent a client where the lawyer was ***personally and substantially*** involved in the matter, unless the government agency gives informed consent. The former government lawyer's firm is ***not disqualified*** if she is ***adequately screened*** from the case, ***shares no fees***, and gives prompt, ***written notice*** to the government agency. This rule is an exception to the rule discussed above about duties to a former client.

b. Confidential Government Information

The lawyer may not represent a private client adverse to another private party about whom the lawyer learned confidential government information while in office, *i.e.,* FBI reports or other information only government officials could obtain.

c. Lawyer Coming to Government from Private Practice

A government lawyer may not work on matters in which she was ***personally and substantially*** involved in nongovernmental employment unless other law expressly permits. In addition, the usual rules governing duties to former clients also apply.

d. Negotiating for Private Employment

Government lawyers may not negotiate for private employment with persons involved in matters on which the government lawyer is working.

2. Federal Statute

The Federal Conflict of Interest Act, 18 U.S.C. § 207, imposes ***criminal sanctions*** for certain representation of private parties after government service.

VI. OBLIGATIONS TO THIRD PERSONS AND THE LEGAL SYSTEM

A. LAWYER'S ROLE AS COUNSELOR

1. Duty to Give Candid Advice

A lawyer must "exercise independent professional judgment and render candid advice," which includes not withholding unpalatable information from the client, and may include advising a client about moral, economic, social, and political factors.

2. Duty Not to Counsel or Assist Illegal or Fraudulent Conduct

A lawyer may ***not*** counsel or assist a client in illegal or fraudulent conduct. The lawyer may, however, assist a client to do an act that will result in a ***good faith testing of the bounds of the law***.

3. Discussing Legal Consequences of Conduct

If requested, a lawyer ***may discuss*** the legal consequences of a client's proposed illegal conduct, as long as the lawyer does not advocate the conduct or advise the client how to avoid detection or escape arrest.

4. Refusal to Assist Client

A lawyer may refuse to assist her client in committing an ***arguable*** crime or fraud.

B. SPECIAL DUTIES WHEN REPRESENTING AN ORGANIZATION

1. Duty to Treat the Entity as the Client

An organization is inherently a bundle of often-conflicting interests that has to operate as if it were of one mind. Lawyers who represent organizations deal with that reality by representing "the organization acting through its duly authorized constituents." We call that representing the organizational "entity."

2. Duty to Clarify Whom the Lawyer Represents

It is possible for a lawyer to represent both the organization and one or more of its constituents if the tests for a conflict of interest and informed consent are met. But organizational lawyers often regularly deal with constituents who come to trust and confide in the lawyers. Because of the potentially serious consequences of a constituent's mistaken believing the lawyer represents her along with the organization, the lawyer must explain the identity of the client when the lawyer knows or reasonably should know that the organization's interests are adverse" to the constituent's interest.

3. Representing an Organization When a Constituent Violates Duties to It

Organizational constituents make decisions within their areas of responsibility. But special obligations arise for a corporation's lawyer who learns that someone is acting ***illegally*** and in a way that will ***significantly injure*** the client corporation.

a. Basic Obligation—Reporting up

The conditions just identified presumptively require the lawyer to refer the situation to higher authority in the organization, even ultimately to the highest authority that can act to correct the situation, typically a corporation's board of directors. The premise of the process is that the organization can correct its own problems.

b. Lawyer's Authority—Reporting out

After enough cases arose in which organizations seemed to have covered up problems rather than dealt with them, the Model Rules now give lawyers permission to disclose to others outside the organization if the lawyer is [i] ***unsuccessful*** in getting the matter resolved by the highest authority in the organization and [ii] the matter is ***clearly a violation of law*** and [iii] ***reasonably certain*** to result in substantial injury to the organization, insofar as the lawyer ***reasonably believes necessary*** to prevent the threatened ***substantial injury***.

c. **Exception—Lawyer Hired to Defend Against Charges**

The Model Rules expressly ***withhold*** this authority to "report out" in cases where a lawyer was retained to investigate or defend the corporation against the charges that would otherwise be reported.

d. **Lawyer's Duty to Report Wrongful Discharge**

A lawyer who "reasonably believes" that she was discharged or had to resign for taking the steps required by Model Rule 1.13(b) or (c) is ***required*** to "proceed as the lawyer reasonably believes necessary to assure that the organization's highest authority" knows what happened to the lawyer, presumably to cause the organization to change its ways.

C. REQUIREMENT OF HONESTY IN COMMUNICATIONS WITH NON-CLIENTS

1. Basic Obligation of Truthfulness

A lawyer may not knowingly make a ***false statement of material fact or law***, even where it would seem to be in the client's interest to do so.

2. Lawyer's Duty in Negotiations

In general, a lawyer has no duty to do the other side's fact research, nor the right to undermine the client's position through such revelations.

a. **Puffing**

A common practice in negotiation is to try to make the opposing person believe your case is stronger than it really is, that your bargaining position is unyielding, and the like. The Model Rules say that reasonable lawyers do not take estimates of value and intentions as to settlement as statements of material fact for purposes of compliance with the rule of truthfulness.

b. **False Assumptions by Opponent**

There is generally ***no duty to correct misapprehensions*** not involving deceit by the lawyer or her client. If a buyer believes the city will build a road to a parcel of land, but the seller did not say that, the seller does not have to correct the buyer's belief.

D. SPECIALLY ASSUMED DUTY OF CANDOR—LAWYER AS EVALUATOR

1. Giving Opinions to Nonclients

Unless contrary to his client's interests, a lawyer may ***certify facts or issues of legal authority*** when requested to do so by the opposing party. That is often done because the lawyer knows the facts while the opposing party would have to do an investigation. However, the lawyer will be ***liable to the third party*** for dishonesty or negligence in preparing the opinion if the lawyer's assertions turn out to be wrong.

2. When Lawyer's Opinion Is to Be Widely Disseminated

When a lawyer agrees to certify facts to a large number of persons who can be expected to rely on the lawyer, the lawyer has a special obligation to be ***complete, accurate, and candid*** (*e.g.*, securities disclosure cases).

E. COMMUNICATING WITH ANOTHER PERSON ON BEHALF OF CLIENT

1. Person Represented by Counsel

A lawyer who ***knows*** that another person is represented by counsel in a matter ***must not communicate*** with that person on any subject of controversy in that matter unless that person's counsel is present or has given prior consent or the communication is authorized by law or court order. This rule prohibits communication with ***any*** person represented by counsel, not just an adverse party. Note that represented persons may communicate with each other.

a. **Corporations and Other Organizations**

When an organization is protected by this rule, a lawyer may ***not*** talk to persons in the organization who ***have authority to settle the matter***, those who ***regularly communicate with the organization's counsel*** about the matter, and those whose ***conduct or statements may be imputed*** to the organization.

(1) **Former Employees**

A lawyer generally ***may contact*** a former employee ***unless*** the employee ***continues*** to regularly communicate with the organization's counsel.

2. **Person Unrepresented by Counsel**

Generally, after clearly stating that he is ***not a disinterested person***, a lawyer may communicate with an unrepresented person but should ***not advise*** the person beyond suggesting that he secure counsel.

3. **Acquisition of Evidence from a Third Party**

Lawyers may not use methods of obtaining evidence that violate the legal rights of another (*e.g.,* illegally recording conversations, seeking privileged information).

4. **Threats of Criminal Prosecution**

Although the Model Rules do not say so, a lawyer ordinarily may ***not*** file or threaten to file criminal charges solely to obtain an advantage for the client in a civil matter. Threats of administrative or disciplinary charges are equally improper.

F. OBLIGATION TO AVOID KNOWING HARASSMENT OR DISCRIMINATION

1. **Lawyers Subject to Antidiscrimination Laws**

Lawyers have long been subject to federal & state antidiscrimination laws and many states already prohibit discrimination in their own Rules of Professional Conduct.

2. **ABA Model Rule 8.4(g) Creates a New Standard**

a. **The Prohibited Conduct**

The new rule makes it professional misconduct for a lawyer to "engage in conduct that the lawyer knows is harassment or discrimination" on the basis of race, sex, religion, national origin, ethnicity, disability, age, sexual orientation, gender identity, marital status, or socioeconomic status as part of "conduct related to the practice of law." Other antidiscrimination laws "may guide application" of the professional standard, but discipline is not expressly limited by such precedent.

b. **Conduct Not Prohibited**

(i) The rule says that it does not change current standards for taking or withdrawing from a case.

(ii) It says it "does not preclude legitimate advice or advocacy consistent with these Rules."

(iii) Lawyers may limit their practice to "members of underserved populations."

(iv) Discrimination in order to promote "diversity and inclusion" is encouraged.

G. ENCOURAGEMENT TO PROVIDE PRO BONO SERVICE

1. Voluntary Duty to Provide Pro Bono Service

The Model Rules assert that lawyers should "aspire" to perform at least 50 hours of pro bono legal service each year, the "substantial majority" of which should be to "persons of limited means" or organizations serving such persons.

2. Accepting Appointment as Counsel

Lawyers have a similar moral duty to accept a court appointment to represent a criminal defendant unless they have a good reason to decline it, such as a conflict of interest, it would impose an unreasonable financial burden, or the lawyer's personal feeling of repugnance at the client or the offense would impair the likelihood of providing effective representation

3. Ethical Duty to Provide Representation Where Needed

Lawyers "should" accept some cases where clients cannot afford legal services, but the failure to do so does not result in discipline. Some states impose an affirmative duty to represent the "defenseless or oppressed."

4. Rights of Lawyer

Some cases have held that it is unconstitutional for a public agency to require representation of an indigent client without ***compensation***. Furthermore, the Supreme Court has held that, while a federal court may request a lawyer to represent an indigent client in a ***civil case***, it cannot order him to do so.

H. OTHER INTERACTIONS BETWEEN LAWYERS AND THE LEGAL SYSTEM

1. Not Claim Ability to Improperly Influence a Government Agency

A lawyer expressly may not assert or imply an ability to influence a government agency or official in a way that would violate the law or legal ethics rules.

2. Disclosure That Legislative Appearance Is in a Representative Capacity

Even if a lawyer personally supports particular legislative action, if the lawyer testifies or otherwise lobbies in support of the action, the lawyer must reveal that he appears in a representative capacity.

3. No Reckless or Knowingly False Criticism of a Judge

A lawyer may speak critically about a judge or judicial decision, but a reckless or knowingly false statement will subject the lawyer to discipline.

4. No "Pay to Play" Political Contributions

A lawyer who makes a political contribution to a judge "for the purpose of obtaining or being considered" for an appointment the judge has power to make is barred from later accepting such an appointment.

VII. SPECIAL OBLIGATIONS OF LAWYERS IN LITIGATION

A. DUTY NOT TO WASTE THE COURT'S TIME

1. Baseless Lawsuits

A lawyer may not file suit on behalf of a client unless it has a ***nonfrivolous*** basis, which includes a ***good faith argument*** for an ***extension, modification, or reversal*** of existing law. A filing is ***not frivolous*** if a lawyer does not have all the facts but expects to determine them ***in discovery***. Note that a lawyer may zealously defend a ***criminal defendant*** whom she believes to be guilty.

2. Abusive Delay in Litigation

Delaying a trial to harass or injure the opponent or failure to appear may subject a lawyer to sanctions by the court. The Model Rules impose an ***affirmative duty*** to expedite litigation.

a. Federal Rule 11

This rule requires a lawyer in federal court to ***sign every pleading***, thus ***certifying*** that the pleading is not filed for the "purposes of delay." Violations may result in a lawyer or client being required to pay attorney's fees and other expenses incurred by the opponent.

3. Discovery Abuse

A lawyer is subject to professional discipline and judicially-imposed compensation to the opponent for making frivolous discovery requests or failing to use diligent efforts to comply with appropriate requests.

B. DUTY OF HONESTY AND CANDOR BEFORE A TRIBUNAL

A lawyer must not knowingly make a false statement of law or fact to a tribunal.

1. In Pleadings

Pleadings must be truthful and accurate. In many states, as well as federal courts, a lawyer must sign every pleading certifying that there are good grounds to support it.

2. Ordinarily No Duty to Disclose Harmful Facts

Generally, a lawyer has ***no affirmative duty*** to disclose facts harmful to his client's case unless the failure to do so would make what the lawyer does say a ***material misstatement***.

3. Duty Not to Misstate Law

A lawyer must not knowingly mislead the judge as to the law and must also correct any previous misstatement of law.

4. Duty to Disclose Adverse Legal Authority

The lawyer owes an affirmative duty to disclose ***applicable law***, including that adverse to the client's case. However, only ***directly*** contrary authority from the ***controlling jurisdiction*** that the opponent has not cited must be disclosed.

5. Duty When a Client or Witness Gives False Evidence

The lawyer has a duty to the court not to rely on false evidence, but also has a duty to minimize injury to the client.

a. False Statement in a Civil Case

A lawyer must correct, or have the witness correct, any false material evidence or material mistakes.

b. Intent to Commit Perjury in a Criminal Case

A criminal defendant has been held to have a constitutional right to testify in his own defense. When a ***client or witness*** intends to commit perjury, however, at minimum, the lawyer must try to persuade the client or witness either not to testify or not to testify falsely. When a lawyer's efforts (*i.e.,* persuasion, attempt to withdraw) are unsuccessful, she may be required to ***reveal*** the situation to the judge.

c. After False Testimony Given in a Criminal Case

Even in criminal cases, a lawyer must ***take reasonable remedial measures***. These include ***urging a client*** to cooperate in withdrawing or correcting the false evidence. Lacking client cooperation, a lawyer should consider seeking ***permission to withdraw***. If not possible or not an effective solution, the lawyer may be required to ***disclose*** the situation to the judge, even if that would breach client confidentiality.

6. Disclosure of Crime or Fraud upon the Court

A lawyer must take reasonable remedial measures, including disclosure, when she learns his client intends to act, is acting, or has acted to corrupt the court proceedings (*e.g.*, jury tampering).

7. Scope and Duration of Requirements

The lawyer's duty ends at the proceeding's conclusion (including appeals). If the lawyer learns of her client's false testimony the day after the time for all appeals are over, she not only need not, she presumably may not, take remedial measures.

8. *Ex Parte* Proceedings

Because in an *ex parte* proceeding, the opposing party is not present, the moving party's lawyer must inform the court of ***all material facts*** known to the lawyer that are likely to be ***relevant,*** even facts that weaken the client's case.

C. OTHER DUTIES OF AN ADVOCATE TO NONCLIENTS AND TRIBUNALS

1. Conduct Affecting Witnesses and Evidence

a. Suppression of Evidence

A lawyer ***may not obstruct*** any party's ***access*** to, or unlawfully ***alter or destroy***, relevant ***evidence***. Neither may a lawyer ask a ***potential witness*** not to talk to the other side ***unless*** the person is a client's relative, employee, or agent, and the lawyer reasonably believes the withholding of information will not adversely affect the person.

b. Inducing Favorable Testimony

A lawyer may not pay any amount to nonexpert witnesses other than ***reasonable*** reimbursements for ***expenses and loss of time***. Under no circumstances may the lawyer agree to pay even an expert witness a fee contingent upon the content of the testimony and/or outcome of the case.

c. "Coaching" Witnesses

While the lawyer may prepare the witness for giving testimony, he may not improperly influence the witness to give certain testimony.

d. Treatment of Adverse Witnesses at Trial

A lawyer may not use cross-examination simply to degrade or harass a witness. It is also ***improper*** for a lawyer to express her ***personal opinion*** as to a witness's credibility.

e. Receipt of Inadvertently Sent Document

Upon receiving a document containing privileged or sensitive information, mistakenly sent by opposing counsel, the receiving lawyer must promptly ***notify the sender***. The burden then is on the sender if he hopes to obtain a judicial order declaring that the item must be returned, remains privileged, etc.

2. Strategy and Tactics in Trial

Procedural and evidentiary rules are means to insure that proceedings are conducted in the interests of justice. Professional standards impose limits on a lawyer's tactics.

a. Reference to Matters Unsubstantiated by Evidence

In court appearances, a lawyer must not state or allude to any matter that he has no reasonable basis for believing is or will be supported by admissible evidence.

b. Personal Knowledge or Opinion of Lawyer

The lawyer is ***prohibited*** from asserting ***personal knowledge*** of the facts in issue or a ***personal opinion*** on the justness of a claim, credibility of a witness, culpability of a civil litigant, or the guilt or innocence of the accused.

c. Appeals to Emotion or Prejudice

A lawyer may not arouse the emotions or prejudices of jurors as to matters that are not supported by admissible evidence.

d. Violation of Rules of Evidence or Procedure

A lawyer must not knowingly violate a rule of procedure or evidence, but a lawyer may, within the framework of the law, test the validity of an order or rule. Intentional violations may subject a lawyer to ***sanctions***, including contempt of court and ***professional discipline***.

3. Requirement of Dignity in Adversary Proceedings

The lawyer has an obligation of courtesy and proper behavior toward ***all*** persons involved in the legal process (including opposing counsel and the court).

4. Settlement Restricting Lawyer's Right to Practice

Settlement agreements that restrict a lawyer's future practice (*e.g.,* an agreement to refrain from filing similar cases) are expressly prohibited.

D. LIMITATIONS ON TRIAL PUBLICITY

1. General Rule

A lawyer may not make an out-of-court statement likely to be reported by the media if he reasonably should know that the statement would have a ***substantial likelihood of materially prejudicing an adjudicative proceeding***.

2. Criminal Proceedings

a. Information that May Be Disclosed

A lawyer associated with the investigation of a criminal matter is forbidden to make any out-of-court statement that does more than state:

(i) the ***crime*** being investigated;

(ii) that an ***investigation is in process***;

(iii) a request for ***assistance*** in apprehending a suspect or other assistance;

(iv) a ***warning*** of danger to the public;

(v) the ***identity*** of the accused;

(vi) ***information about an arrest***, if any; and

(vii) any information in a ***public record***.

b. Matters that Should Not Be Disclosed

The rules expressly prohibit disclosure of: (i) ***prior arrest record*** of the accused; (ii) a ***confession*** or the ***possibility of a guilty plea***; (iii) ***test results*** or a ***refusal to submit*** to tests; (iv) any ***opinion as to the guilt*** of the accused; and (v) information that would be ***inadmissible at trial***.

c. Special Duty of Prosecutors

In addition to the above rules, prosecutors must not make extrajudicial statements that have a ***substantial likelihood of heightening public condemnation*** of the accused.

d. Defense Lawyers

A defense lawyer may make statements reasonably believed necessary to protect a client from the substantial prejudicial effect of recent publicity not initiated by the lawyer or her client, *e.g.*, leaks from police officers.

e. Proceedings Subject to Limitations

The public statement rules applicable to criminal proceedings also apply to ***professional disciplinary*** and juvenile proceedings.

3. Civil and Administrative Proceedings

Most of the above pretrial limitations also apply to civil litigation. However, the number of civil cases in which publicity causes "material prejudice" is probably much less than in criminal cases and some courts have found constitutional limits on the right to regulate lawyer speech about civil cases.

E. LIMITATIONS ON ADVANCING MONEY TO CLIENT

In general, a lawyer may not pay any of a client's personal expenses, even those caused by the client's poverty or inability to work. The ***Model Rules***, however, do allow the payment of litigation expenses, repayment of which are ***contingent*** on the outcome of the case or ***waived for indigent clients***.

F. LAWYER AS WITNESS AND ADVOCATE

An advocate-witness is forced to argue her own credibility, is more easily impeached, and may therefore be less effective both as counsel and witness. Thus, the general rule is that a lawyer may ***neither accept nor continue employment*** if she knows or it is obvious that she may be called as a witness during the proceedings.

1. Exceptions to General Rule

The lawyer ***may*** appear as a witness and continue to serve as advocate where:

a. Testimony is on an ***uncontested matter;***

b. Testimony is on the ***nature and value of legal services;* or**

c. Testimony is necessary to ***prevent substantial hardship to the client.***

2. Lawyer Called as Witness by Opposing Party

A lawyer called as a witness other than on behalf of the client may not continue representation if the testimony might conflict with the client's case, unless the client gives his informed consent.

3. Representation by Another Lawyer in Witness-Lawyer's Firm

The Model Rules provide that disqualification is ***not imputed*** to other lawyers in the witness-lawyer's firm. Unless the firm itself would have a conflict of interest in doing so, another lawyer in the witness-lawyer's firm may act as advocate in the case.

G. IMPROPER CONTACTS WITH COURT OFFICIALS AND JURORS

1. No Gifts or Loans to Court Personnel

A lawyer should never make a gift or a loan to a judge, hearing officer, or other employee of a tribunal unless permitted by law (*e.g.,* there is a personal or family relationship). Lawyers ***may*** contribute ***campaign funds*** to candidates for judicial office.

2. Communication with Judge or Hearing Officer

In an adversary proceeding, the lawyer may communicate with a judge regarding the ***merits of the case*** only in the course of the proceedings. The limited exceptions to this rule require that ***copies of written communications*** and ***prior notice of proposed oral communications*** be given to opposing counsel.

3. Contacts with Jurors

A lawyer owes a duty to the legal system to avoid improper contact with jurors.

a. Communications Before Trial

Lawyers ***must not communicate*** with persons known to be members of the panel for the case.

b. Contacts During Trial

Only "official" communications (*e.g.,* voir dire) are permitted.

c. Communications After Trial

These are proper to: (i) determine a basis for ***challenging the jury verdict***; or (ii) to ***improve advocacy skills*** (becoming informed of factors that led to the verdict). But a lawyer may not ***harass or embarrass*** the jurors or try to influence their conduct in future jury service.

d. Communications with Members of Juror's Family

The same restraint on communications with jurors and prospective jurors applies to contacts with jurors' family members.

H. SPECIAL DUTIES OF PROSECUTORS AND OTHER GOVERNMENT LAWYERS

The "client" of government lawyers is the state. A prosecutor's duty is to ***seek justice*** rather than solely to convict.

1. Special Limitations on Prosecutorial Function

The prosecutor must: (i) use ***restraint*** in the exercise of governmental power (*e.g.,* charges filed must be supported by ***probable cause***; no urging an unrepresented accused to ***waive important pretrial rights***); (ii) help the accused ***retain counsel***; and (iii) perform the ***dual role*** of advocate and representative of the broad public interest at trial.

2. Duties Respecting Witnesses and Evidence

The prosecutor must make timely disclosure to the defense of any available evidence known to the prosecutor that may negate guilt, mitigate the degree of the offense, or reduce the appropriate punishment. Other duties include the obligation to pursue ***evidence harmful*** to the government's case and to allow defense counsel ***access*** to government witnesses.

3. Defense Records

Prosecutors are normally ***prohibited*** from ***subpoenaing defense records*** (or calling defense lawyers before a grand jury) unless the information is not privileged and is essential to the investigation or prosecution, and there is no other feasible way to obtain the information.

4. Duty to Correct Prior Injustice

A prosecutor who learns of "new, credible and material evidence creating a reasonable likelihood that a convicted defendant did not commit" the offense for which he was convicted must (i) promptly disclose the evidence to an appropriate court or prosecutor, and (ii) if the conviction was in the prosecutor's jurisdiction, promptly notify the defendant and investigate whether the defendant was wrongly convicted. If there is clear and convincing evidence of a wrongful conviction, the prosecutor must seek to "remedy the conviction."

I. ADVOCATE IN A NONADJUDICATIVE PROCEEDING

1. Duty to Disclose Representative Capacity

Even if a lawyer personally agrees with her client's position on an issue, when acting as a retained lawyer on behalf of a client, the lawyer must disclose that she appears in a representative capacity.

2. Substantive Rules that Regulate the Lawyer's Behavior

In her work before a legislature or in any other non-adjudicative role, the advocate must obey the requirements for honesty and candor, non-obstruction of access to evidence and the same prohibitions of improper influence that apply in litigation.

VIII. THE BUSINESS OF PRACTICING LAW

A. ASSOCIATIONS OF LAWYERS FOR THE PRACTICE OF LAW

1. Law Firm

a. Roles in a Traditional Law Firm

(1) Partners

Partners are the principals in a traditional firm.

(2) Associates

Normally, associates perform legal services as salaried employees of the firm.

(3) "Of counsel"

This signifies a lawyer's continuing relationship with a firm other than as partner or associate.

(4) Paralegals

These are nonlawyer legal assistants. For purposes of the Model Rules, the term paralegal describes all non-lawyer employees in the firm.

b. Practice Through Professional Law Corporations

In most states, lawyers may form a corporation or limited liability company to carry on the practice of law. Principals in such organizations are typically protected from personal liability for the malpractice of others in the firm. Such organizations are treated as firms in the Model Rules.

c. **Supervisory Relationships**

Under the Model Rules, partners and other principals in a firm must make reasonable efforts to assure that all lawyers in the firm conform to ethical standards.

(1) **Responsibility for Another Lawyer's Conduct**

A lawyer is personally responsible for another lawyer's ethical violation if the lawyer ***ordered***, or with knowledge, ***ratified*** the conduct, or if she is a ***partner*** in the firm or a ***direct supervisor*** of the other and ***failed*** to take reasonable ***remedial action***.

d. **Subordinate Lawyers**

The Model Rules specifically require all lawyers in a firm to obey the Rules, even when directed to act contrary to the standards by a supervisor. But a subordinate lawyer may comply with a supervising lawyer's "reasonable resolution of an arguable question of professional duty."

e. **Name of Firm or Corporation**

Under the Model Rules, trade names are now allowed if they are ***not misleading*** and do ***not imply connection with a government agency*** or legal services organization. The firm name may contain the names of deceased or retired members, but the name of a lawyer who has left the firm for public service for a substantial period must be removed.

f. **Association with Nonlawyers in Practice**

(1) **Partnerships with Nonlawyers Prohibited**

A lawyer ***may not*** become a partner of a nonlawyer if ***any*** of the partnership activities includes the ***practice of law***.

(a) **Partnerships Not Involving the Practice of Law**

These are permissible if confined ***solely to nonlegal*** activities.

(b) **Law Corporations**

All officers, directors, and shareholders must be licensed to practice law.

(2) **Sharing Fees with Nonlawyer Prohibited**

Both the ABA Code and Model Rules prohibit the sharing of legal fees with a nonlawyer, subject to the following exceptions:

(a) **Permissible Fee Sharing**

Fee income may be used to: (i) employ nonlawyers on a flat salary basis; (ii) fund profit-sharing and retirement plans; (iii) make payments to the estate of a deceased lawyer; and (iv) share court-awarded fees with a nonprofit organization that hired or recommended the lawyer.

g. **Noncompetition Agreements**

Agreements restricting the right of a lawyer to practice after termination of a relationship are ***prohibited*** (except as a condition for payment of retirement benefits). Thus, a firm's employment agreement may not provide that the lawyer will not practice in competition with the firm for a period of time after leaving the firm.

h. Law-Related Services

A lawyer is subject to the Model Rules while providing law-related services (*e.g.*, financial planning, lobbying) if the services are rendered as part of the provision of legal services. The Rules are also applicable even if the lawyer is not providing legal services, unless the client has been informed and advised that certain protections (*e.g.*, attorney-client privilege) do not apply.

2. Group and Prepaid Legal Services Plans

The organized bar traditionally opposed such plans, but the Supreme Court has held that the right to furnish such services is constitutionally protected. Participation in such plans is now permissible (with some limitations imposed by the ABA Model Rules).

B. REGULATION OF THE MANNER OF LAWYERS SEEKING EMPLOYMENT—SOLICITATION AND ADVERTISING

1. Traditional Position of Organized Bar

The organized bar traditionally did not permit a lawyer to publicize his or her services. However, this position was criticized and eventually held unconstitutional.

2. Lawyer Advertising and Publicity—Current Status of the Law

a. Relaxation of Traditional Standards—*Bates v. State Bar of Arizona*

The Supreme Court held that ***truthful advertising*** by lawyers is protected by the First Amendment but that ***reasonable time, place, and manner restrictions*** were acceptable, and false or misleading advertising is subject to restraint.

b. ABA Reactions to *Bates*

The Model Rules ***prohibit only false and misleading advertising*** and permit advertising through any public medium or written communication that does not involve in-person solicitation.

c. Additional Limits on State Regulation

The Supreme Court has upheld the Model Rules ban on false and misleading advertising and protected the use of accurate illustrations as well as text in lawyer advertising.

d. Went for It case

The Court, however, in a split decision, ***upheld state limits*** on lawyer advertising in the *Went For It* case by letting stand a state law barring direct mail advertising within 30 days of an accident or disaster. The regulation was valid based, in part, on a state's substantial interest in protecting the "flagging reputation" of the legal profession.

3. Solicitation

Solicitation is ***direct contact*** with a potential client that is not protected as advertising.

a. Model Rules

The Model Rules prohibit in-person or live telephone, or real-time electronic contact with strangers where a ***significant motive*** is the ***lawyer's personal gain***. The Model Rules also forbid contact if a person has informed the lawyer that he does ***not desire to be solicited*** or if the solicitation involves duress, and the Rules require that written materials or recorded messages directed at persons known to be in need of services be ***labeled "Advertising Material."***

b. Constitutionality

The Supreme Court has upheld regulation of in-person solicitation, at least where a fee will be charged and deception or improper influence is involved.

c. Exceptions to General Prohibition on Solicitation

There are certain situations where contact otherwise prohibited as solicitation is allowed:

(1) Advice to close friend, relative, or present or former client;

(2) Contact with another lawyer;

(3) Request for referrals from lawyer referral service or legal aid organization;

(4) Free services offered to persons in need; and

(5) Certain class action situations.

C. SPECIALIZATION AND LIMITATION OF PRACTICE

1. Introduction

Present rules tend to limit dissemination of specialization information to prospective clients.

2. Exceptions

Patent lawyers, ***certified specialists***, and ***admiralty*** lawyers may designate their specialization areas. Certification must be by an appropriate authority. These consist of ***state certification agencies*** and, pursuant to a Supreme Court ruling, certification by a ***private organization*** if the lawyer's claim is both ***verifiable and true***. The Model Rules provide that the certifying organization must be identified and have been approved by the state or ABA.

3. Limitation of Practice

The Model Rules also let a lawyer "limit practice" to particular subjects, which is said to carry no implication of special skill. Such designations are subject to the requirement that they not be false or misleading.

D. DIVISION OF FEES WITH LAWYERS OUTSIDE ONE'S FIRM

1. Referral Fees

The Model Rules prohibit referral fees unless they are expressed in terms of fee sharing among lawyers with joint responsibility.

2. Joint Responsibility

Lawyers assuming ***joint responsibility*** may share the fee in whatever proportions to which they agree, as long as the total fee is ***reasonable*** and the client ***agrees in writing*** to the share each lawyer will receive.

3. Distinguish—Reciprocal Referral Arrangements

Referrals between lawyers (and between a lawyer and a nonlawyer) are permitted if the arrangement is ***not exclusive*** and clients are informed of the ***existence and nature*** of the arrangement.

4. Fee Sharing with Former Partners and Associates

This is permitted, but only pursuant to a separation or retirement agreement.

5. Purchase of Lawyer's Practice

Sales of "***goodwill***" were once prohibited, but the Model Rules permit them if: (i) the selling lawyer ***ceases practice*** in the jurisdiction in the subject matter area or areas being sold; (ii) the practice is ***sold in its entirety or the entire subject matter area is sold***; (iii) ***written notice*** is given to each client; and (iv) ***fees are not increased*** as a result of the sale.

IX. THE SPECIAL RESPONSIBILITIES OF JUDGES

A. INTRODUCTION

The ABA Model Code of Judicial Conduct ("CJC"), as amended in 2007, establishes the special rules pertaining to state judges and becomes legally binding on judges as it is adopted by individual states. It does not apply to third-party neutrals. The content of the CJC is tested on the Multistate Professional Responsibility Examination.

B. GENERAL NORMS

1. Maintain High Standards of Conduct

A judge must establish, maintain, enforce and observe high standards of personal conduct.

2. Promote Public Confidence in Judiciary

Judges must ***obey the law*** and behave in a manner promoting public confidence in the ***integrity and impartiality*** of the judiciary.

3. Avoid Using Influence or Being Influenced

A judge must not let anyone influence judicial conduct; she may not advance others' interests in her judicial capacity, nor may she be a ***character witness unless subpoenaed***.

4. Avoid Memberships in Discriminatory Organizations

Judges are barred from membership in organizations that invidiously discriminate on the basis of race, sex, religion, or national origin. Upon learning of discrimination, a judge must ***promptly resign*** or endeavor to ***end the discriminatory practice***. On the other hand, a judge may belong to a ***completely private*** organization whose membership limitations cannot be constitutionally prohibited ***or*** to one that is "***dedicated to the preservation of religious, ethnic, or cultural values***."

C. JUDGE'S OFFICIAL ACTIONS

1. Priority of Judicial Duties

Judges should put judicial duties ahead of other activities.

2. Behavior on the Bench

A judge must be ***faithful to the law, remain competent***, and be ***unswayed*** by outside pressures.

a. In General

A judge must hear all cases assigned (unless disqualified), give every person with a legal interest in a proceeding the right to be heard, maintain order in the court, and be courteous to others.

b. Bias or Prejudice

A judge must not exhibit bias or prejudice on the basis of race, sex, gender, religion, national origin, ethnicity, disability, age, sexual orientation, marital status, socioeconomic status, or political affiliation. Further, the judge must require her staff and lawyers appearing before the court not to manifest such bias.

3. *Ex Parte* Contacts

Ex parte contacts, except where they deal with scheduling matters, emergencies, settlement discussions, or are otherwise authorized by law, are generally prohibited. If a judge requests proposed findings of fact and conclusions of law from one party, he must permit other parties to respond. However, a judge ***may consult with disinterested legal experts***, if he advises the parties thereof, and he may discuss a case with his law clerks and fellow judges.

4. Independent Investigation of Facts

A judge ***must not*** independently investigate facts of a case and must consider only the evidence presented.

5. Disposition of Matters

Matters must be handled promptly, efficiently, and fairly.

6. Comments About Jurors

Except in an order or opinion, a judge ***may not commend or criticize*** jurors for their verdict.

7. Relations with News Media

Judges, and other court personnel, ***may not comment*** to the media about pending or impending matters.

8. Nonpublic Information

Nonpublic information learned in a judicial capacity ***may not be disclosed***.

9. Administrative Duties

A judge must discharge administrative duties ***diligently, competently, cooperatively, and without discrimination***. This includes reporting lawyer misconduct and making no unnecessary appointments.

10. Disciplinary Duties

A judge must take or initiate appropriate action against a judge or lawyer upon receiving information indicating a "substantial likelihood" of misconduct. The judge is ***absolutely privileged against retaliation*** by the accused lawyer or judge.

D. JUDICIAL DISQUALIFICATION

1. Bases for Disqualification

A judge is disqualified when her ***impartiality*** might reasonably be questioned. Bases of disqualification include:

a. The judge's ***personal bias*** concerning a party that comes from an extrajudicial source;

b. The judge's ***knowledge of disputed evidentiary facts***;

c. The judge's ***prior involvement*** in the matter;

d. The ***financial interest*** of judge (or judge's spouse, parent, child, or any family member residing in the judge's household) in a party or in the subject matter of litigation, although the following are usually ***not*** disqualifying interests: mutual fund ownership, office in an educational, charitable, fraternal, or civic organization, interest as a policyholder in an insurance company or depositor in a bank, or ownership of government securities;

e. The judge's ***relative's involvement in the case*** (as a likely witness, a party, an officer or director of a party, or a lawyer) or when a relative has an interest that could be substantially affected; and

f. ***Contributions from a party or a party's lawyer*** to the judge's election campaign if the contributions were made within a designated number of years and exceed the jurisdiction's specified amount.

2. Disclosure by Judge

Even if a judge believes there is no reasonable ground for disqualification, she should disclose, on the record, information that she believes the parties or their lawyers might consider relevant to the issue of impartiality.

3. Remittal of Disqualification

If a judge is disqualified for any reason "***other than personal bias or prejudice*** concerning a party," the parties and their lawyers may ***waive*** the disqualification if ***all*** agree that the interest has an insubstantial effect and ***each*** person then indicates in writing a waiver of the disqualification.

4. Rule of Necessity

The rule of necessity, created by case law, ***overrides disqualification rules***. It applies when a judge would otherwise be disqualified on a conflict of interest basis, but there is no other way for the case to be heard (e.g., challenge to judicial salaries; no judge would be unaffected by the decision).

E. EXTRAJUDICIAL ACTIVITIES OF THE JUDGE

1. In General

A judge's extrajudicial activities ***must not***: (i) cast doubt on the judge's impartiality, (ii) demean the judicial office, or (iii) interfere with proper performance of judicial duties.

2. Speak, Write, Lecture, and Teach

These are proper activities for a judge. Teaching may be about both legal and nonlegal subjects.

3. Consult with Legislators and Executive Officials

A judge may do so only on subjects of the law, the legal system, or administration of justice.

4. Serve on Government Commissions

Such service is ***limited*** to the ***law, legal system, or administration of justice,*** but a judge may serve as an official representative at certain ceremonial occasions.

5. Officer of Organizations

A judge ***may*** be a member, officer, trustee, director, or nonlegal advisor to ***nonprofit*** agencies or educational, religious, charitable, fraternal, or civic groups. But service on the board of a public educational institution other than a law school is prohibited, while service on the board of a private educational institution is generally permitted.

a. Restrictions

A judge ***may not serve*** as an officer of an organization that ***frequently litigates*** in her court, nor may she personally ***raise money*** for organizations, although she may participate in investment decisions.

F. MONEY-MAKING ACTIVITIES OF THE JUDGE

1. In General

Financial activities of a judge must not affect her impartiality, interfere with judicial duties, exploit the office, or involve her with persons likely to come before the court.

2. Investments

Subject to the above qualifications, a judge ***may*** hold and manage investments, including real estate.

3. Participation in a Business

A judge ***may not*** be an officer, director, manager, advisor, or employee of any business (***except*** a closely-held family business or investment trust).

4. Gifts, Bequests, Favors, or Loans

A judge and family members residing in his household must be careful about accepting gifts, etc. The CJC enumerates the types of gifts a judge may accept.

5. Fiduciary Activities

A judge ***may not*** serve as a fiduciary (*e.g.*, executor, guardian) ***except for family members***, and even this is forbidden if the matter is likely to proceed in the judge's court or under its appellate jurisdiction.

6. Arbitrator or Mediator

Unless sanctioned by law, a judge ***may not*** serve as an arbitrator or mediator.

7. Practice Law

A judge ***may not*** practice law (but he may give uncompensated legal advice to family members without compensation).

8. Receiving and Reporting Compensation

All judges ***must report*** compensation and reimbursement of expenses as required by law, and compensation must be ***reasonable*** in amount. The CJC requires at least an annual public reporting. Other disclosures of assets need only be made as required by law or specific provisions of the CJC.

G. INVOLVEMENT OF JUDGES AND JUDICIAL CANDIDATES IN POLITICAL ACTIVITIES

1. General Principles Applicable to Judges and Judicial Candidates

Subject to a few exceptions, the following rules apply to judges and also to lawyers running for judicial offices:

a. ***No office in political organizations;***

b. ***No endorsements of political candidates;***

c. ***No speeches for political organizations;***

d. ***No political fund-raising;***

e. ***No running for nonjudicial office*** (a judge must resign if runs);

f. ***No other political activity***—An incumbent judge (but not a judicial candidate) must avoid all other political activity ***except*** those (i) designed to improve the law, the legal system, or the administration of justice; (ii) specifically authorized by law; or (iii) otherwise permitted under the CJC; and

g. ***No misrepresentations or specific campaign promises.***

2. Judicial Candidates Subject to Public Election

a. All Judicial Candidates Subject to Public Election

All such candidates (or a judge subject to election for a nonjudicial position) ***may buy tickets*** for political functions, ***attend*** political events, ***identify*** their political party, and ***contribute*** to a political organization.

b. Judicial Candidates Running for Public Election

When actually running for public election, a judge or candidate ***may*** also ***speak to gatherings*** on her own behalf, appear in ***media advertising*** and distribute her ***promotional literature*** supporting her candidacy, and ***publicly endorse or oppose candidates*** for the same office.

c. Solicitation of Campaign Contributions

Candidates ***may not personally*** solicit campaign contributions. Properly constituted committees may solicit contributions during a period one year before and up to 90 days *after* the election.

3. Candidates Seeking Appointment to Judicial Office

a. No Personal Solicitation of Funds

A person seeking appointment to judicial office ***may not solicit*** or accept funds—even through a committee.

b. Other Political Activity

Political activity to secure appointment is barred, except: (i) ***communicating with the nominating authority***; (ii) ***seeking endorsements from organizations*** that regularly make recommendations for such appointments; (iii) ***providing information*** about qualifications to the appointing authority; and (iv) if the person is ***not currently a judge***, he may continue to be active and ***hold office*** in his political party.

c. Judge Seeking Other Government Office

The ***same rules*** apply to an incumbent judge who is seeking another government office.

4. Sanctions for Violations

A ***successful*** judicial candidate who violates the political activity rules is subject to ***judicial discipline***. An ***unsuccessful lawyer*** candidate who violates the rules is subject to ***lawyer disciplinary rules***.

H. STANDARDS APPLICABLE TO FEDERAL JUDGES

1. No Practice of Law

Federal statute defines a federal judge or justice who engages in the practice of law as guilty of a "high misdemeanor."

2. Circumstances in Which Disqualification Required

Most of the disqualification standards for federal judges are ***substantially the same*** as rules under the CJC (*e.g.*, personal bias, financial interest in the matter). However, a few rules are different or are stated differently:

a. A federal judge must recuse himself upon a ***litigant's filing*** of a "timely and sufficient affidavit" asserting ***personal bias or prejudice***.

b. A federal judge, including a Supreme Court justice, must recuse herself whenever her "***impartiality*** might reasonably be questioned."

c. Disqualification is required whenever a federal judge ***participated***, as counsel, adviser, or witness, in the case ***or expressed an opinion*** concerning the merits of the case; and

d. If a ***disqualifying financial interest*** is discovered only after a judge has spent substantial time on a case, he may ***avoid disqualification by disposing*** of the interest.

3. Discipline of Federal Judges

Federal judges are appointed for life but can be removed from office through impeachment by the House of Representatives and conviction by the Senate. Also, the judicial council of each circuit may impose less severe discipline on federal judges.

Approach to Exams

A. INTRODUCTION

Legal Ethics concerns the law governing legal practice. To protect the public and maintain the integrity of the legal profession, rules have been established to prohibit the unauthorized practice of law, set standards for admission to the practice of law, and regulate the conduct of lawyers after admission. Most states have adopted some version of the American Bar Association ("ABA") Model Rules of Professional Conduct. Thus, the ABA Model Rules form an ***indirect*** basis for regulation of much of the legal profession, and they are the subject of the Multistate Professional Responsibility Exam ("MPRE").

B. APPROACH

In analyzing Legal Ethics problems, begin by asking whether the question relates to the lawyer's responsibilities to a client, a person with whom the lawyer deals on the client's behalf, the court, or others. Then consider what duties the lawyer owes to the other person and whether the lawyer violated the rules detailing those duties. This will help you to determine whether the lawyer may be subject to discipline and to identify the remedies.

C. LAWYER'S DUTIES TO CLIENTS—IN GENERAL

A lawyer must protect a ***prospective*** client's confidential information and property and must use reasonable care in giving the person any legal advice. ***After termination*** of the lawyer-client relationship, the lawyer still must not reveal confidential information of the former client or represent interests that conflict with the former client's interests in a substantially related matter. Moreover, a lawyer owes these additional duties to ***current*** clients:

1. Competence

A lawyer must act with the knowledge, skill, thoroughness, and preparation reasonably necessary for the representation.

2. Diligence

A lawyer should pursue a matter on the client's behalf with zeal and promptness.

3. Communication

A lawyer must explain the matter to the client and keep the client informed.

4. Confidentiality

A lawyer must not reveal client information.

5. Loyalty

A lawyer must avoid conflicts of interest.

6. Protection of Client Property

A lawyer must safeguard the client's money and property and keep them entirely separate from the lawyer's assets.

D. DUTY TO PROTECT CLIENT'S CONFIDENTIAL INFORMATION

The three most important doctrines that govern a lawyer's dealing with confidential information are the attorney-client privilege, the work product doctrine and the duty of confidentiality.

1. Attorney-Client Privilege

The attorney-client privilege is the narrowest of the two doctrines. It is a rule of evidence that prevents a court from compelling the revelation of confidential communications between a lawyer and a client that were made in order to give or obtain legal advice or assistance.

2. The Work Product Doctrine

Work product is a discovery doctrine that says materials collected or prepared in anticipation of litigation need not be turned over to the other side unless the other side cannot obtain them otherwise. The material need not have been revealed by the client. Opinion work product that reveals the thought process of the lawyer is unlikely to meet the standard for disclosure; ordinary work product is more likely to do so.

3. Duty of Confidentiality

The duty of confidentiality prohibits a lawyer from disclosing any information related to the representation of a client, a prospective client, or a former client. It also prohibits a lawyer from using this information to the disadvantage of the client. This concept covers virtually everything the lawyer knows about the case, even if it is known to others as well.

E. DUTY OF UNIMPAIRED LOYALTY—CONFLICT OF INTEREST

A lawyer must not represent a client if there is an ***actual or potential*** conflict of interest, unless the client gives informed consent. The four major conflicts are:

1. Conflicts between the lawyer's ***personal interest*** and the interest of the client;
2. Conflicts between the interests of ***two or more clients*** that the lawyer is concurrently representing;
3. Conflicts between the client's interest and that of a ***third party***; and
4. Conflicts between the lawyer's duties to a present client and the lawyer's continuing duties to a ***former client***.

F. DUTIES TO THIRD PERSONS

A lawyer must represent the client zealously, but the law imposes important limitations on what a lawyer may do on the client's behalf.

1. Duty as Counselor Not to Assist Client in a Crime or Fraud

A lawyer may advise a client as to the legal consequences of the client's intended conduct and may assist a client to commit an act that will, in good faith, test the validity, scope, meaning, or application of the law. However, a lawyer must not counsel or assist a client to engage in conduct that the lawyer knows is illegal or fraudulent.

2. Duty of Honesty

The lawyer must be honest with others and sometimes must also affirmatively disclose matters to the court or the other party.

3. Duty to Communicate with Another Person's Lawyer

A lawyer must not communicate about the subject of a controversy with a person the lawyer knows is represented by counsel, unless that person's counsel consents or the communication is authorized by law.

G. DUTIES OF LAWYERS IN LITIGATION

A lawyer must not abuse the litigation process, and thus:

1. A lawyer has a duty not to bring ***frivolous claims***.

2. A lawyer has a duty to ***expedite litigation***.

3. A lawyer has a duty of ***candor to the tribunal*** and must ***disclose directly adverse legal authority from the controlling jurisdiction***.

4. A lawyer has a duty to ***deal with the opposing party and counsel with integrity***.

5. A lawyer has a duty to ***preserve the impartiality and decorum of the tribunal***.

6. A lawyer must ***restrict out-of-court comments about a case*** that are likely to be widely disseminated.

7. A lawyer ***may not give or lend money*** to the client except for litigation expenses.

8. A lawyer ordinarily ***must not act as both an advocate and a witness***.

9. A lawyer ***must not make gifts or loans to court personnel***, ***contact the judge*** without notice to the other party, or ***contact jurors*** during the trial.

10. A ***public prosecutor or government attorney*** has a duty, beyond those above, to ***seek justice*** in the proceeding, not just to represent the state or government.

H. DUTIES RELATED TO THE PRACTICE OF LAW

1. Duties of Partners and Supervisory Lawyers

Partners and supervisory lawyers must make reasonable efforts to ensure that other lawyers in their organization adhere to the Model Rules.

2. Duties of Subordinate Lawyers

A subordinate lawyer will be subject to discipline if he carries out a supervisory lawyer's order that is a clear ethics violation.

3. Duties Regarding Nonlawyers

Partnerships between lawyers and nonlawyers are prohibited if any of the partnership activities include the practice of law. When a lawyer employs nonlawyer assistants, the lawyer must instruct the nonlawyers about legal ethics and should ensure that they act in conformity with professional standards.

4. Advertising and Solicitation

As a general rule, advertising is permitted as long as it is not false or misleading. On the other hand, solicitation (*i.e.*, direct contact with a potential client for the lawyer's personal gain) is generally not allowed unless the potential client is a close friend, a relative, a current or former client, or another lawyer.

5. Specialization

A lawyer may not identify herself as a specialist unless she is a patent or admiralty lawyer or a certified specialist.

6. Fee Sharing

When two or more lawyers from different firms work together on a case, they may split the fee if the total fee is reasonable, the lawyers assume joint responsibility, and the client agrees to the split in writing. Sharing fees with a nonlawyer is prohibited unless shared on a flat salary basis, in a retirement or profit-sharing plan, as payments to the estate of a deceased lawyer, or as court-awarded fees shared with the nonprofit organization that hired or recommended the lawyer as counsel in the matter.

I. REMEDIES

The remedies for lawyer misconduct are:

1. Professional Discipline by the State

A lawyer may be subject to disbarment, suspension, reprimand, or admonition for a violation of professional ethics.

2. Malpractice Liability

A lawyer may have to pay damages for harm to a client due to negligence, intentional tort, breach of contract, or breach of fiduciary duty.

3. Other Sanctions

A lawyer may be punished for failure to adhere to proper standards of conduct through contempt sanctions, disqualification, exclusion of evidence, or other remedies short of traditional professional discipline.

J. JUDICIAL ETHICS

1. Code of Judicial Ethics

The ABA's Code of Judicial Conduct ("CJC") serves as a model for the ethical conduct of judges. As with the Model Rules, the content of the CJC is tested on the MPRE. The CJC is intended to ensure the ***integrity and independence*** of the judiciary. Its standards apply to a judge's official actions, unofficial and money-making activities, and political activities.

2. Judge's Official Actions

Judicial duties should take precedence over all of a judge's other activities. A judge must maintain competence, be faithful to the law, and be unswayed by outside influences. If the judge's impartiality might reasonably be questioned, she must recuse herself.

3. Judge's Extrajudicial Activities

A judge's extrajudicial activities may not cast doubt on her impartiality, demean the judicial office, or interfere with her official duties.

4. Judges and Politics

Generally, a judge must avoid involvement in politics. However, a judge may participate if the political activities are specifically authorized by law or permitted by the CJC.

5. Federal Judges

Federal judges are subject to rules that are similar, but not identical, to those for state judges. Federal judges hold office for life, during good behavior, but can be removed by impeachment. Also, the judicial council of each circuit may discipline federal judges in less severe ways (*e.g.*, by admonishment).

Legal Ethics

Ninth Edition

Chapter One

Regulating the Right to Practice Law

Chapter One

CONTENTS	PAGE

Chapter Approach

Welcome to the study of a regulated industry. Lawyers act on behalf of clients who need help but who often are not in a position to know whether they have been well or badly represented. Thus, the practice of law is a classic subject for regulation. "Legal Ethics," "Professional Responsibility," and "Law Governing Lawyers" are all names given to these regulations. States determine who may become licensed to practice law in the state; they prohibit "unauthorized" practice by those not licensed; and they prescribe the conduct required of lawyers in the course of their practice.

As you look at the material in this chapter, think about the following issues:

1. ***What does it mean to "practice law,"*** *i.e.,* to engage in the activity that is reserved to lawyers?
2. What standards determine a person's eligibility for ***admission to the bar,*** i.e., the right to practice law?
3. What are the sources of the ***standards that govern a lawyer's conduct*** in the practice of law?
4. How are the standards governing lawyer conduct enforced?

The sources of most of the principles in this chapter are Restatement §§ 1–13 & 48–58 and Model Rules 5.5 and 8.1–8.5.

A. Reserving the Practice of Law to Lawyers

1. Basic Principles

a. Lay Persons May Represent Themselves

A lay person is not required to seek legal assistance and may appear in court "pro se." [Restatement § 4, comment d] The lay person may be said to be exposing only him- or herself to possible injury.

b. But Only Lawyers May Represent Persons Other than Themselves

What a lawyer has that a non-lawyer does not is the privilege of "practicing law" on behalf of others. This privilege is said to be based upon the two attributes for which persons admitted to the legal profession are examined: (i) ***competence*** and (ii) ***integrity.*** [Restatement § 1; **Lawline v. American Bar Association,** 956 F.2d 1378 (7th Cir. 1992)]

2. Activities That Constitute the "Practice of Law"

a. Tests Applied—In General

The definition of the term "practice of law" varies among jurisdictions. The courts have had to attach meaning to the term in specific situations. [Restatement § 4, comment c]. Two tests stand out.

(1) "History and Custom"

Some cases turn on whether the activity ***traditionally*** has been handled by lawyers. But that test tends to ignore changing conditions and privilege lawyer vested interests over client needs.

(2) "Need for Professional Judgment"

A better test asks whether a given activity requires a lawyer's "professional legal judgment"—*i.e.*, bringing trained ***judgment*** to bear on ***specific facts*** based on a knowledge of the general body and philosophy of law. [ABA Model Code of Professional Responsibility, Ethical Consideration 3–5]

EXAM TIP GILBERT

If you get an exam question that requires you to determine whether the practice of law is involved, ask yourself whether the activity: (i) is one ***traditionally performed by lawyers,*** (ii) involves ***legal knowledge*** beyond that which the average layperson possesses, and (iii) involves applying the law to a ***specific situation*** (as opposed to writing a book, for example).

---

b. Application of These Principles to Recurring Situations

(1) Appearance in Judicial Proceedings

Typically, in an effort to keep court proceedings running smoothly, representation of others in court proceedings has been solely the privilege of lawyers.

(a) Distinguish—Specialized Courts and Agencies

However, in an effort to make needed assistance more widely available, state and federal administrative agencies increasingly permit specially qualified laypersons to represent clients before them, and some courts are beginning to do so, *e.g.*, the Washington Limited License Legal Technician program.

(b) Prisoner Legal Assistance by Lay Prisoners

The activities of "jailhouse lawyers" to assist fellow inmates in seeking post-conviction relief are clearly the unauthorized practice of law. However, the Supreme Court has struck down state regulations designed to suppress this assistance where ***the state has not provided reasonable alternative forms of legal aid for prisoners.*** [**Wolff v. McDonnell,** 418 U.S. 539 (1974); *and see* Constitutional Law Summary]

(2) Giving Advice

Giving individualized advice about legal rights and obligations is usually regarded as the practice of law, whether or not a fee is charged for such advice.

(a) Distinguish—General Publications

On the other hand, the publication by a layperson of ***a book or pamphlet*** containing ***general*** advice and forms (*i.e.*, not directed at the needs of a particular individual) does not constitute the practice of law. [**New York County Lawyers Association v. Dacey,** 21 N.Y.2d 694 (1967)—"do-it-yourself" probate kit permissible because people have right to prepare their own documents if they choose to do so]

(3) Drafting Documents

The drafting of documents that ***affect substantial legal rights or obligations*** of others is generally considered the practice of law. Preparing a will for another person, for example, is traditionally seen as the practice of law.

(a) Distinguish—Filling in Blanks on Forms

While drafting instruments or agreements may be the practice of law, filling in blanks on standard forms is typically seen as a clerical function (for "scriveners"), and as such may be performed by laypersons. The difficult issue, of course, is defining the point at which clerical work by laypersons becomes prohibited "drafting."

(b) Computer-Assisted Drafting Programs

Today, issues frequently involve document companies such as LegalZoom.com whose computer programs take information entered directly by customers and turn it into completed legal documents that are ready to be executed. States have challenged at least the portion of that service in which the company's lay employees verify that the finished documents are printed correctly. Cases have been settled with LegalZoom agreeing to give clients the names of lawyers who could review their documents.

(4) Law Students and Law Clerks

Clerks and students not admitted to practice may perform research or administrative tasks in a law firm, but they may not perform acts that would be the practice of law, *e.g.*, advising clients or appearing in court.

(a) Distinguish—Student Training Programs

Several states have authorized law students to engage in a variety of legal activities. These often include preparation of pleadings or briefs, interviewing clients and witnesses, participation in negotiations, and appearances in court. [*See, e.g.,* Ill. Sup. Ct. R. 711] However, such activity typically must take place under the ***guidance and supervision*** of a licensed lawyer, and the lawyer must assume ***personal*** responsibility for the student's work.

(5) No Corporate Self-Representation

In most states, a corporation may not represent ***itself,*** *i.e.,* it may not appear in court through nonlawyer officers and directors. Thus, for example, a corporation must hire a lawyer to file suit to collect its bills. **[Remole Soil Service v. Benson,** 215 N.E.2d 678 (Ill. App, 1966)].

(a) Distinguish—Professional Law Corporations

The absolute prohibition of the corporate practice of law has now been significantly modified as most states' statutes expressly allow lawyers and law firms to practice as professional corporations. (*See infra*, p. 151.)

(b) Distinguish—Group Legal Services

Another important exception to the general rule allows legal clinics and similar organizations to deliver group legal services. (*See infra*, p. 156.)

3. Efforts to Prohibit Practice of Law by Nonlawyers

a. Sanctions Faced by the Nonlawyers

Sanctions against a nonlawyer who practices law include ***injunctions, criminal prosecution, or denial of the right to fees*** for the unauthorized services.

b. Obligations of Attorney in Preventing Unauthorized Practice

ABA Model Rule 5.5 requires lawyers not to aid a nonlawyer in the unauthorized practice of law. [Model Rule 5.5(a); Restatement § 4, comment f]

EXAM TIP GILBERT

Note that the above rule does not prohibit a lawyer from delegating tasks to a paralegal, law clerk, student intern, or other such person, but the lawyer must ***supervise*** the delegated work carefully and must be ***ultimately responsible*** for the results.

(1) Not Share Legal Fees with a Nonlawyer

In furtherance of this principle, a lawyer may not (with certain limited exceptions) ***share legal fees with a nonlawyer.*** [Model Rule 5.4(a); Restatement § 10; *and see infra*, pp. 152–153]

(2) Not Enter into a Partnership with a Nonlawyer

Likewise, a lawyer may not enter into a partnership with a nonlawyer if any of the partnership activities include the practice of law. [Model Rule 5.4(b); Restatement § 10; *and see infra*, p. 152]

c. Need to Expand Availability of Legal Services

However, related to the expansion of activity by nonlawyers is the increasing public demand for services historically considered to be the "practice of law." Such services may range from appearances before courts or administrative agencies to counseling on leases, contracts, and other legal instruments. The bar has been criticized for devoting more attention to unauthorized practice issues than to the need for legal help among large groups of citizens.

d. Bar Opinions on What Constitutes Unauthorized Practice

Traditionally, the bar's unauthorized practice committees have stipulated what is and is not the unauthorized practice of law, and lawyers have felt constrained to follow these decisions. Now, however, such opinions from unofficial state or local bar association may be alleged to deter competition in violation of the antitrust laws. [*Cf.* **NC State Board of Dental Examiners v. FTC,** 135 S.Ct. 1101 (2015)]

UNAUTHORIZED PRACTICE OF LAW—EXAMPLES OF WHEN PROFESSIONAL JUDGMENT REQUIRED	GILBERT
PERMISSIBLE LAY ACTIVITIES	**IMPERMISSIBLE LAY ACTIVITIES**
Real estate broker/agent filling in blanks on standard sales contract	Real estate broker/agent drafting sales contract
Tax adviser preparing tax returns	Tax adviser giving advice on tax law and resolving legal tax questions
Estate planner disseminating general information to the public on estate planning	Estate planner drafting wills or preparing estate plans for specific individuals

4. Practice in Jurisdictions Where a Lawyer Is Unlicensed

a. Introduction

Each state determines the conditions for admission to its bar. There is no constitutional duty to permit out-of-state lawyers to practice within the state, but the needs of clients and ease of transportation and communication have led to lawyers engaging in the practice of law even in jurisdictions in which they have not become licensed.

b. Admission to General Practice

Requirements for an out-of-state lawyer to be admitted to general practice within another state vary widely. [Restatement § 2]

(1) Admission by Reciprocity

A number of states admit practicing lawyers from other states without a bar exam, provided the lawyer has actively practiced in the first state for a certain period of time (usually four to six years). Most of these states limit such admission to lawyers from ***other states that allow reciprocity***, disqualifying lawyers from states that do not grant such rights. Such a limitation does not violate the Equal Protection Clause. [**Schumacher v. Nix,** 965 F.2d 1262 (3d Cir. 1992)]

(2) Separate Examination

Other states require lawyers to pass a written examination in addition to having practiced in the first state for the requisite period. [*See* Cal. Bus. & Prof. Code § 6062]

c. Unauthorized Practice of Law

A lawyer may be guilty of the unauthorized practice of law if the lawyer practices in a jurisdiction in which the lawyer is unlicensed. [Model Rule 5.5(a); Restatement § 3]

e.g. **Example:** In the case in which this principle was made most real to lawyers, a New York law firm was ***denied the right to collect its fee*** for initiating arbitration proceedings and negotiating a settlement in California at the request of its California client. [**Birbrower, Montalbano, Condon & Frank, P.C. v. Superior Court,** 17 Cal. 4th 119 (1998)]

5. Temporary Multi-Jurisdictional Practice

Many clients ask law firms to conduct such activities on a limited basis in other jurisdictions [*see* Restatement § 3, comment e] ABA Model Rule 5.5 now provides that lawyers may "provide legal services on a temporary basis" in jurisdictions in which they are not licensed under four circumstances:

a. Association with Local Lawyer

Temporary practice is allowed if the lawyer associates with "a lawyer who is admitted to practice in the jurisdiction and who actively participates in the matter." [Model Rule 5.5(c)(1)]

b. Litigated Matter

Temporary practice is also allowed if the services "are in or reasonably related to a pending or potential proceeding before a tribunal . . . if the lawyer, or a person the lawyer is assisting, is authorized by law or order to appear in such proceeding, or reasonably expects to be so authorized." [Model Rule 5.5(c)(2)]

(1) Admission Pro Hac Vice

This part of the rule simply adopts the longstanding principle that an out-of-state lawyer may obtain permission to appear in the courts of a sister state in a ***particular*** case ("pro hac vice"). While such permission is technically discretionary, most courts will allow an out-of-state lawyer to appear and litigate a particular case as a matter of reciprocity or comity with the courts of the state in which the lawyer is admitted.

(2) Inadequate Local Counsel

The discretion to limit appearances pro hac vice was sometimes used to block adequate representation in local civil rights cases, and ***where adequate local counsel is unavailable*** due to racial bias or prejudice, the courts have invalidated local rules that would exclude out-of-state lawyers from appearing in such cases. [*See, e.g.*, **Sanders v. Russell,** 401 F.2d 241 (5th Cir. 1968)]

c. Arbitration or Other Alternative Dispute Resolution Proceeding

The out-of-state lawyer may provide services if they are in the course of or reasonably related to an alternative dispute resolution proceeding that is reasonably related to the lawyer's practice in a state where he is admitted and if the forum does not require pro hac vice admission for those services. [Model Rule 5.5(c)(3)]

d. Reasonable Relation to Lawyer's Usual Practice

The lawyer may provide services that "arise out of or are reasonably related to the lawyer's practice in a jurisdiction in which the lawyer is admitted to practice." This is likely to be the most common basis for a lawyer to provide non-litigation legal services to a regular client. [Model Rule 5.5(c)(4)]

CHECKLIST FOR TEMPORARY MULTI-JURISDICTIONAL PRACTICE GILBERT
A LAWYER MAY PROVIDE LEGAL SERVICES ON A TEMPORARY BASIS IN A JURISDICTION IN WHICH THE LAWYER IS NOT ADMITTED IF:
☑ The out-of-state lawyer ***associates with*** a lawyer who is admitted to practice in the jurisdiction and who is actively participating in the matter;
☑ The out-of-state lawyer, or a person the lawyer is assisting, received or expects to receive ***special permission*** from a local court, administrative agency, or other tribunal to handle that ***particular matter*** in that tribunal ("pro hac vice");
☑ The out-of-state lawyer is engaging in ***alternative dispute resolution*** that arises out of or is reasonably related to his practice in a state in which he is admitted; or
☑ The services are ***reasonably related to the lawyer's home-state practice.***

6. Prohibition of Continuous Practice Where Unlicensed

In spite of the authority to conduct a temporary practice, a lawyer may not "establish an office or other systematic and continuous presence . . . for the practice of law" in a jurisdiction in which the lawyer is unlicensed. [Model Rule 5.5(b)(1)]

a. Prohibition of Holding out

In addition, a lawyer may not "hold out to the public or otherwise represent that the lawyer is admitted to practice" in a jurisdiction in which that is untrue. [Model Rule 5.5(b)(2)]

b. Corporate Counsel Exception

Because an in-house lawyer for a corporation, government, or other organization has a single client that can presumably assess the lawyer's competence, such lawyers usually may work permanently, even in states in which they are not licensed. [Model Rule 5.5(d)(1); Restatement § 3, comment f]

7. Admission to Practice in the Federal System

a. Separate Requirements for Admission

Admission to the bar of a state does not confer the right to practice in federal courts. Rather, ***each*** court at ***each level*** of the federal judicial system independently grants admission pursuant to its own rules.

(1) No Separate Examination

Most federal courts do not require passage of a federal bar examination in order to practice in the system. They simply require that the candidate be a member of the bar of the state in which the court sits—although a separate application for admission still must be made.

(2) Course Requirements

In response to concerns about the competency of trial lawyers, however, federal courts may require that applicants complete certain courses relevant thereto (*e.g.*, trial advocacy, professional responsibility, and federal civil and criminal procedure). [**Brown v. McGarr,** 583 F. Supp. 734 (N.D. Ill. 1984)]

(3) **May Not Require Local Office**

A federal court may not deny admission to an otherwise qualified lawyer because she does not maintain an office in the state where the court is located. [**Frazier v. Heebe,** 482 U.S. 641 (1987)]

b. Validity of State Regulation Applied to Those Engaged Exclusively in "Federal" Practice

The question has arisen whether a person who is engaged exclusively in a "federal" practice (*e.g.*, bankruptcy, antitrust) must be admitted to the bar in the state in which she practices.

(1) Where Specific Federal Regulation of Practice Exists

If federal legislation provides for admission to and regulation of a particular area of practice, federal law ***preempts*** any state regulation of that practice.

e.g. **Example:** State statutes barring "nonlawyers" from practicing law within the state cannot be applied to a nonlawyer ***patent agent*** who is admitted to practice before the United States Patent Office and who ***limits practice*** to patent law. [**Sperry v. State of Florida *ex rel.* Florida Bar,** 373 U.S. 379 (1963); *and see* Model Rule 5.5(d)(2) and Restatement § 3, comment g]

(2) Where No Federal Regulation Exists

The rule is less clear where no federal regulation specifically authorizes the practice, but there is authority for saying that states may not prevent out-of-state lawyers from practicing federal law in the jurisdiction. [***In re* Desilets,** 291 F.3d 925 (6th Cir. 2002)—bankruptcy practice]

c. Appearances Pro Hac Vice

Where an out-of-state lawyer seeks to appear in ***federal court*** on a particular matter involving federal law, the state in which the federal court is located may ***not*** deny admission pro hac vice to a lawyer ***admitted*** to and in good standing with a ***state bar,*** absent a showing of misconduct that would justify disbarment of one already admitted to practice before the court. [***In re* Admission of Lumumba,** 526 F. Supp. 163 (S.D.N.Y. 1981)—citing the Privileges and Immunities Clause of the U.S. Constitution]

8. Practice of International Law

A foreign lawyer engaged in international practice has ***no*** general right to practice in a particular U.S. jurisdiction or forum.

a. Foreign Legal Consultant Rules

However, several states (*e.g.*, New York) now specially license foreign lawyers as "legal consultants" to enable them to render advice as to the law of countries in which they are admitted to practice. [Restatement § 2, comment g; N.Y. Ct. Appeals R. 521]

b. Supreme Court Practice

The United States Supreme Court rules provide that a foreign lawyer may appear before it ***pro hac vice*** at the discretion of the Court, and if associated with an American lawyer, may be admitted to practice before the Supreme Court. [Sup. Ct. R. 6]

B. State Court Regulation of Admission to Practice Law

1. Introduction

States require that candidates for "admission to the bar," i.e., the right to practice law, meet certain standards. Each state establishes its own standards, the usual constitutional limit on which being only that the requirements imposed have some ***rational connection*** with the applicant's ***fitness or capacity*** to practice law. [Restatement § 2; **Schware v. Board of Bar Examiners,** 353 U.S. 232 (1957)]

a. U.S. Citizenship Not a Valid Requirement for Admission

A state may ***not*** constitutionally require that a person be a United States citizen in order to be admitted to practice law within the state. The fact that a person is not a citizen bears ***no rational relationship*** to the person's fitness to practice law, so there is no state interest in excluding aliens from practicing law if they meet all other admission requirements. [Restatement § 2, comment f; ***In re*** **Griffiths,** 413 U.S. 717 (1973)]

b. Residency Not a Valid Requirement for Admission

The requirement that a bar applicant be a resident of the licensing state has also been struck down. [Restatement § 2, comment f; **Supreme Court of New Hampshire v. Piper,** 470 U.S. 274 (1985)]

c. Undocumented Immigrant May Be Admitted

Federal law makes an undocumented immigrant ineligible for many state benefits, including a "professional license." But states may enact laws overriding that rule. California and some other states have passed such laws and have admitted undocumented immigrants. [*See* ***In re*** **Sergio C. Garcia,** 315 P.3d 117 (Cal. 2014)]

2. Determination of Intellectual Capability

a. Educational Requirements

Practically all states require an applicant to complete a prescribed period of college work, followed by a period of law school study, as a means of demonstrating sufficient training to practice law. [Restatement § 2, comment c]

(1) ABA Accreditation of Law Schools

Many states also require graduation from a law school ***accredited*** by the ABA. This requirement has been upheld by state and lower federal courts as bearing a "rational relationship" to fitness to practice. [**Massachusetts School of Law at Andover v. American Bar Association,** 107 F.3d 1026 (3d Cir. 1997); ***In re*** **Brooks,** 11 S.W.3d 25 (Ky. 2000)]

(2) Some States Accredit Law Schools Themselves

A few states, most notably California, allow graduates of their state-accredited law schools to take the bar examination in their state, but education at those schools is typically not sufficient for admission to the bar in other states.

b. Examination by State Bar

In addition to formal training, nearly all states require the candidate to pass an examination prepared and administered by the state bar. [Restatement § 2, comment e] Each state adopts its own test, although the National Conference of Bar Examiners recommends standards to be followed in such examinations and prepares exams such as the Multistate Bar Exam and the new Uniform Bar Exam that are used as at least part of the examination process in a majority of states today. The constitutionality of fairly administered exams has been repeatedly upheld by the courts. [*E.g.*, **Jones v. Board of Commissioners of Alabama State Bar,** 737 F.2d 996 (11th Cir. 1984)]

3. Determination of "Good Moral Character"

A more troublesome step in the admission process involves the investigation of an applicant's moral character. The state clearly has a valid interest in insuring that persons admitted to practice possess high moral standards, including mental and emotional stability. [*See* Model Rule 8.1; Restatement § 2, comment d] On the other hand, the constitutional rights of applicants must also be protected against ***unwarranted*** infringement by the state.

a. Investigative Procedure

The investigation of a candidate's moral fitness to practice law is generally conducted by a committee of bar examiners on behalf of the state's highest court. Usually the applicant is required to fill out a detailed questionnaire, list a number of references, and submit fingerprints and photographs for identification purposes. The information obtained is then checked by letter or personal investigation.

b. Hearing Before Committee

If the committee feels that a question exists regarding moral fitness, the applicant is requested to appear at a hearing before the committee.

(1) Issue Same as for Disbarment

The question before the committee of bar examiners has been ***equated with*** the question before a ***discipline*** committee—namely, "is the applicant a fit and proper person to practice law?" [**Hallinan v. Committee of Bar Examiners,** 65 Cal. 2d 447 (1966)]

(2) Burden of Proof on Applicant

The burden of coming forward with evidence and establishing good moral character is on the applicant, who is deemed to be in the best position to know the pertinent facts. The applicant owes a ***duty to cooperate*** in reasonable investigations by the state bar and ***to make disclosures*** relevant to fitness to practice. [***In re*** **Anastaplo,** 366 U.S. 82 (1961)]

(3) Applicant's Procedural Rights

At the same time, the applicant is entitled to procedural due process in committee proceedings—which includes the right to know the charges, to explain away derogatory information, and to confront critics or objectors. [**Willner v. Committee on Character & Fitness,** 373 U.S. 96 (1963)]

(4) Judicial Review of Adverse Determination

An applicant who is denied admission on the ground of bad moral character is also entitled to judicial review, usually by the highest court of the state.

c. Conduct Relevant to Determination of "Good Moral Character"

The bar committee has the right (indeed the obligation) to investigate all aspects of an applicant's past conduct that may reflect upon the applicant's honesty and integrity. [Restatement § 2, comment d; **Konigsberg v. Board of Bar Examiners,** 353 U.S. 262 (1957)]

(1) Any Past Conduct Relevant

The committee's investigation of the applicant is not limited to criminal convictions. Rather, the committee may consider ***any conduct*** of the applicant.

e.g. **Example:** Filing for bankruptcy so as to default on student loans three days before law school graduation was found to show a student's lack of sensitivity to his "moral responsibility to his creditors" and thus led to denial of his admission to the bar. [***Re*** **G.W.L.,** 364 So. 2d 454 (Fla. 1978)]

(2) Conviction of Crime Involving "Moral Turpitude"

Conviction of certain crimes may be enough by itself to show lack of good moral character. Traditionally, such crimes have been said to involve "moral turpitude." So as not to make the concept open-ended, the courts focus on traits of particular importance for lawyers, the crimes primarily include those involving an ***intent to defraud*** or ***intentional dishonesty for the purpose of personal gain***—*e.g.*, forgery, bribery, perjury, theft, robbery, extortion, etc.

(3) Not All Crimes Necessarily Establish a Lack of Good Moral Character

Many crimes do not involve "moral turpitude," and conviction of such crimes is often ***not*** enough by itself to disqualify the applicant. Whether moral turpitude exists will depend on both the ***nature*** of the offense and the ***motivation of the violator.***

(a) Application—"Adolescent Misbehavior"

Arrests for fistfighting and the like during youth may ***not*** be enough to establish "moral turpitude" sufficient to disqualify an applicant. Rather, this can be viewed as "adolescent behavior" which does not necessarily bear on the applicant's present fitness to practice law. [**Hallinan v. Committee of Bar Examiners,** 65 Cal. 2d 447 (1966)]

(b) Application—Civil Disobedience

Nonviolent civil disobedience may also be insufficient grounds for denying admission to practice, since such conduct often may be committed by "persons of the highest moral courage," and therefore may not affect their qualification to practice law. [*See* **Hallinan v. Committee of Bar Examiners,** *supra*]

(4) Effect of Concealment

Even when conduct by the applicant does not itself demonstrate a lack of good moral character, it still must be disclosed in response to inquiry by the bar examiners.

(a) Concealment or False Statements

Concealment or false statements by the applicant in response to such inquiry is ***itself*** evidence of sufficient lack of moral character to justify denial of the application. It makes no difference that the concealment is not discovered until after the applicant is admitted to practice, because a lawyer is subject to disciplinary sanctions (*e.g.*, disbarment) for making a ***materially*** false statement or for deliberately failing to disclose a ***material*** fact in her application for admission. [Model Rule 8.1]

(b) Limitations on Questions That May Be Asked

As part of the sensitive process requiring complete disclosure of what is asked, most states now try to carefully limit the information they seek to that which is directly relevant to the ability to practice law going forward. Questions about mental health treatment, for example, tend to be limited to conditions not subject to treatment or not now being treated.

(5) Rehabilitation as Mitigating Factor

An applicant whose past record contains acts of moral turpitude may still gain admission by demonstrating ***sufficient rehabilitation*** of character. The courts reward self-improvement by the applicant—especially where other evidence indicates that the applicant is presently fit to practice law. [**March v. Committee of Bar Examiners,** 67 Cal. 2d 718 (1967)]

(6) Political Activity

A lawyer is sworn to uphold the Constitution and laws of the United States and the state in which the lawyer is admitted to practice.

(a) Refusal to Take Oath to Support Constitution

An applicant who refuses to take the ***required oath*** to support the federal and state constitutions may be ***denied admission***, since there has been held to be a rational connection between this requirement and the practice of law. [**Law Students Research Council v. Wadmond,** 401 U.S. 154 (1971)]

(b) Distinguish—Membership in Communist Party

However, even ***actual*** membership in the Communist Party was held not to be a sufficient inference of "bad moral character" per se to permit exclusion from the practice of law. [**Schware v. Board of Bar Examiners,** 353 U.S. 232 (1957)]

EXAM TIP GILBERT

When answering a question involving an investigation of an applicant's moral character during the admission process, remember that:

- ***Any past conduct*** that reflects on an applicant's ***honesty and integrity*** is relevant to an evaluation of moral character. This includes charges of which the applicant was acquitted and any litigation to which the applicant was a party.
- On the other hand, mere conviction of a crime is ***not*** necessarily sufficient to deny the applicant admission to practice law. To cause disqualification of an applicant, the crime in question must involve ***moral turpitude***, such as a crime involving intentional dishonesty for the purpose of personal gain.
- Despite past conduct involving moral turpitude, an applicant may still gain admission to the legal profession if he can ***demonstrate sufficient rehabilitation*** of his character and a present fitness to practice law.

4. Duty of Lawyers Not to Aid Admission of the Unqualified

Many states require an applicant to submit letters of reference from lawyers as part of the application for admission to the bar. The Model Rules prohibit a lawyer writing a letter of reference from:

(i) Knowingly ***making a false statement*** of material fact;

(ii) ***Failing to disclose a fact*** necessary to correct a misapprehension known to have arisen in the matter; or

(iii) Knowingly ***failing to respond to a lawful demand for information*** about an applicant that is not privileged or otherwise confidential under Model Rule 1.6.

[ABA Model Rule 8.1]

C. Rules of Conduct Regulating Lawyers Admitted to Practice

1. State Regulation

Most of the substantive rules found in the remainder of this Summary reflect state regulation of lawyers who are already admitted to practice law. Like many other professions or businesses, the practice of law affects the public interest and is subject to regulation by the states. [**Bates v. State Bar of Arizona,** 433 U.S. 350 (1977)]

a. Inherent Judicial Power to Regulate

Unlike other professions, however, ultimate regulatory power over the legal profession typically rests with the courts, not the legislature. The practice of law is said to be so intimately concerned with the administration of justice that the judicial branch is often deemed to have ***inherent*** regulatory power over the practice of law (whether in or out of court). [Restatement § 1, comment c; **Shaulis v. Pennsylvania State Ethics Commission,** 833 A.2d 123 (Pa. 2003)]

(1) Lawyers as Officers of the Court

In recognition of the judicial source of their authority, lawyers are often called ***"officers of the court."*** This designation does not significantly alter a lawyer's substantive obligations, but courts invoke the principle to hold lawyers to standards of honesty and fair dealing in the judicial process. [**Newby v. Enron Corp.,** 302 F.3d 295 (5th Cir. 2002)]

(2) Regulation by State's Highest Court

The most pervasive form of regulation is typically that imposed by the highest court of the state in which a lawyer is licensed to practice. [**Hoover v. Ronwin,** 466 U.S. 558 (1984)]

b. Regulation by State Legislature

In many states, however, legislatures also have power to enact statutes regulating the legal profession. [*See, e.g.*, Cal. Bus. & Prof. Code § 6146]. Statutory regulation is most often upheld where lawyers are not singled out but are within the reach of a general regulation. [**Maunus v. State Ethics Commission,** 544 A.2d 1324 (Pa. 1988)]

c. Regulation by "Integrated" Bar

Many states today have "integrated" bar systems created by state statute or judicial decision. In an integrated bar system, all lawyers licensed by the state are ***required*** to join the state bar association and become subject to its rules (including its rules of professional conduct). [Restatement § 1, comment d] Membership in an integrated state bar association is mandatory, while membership in any other bar association (including the American Bar Association and all city and county bar associations) is voluntary.

(1) Constitutionality

The compulsory membership requirement of integrated bar systems has been upheld against attacks that it violates rights of free association. [**Lathrop v. Donahue,** 367 U.S. 820 (1961)]

(2) Use of Membership Dues

However, mandatory membership dues may be used only to support legislative proposals of direct interest to the bar. They may not be used to support legislation favored by a majority of the bar but unrelated to the practice of law. [**Keller v. State Bar of California,** 496 U.S. 1 (1990)]

(3) Antitrust Exposure

Compliance with regulatory rules adopted and enforced by the state's highest court does not violate the federal antitrust laws, but rules issued by voluntary bar associations do not have the same immunity. [**Goldfarb v. Virginia State Bar,** 421 U.S. 773 (1975); *cf.* **NC State Board of Dental Examiners v. FTC,** 135 S.Ct. 1101 (2015)]

d. Regulation by Multiple States

A lawyer is subject to regulation by ***each*** state in which the lawyer is ***admitted*** to practice, regardless of where the lawyer has an office or commits a regulatory violation. A lawyer is *also* subject to regulation by any state in which the lawyer commits a ***regulatory***

violation while providing legal services, even if the lawyer is not admitted to practice there. [ABA Model Rule 8.5(a)]

e. No Preclusion of Federal Regulation

The fact that a lawyer is qualified to practice under state law does not preclude ***additional*** federal regulation where the lawyer's activities are within the scope of applicable federal law.

(1) Practice Before Federal Courts

Each federal courts typically requires a separate license for admission to practice before it. Most require an applicant to be a member of at least one state bar as well, and many adopt by reference the local state's rules of lawyer professional conduct. But ultimately, federal courts decide the standards of practice before them.

(2) Practice Before Federal Agencies

Lawyers who wish to practice before some federal agencies and their tribunals are required to have special qualifications, and increasingly, federal agencies are imposing regulatory requirements on lawyers who "appear and practice" before them. [*See, e.g.*, 17 C.F.R. §§ 205.1–.7—SEC regulations issued pursuant to the Sarbanes-Oxley Act]

2. American Bar Association as a Source of Model Regulation

Voluntary bar associations have no formal role in lawyer regulation, but "models" for many standards for the practice of law come from the American Bar Association ("ABA").

a. Composition of the ABA

The ABA is a voluntary association whose members are fewer than 50% of lawyers practicing in the United States, but it purports to be the national representative of lawyers from all geographic areas and types of practice.

b. Articulating Standards of Conduct

Since it first published its Canons of Professional Ethics in 1908, the ABA has formulated standards of conduct which serve as a guide to state supreme courts in adopting professional regulations. [Restatement § 1, comment b]

c. ABA Model Code of Professional Responsibility (1969)

In 1969, the ABA replaced the Canons of Ethics with a comprehensive Model Code of Professional Responsibility. The ABA Code contained nine brief Canons, or "axiomatic norms," defining a lawyer's responsibilities. Each of the Canons was supplemented by ***Ethical Considerations*** ("ECs") and ***Disciplinary Rules*** ("DRs"). These were substantially more detailed than the Canons and were designed to implement the general concepts expressed in the Canons and relate them to the situations encountered in everyday practice. The ECs were ***"aspirational"***—*i.e.*, they represented objectives that a lawyer should ***strive*** to meet in specific situations. The DRs were ***mandatory*** and stated the minimum level of conduct below which a lawyer could not fall without being ***subject to disciplinary action.***

d. ABA Model Rules of Professional Conduct (1983)

In response to criticism of the ABA Code, in 1983, the ABA approved a new, "Restatement-type" format for what are called the ABA Model Rules of Professional

Conduct. These Model Rules are stated in "black letter" provisions, followed by sometimes extensive "Comments" that explain the provisions.

(1) The Four Roles of a Lawyer

The Preamble to the Model Rules says that lawyers have four professional roles—a ***"client representative,"*** an ***"officer of the legal system,"*** and a ***"public citizen"*** with responsibilities for the quality of justice, and sometimes a ***"third-party neutral"*** role helping to resolve disputes. Many challenges of being a lawyer arise because the four roles do not all lead a lawyer to do the same thing in particular situations. [Model Rules, Preamble §§ 1–3]

(2) The Model Rules Give Special Meaning to the Words "Shall," "Must," "May" and "Should"

When the word "shall" or "must" appears in one of the Model Rules, it means conduct is mandatory. Likewise, "shall not" or "must not" means conduct is prohibited. When the lawyer "may" or even "should" do something, however, it means the lawyer has a choice whether to do it or not, and no discipline is associated with either choice. [Model Rules, Scope § 14]

(3) Difference Between a Rule and a Comment

The Model Rules declare that any "Comments" to a Rule "are intended as guides to interpretation, but the text of each Rule is authoritative." [Model Rules, Scope § 21] Realistically, however, guidance on many points appears almost exclusively in a Comment, and lawyers in this field commonly take such Comments as also authoritative.

e. Restatement of the Law Governing Lawyers (2000)

Recognizing that even the 1983 Model Rules often reflected what lawyers preferred the rules to be rather than what courts had actually imposed, after a lengthy process reviewing case law around the country, the American Law Institute ("ALI") published its *Restatement of the Law (Third): The Law Governing Lawyers* (2000) to stand alongside other ALI Restatements, such as those on Torts and Contracts. References in this Summary to the "Restatement" will be to this influential ALI document on which courts increasingly rely.

(1) Not a "Model" to Be Adopted with Regulatory Effect

Unlike the ABA Model Rules, the Restatement is not intended to be adopted as positive law to "regulate" lawyers. Instead, the Restatement collects rules and cases from all over the country, whether involving professional regulation, malpractice liability or fiduciary duty, and it distills them into 135 black letter sections with related comments and examples.

(2) But a Document Influential in the Courts and on the ABA Model Rules

The Restatement's principal impact has been on courts that regularly cite it when addressing some of the many issues not addressed by state regulatory rules. But the Restatement has also had an effect on the ABA itself, which appointed an "Ethics 2000" Commission to consider how the law revealed in the Restatement affected the rules adopted in the 1983 ABA Model Rules.

3. Current Form of the ABA Model Rules of Professional Conduct

a. Work of the ABA "Ethics 2000" Commission (2002–2003)

The ABA did not change the Model Rules' format, but it extensively revised the substance of the standards when it received the report of its "Ethics 2000" Commission in 2002. The source of many of the changes were insights and language found in the ALI Restatement. Where principles discussed in this Summary are reflected in the Restatement or the ABA Model Rules of Professional Conduct, reference will be made to the relevant Restatement provision and to the Model Rules as they stand after the revisions made in 2002 and thereafter.

b. Impact of the ABA Model Rules on State Regulation of Practice

(1) Diversity Among State Rules of Professional Conduct

The ABA Model Rules do not regulate the legal profession in any state until adopted by a state's highest court, but some form of the ABA Model Rules has been adopted in almost all U.S. jurisdictions. Many have adopted the 1983 rules and most of the 2002–2003 revisions, but states take the rule adoption process seriously, and there is now more variation among particular state professional standards than probably ever before.

(2) California Approach

The California Rules of Professional Conduct represent the only major jurisdiction to truly "go it alone" and not rely on ABA Model Rule standards. However, they do say that "ethics opinions and rules and standards promulgated by other jurisdictions and bar associations may also be considered." [Cal. Rule 1–100] Even in California, ABA Model Rules principles can have some influence and effect.

c. Interpretation of the ABA Model Rules

The meaning of the ABA Model Rules is most authoritatively be determined from ***judicial opinions*** imposing sanctions for the conduct of particular lawyers. However, the ABA Standing Committee on Ethics and Professional Responsibility also issues ***advisory opinions*** as a guide to applying the Model Rules in particular fact situations. State bar associations (and sometimes state courts) often provide similar opinions construing a particular state's rules. All references in this Summary to ***"ABA Opn."*** will be to ***Formal Opinions*** published by the ABA.

4. Role of the Restatement and Model Rules in the Multistate Professional Responsibility Exam

The most significant practical reason for law students to care about the ABA Model Rules is that they are the controlling authority for the Multistate Professional Responsibility Exam ("MPRE"). Applicants for the bar in many states must get a satisfactory score on that exam in order to be admitted. In a world in which actual state rules differ, the MPRE oversimplifies the law and treats the Restatement and the current version of the ABA Model Rules as stating principles of the law governing lawyers in every jurisdiction across the country. Thus, this Summary takes the same approach. The MPRE tests amendments to the Model Rules one year after they become effective.

D. Enforcing Lawyer Standards Using the Disciplinary Process

1. General Grounds for Discipline

A lawyer may be disciplined on any of the following grounds:

a. Violation of Professional Standards

Violating, or ***attempting*** to violate, a state version of the ABA Model Rules is the principal basis for imposing professional discipline. Furthermore, a lawyer must not knowingly ***assist or induce*** another person to violate professional rules nor ***use the acts of another person*** to commit a violation. [Model Rule 8.4(a); Restatement § 5 and comment b]

(1) Disciplinary Jurisdiction Wherever Lawyer Practices or Is Licensed

A lawyer may be disciplined in ***each*** state in which the lawyer is licensed, no matter where the conduct occurs. Indeed, if the conduct takes place in a state in which the lawyer is not licensed at all, discipline may be imposed there as well. [Model Rule 8.5(a); Restatement § 5 and comment h]

(2) Law to Be Applied

In principle, no matter where the lawyer is subject to discipline, the same conduct standard should be applied; *i.e.*, the choice of law rule in each state should yield the same result.

(a) Litigation Matters

In cases seeking discipline for acts done in cases pending before a tribunal, the disciplinary standard applied is that of ***the state in which the tribunal sits.*** [Model Rule 8.5(b)]

(b) Nonlitigation Matters

For all other acts, the law to be applied is that of ***the state in which the conduct occurred.*** But if the ***predominant effect*** of the act is in another state, the professional standards of ***that state*** are to govern. [Model Rule 8.5(b)]

(c) Lawyer's Reasonable Belief

If the lawyer's conduct conforms to the law of a jurisdiction in which the lawyer ***reasonably believes*** the predominant effect of the conduct will occur, the lawyer will not be subject to discipline. [Model Rule 8.5(b)]

EXAM TIP GILBERT

Choice of law questions involving litigation matters do not pose a problem—a lawyer is subject to the disciplinary rules of the forum state. In ***nonlitigation*** matters, the rules of the ***jurisdiction in which the conduct occurred*** usually should be applied, but remember the exceptions: If the ***predominant effect*** of the conduct is in another jurisdiction, ***that jurisdiction's rules apply.*** However, if a lawyer's conduct is ***proper*** in the jurisdiction which he ***reasonably believes*** is most affected by his conduct, he will ***not*** be subject to discipline.

b. Commission of a Crime

Under the Model Rules, a lawyer is subject to discipline for crimes that reflect adversely on the lawyer's ***"honesty, trustworthiness, or fitness as a lawyer in other respects."*** The Model Rules state the principle in this way to avoid imposing discipline for matters of personal morality, such as adultery, that used to be reached under the heading of "crimes involving moral turpitude." [Model Rule 8.4(b) and comment 2; Restatement § 5 and comment g]

(1) Crime Need Not Have Been Committed While Acting as a Lawyer

The crime need not have been connected with the lawyer's professional activities; criminal acts ***wholly unrelated*** thereto, such as fraud on a personal income tax return or domestic violence, are proper grounds for discipline. [*See* **People v. Musick,** 960 P.2d 89 (Colo. 1998)]

(2) Effect of Acquittal, Reversal of Conviction or Pardon

The fact that the conviction has been reversed on appeal, or even pardoned, does ***not affect the power of the court*** to impose discipline. Indeed, a lawyer may even be disciplined for conduct as to which he was ***acquitted*** in a criminal proceeding. [*See, e.g.,* ***In re*** **Segal,** 719 N.E.2d 480 (Mass. 1999)—acquittal; *and see* ***In re*** **Abrams,** 689 A.2d 6 (D.C. 1997)—pardon]

c. Engaging in Conduct Involving Dishonesty, Fraud, Deceit, or Misrepresentation

A lawyer may be disciplined for her involvement in conduct involving dishonesty, fraud, deceit, or misrepresentation. The act ***need not be a crime*** to justify a lawyer's disbarment or other discipline. [Model Rule 8.4(c)]

e.g. **Example:** A lawyer who impersonated her husband and took the bar exam for him was disbarred. The court concluded that disbarment was warranted because the lawyer's dishonesty could have significantly harmed the public by enabling an unqualified person to practice law. [***In re*** **Lamb,** 49 Cal. 3d 239 (1989)]

d. Engaging in Conduct Prejudicial to Administration of Justice

This basis for discipline is very broad but requires some connection between the conduct and a pending judicial proceeding. [Model Rule 8.4(d)]

e.g. **Example:** A lawyer violated this rule by stealing the opposing lawyer's notes while that lawyer was outside the room talking with his client during a break in a deposition. [***In re Winkler,*** 834 N.E.2d 85 (Ind. 2005)]

e. California Statutory Grounds for Discipline

A lawyer in California may be disbarred or suspended from practice for: (i) violating the attorney's oath [Cal. Bus. & Prof. Code § 6103], (ii) appearing for another as attorney without authority [Cal. Bus. & Prof. Code § 6104], (iii) advocating the violent overthrow of government [Cal. Bus. & Prof. Code § 6106.1], or (iv) switching from prosecution to defense in a criminal case [Cal. Bus. & Prof. Code § 6131].

f. Discipline of a Law Firm

Most states impose discipline only on individual lawyers, but in New York and New Jersey, a law firm is subject to discipline, *e.g.*, for failure to supervise associates and for other institutional failings. [*e.g.,* N.Y. Rules of Professional Conduct, Rule 8.4]

CHECKLIST OF GROUNDS FOR DISCIPLINE GILBERT

A LAWYER MAY BE SUBJECT TO PROFESSIONAL DISCIPLINE FOR:

- ☑ ***Violation of a professional ethics rule;***
- ☑ Commission of some ***crimes;***
- ☑ Conduct involving ***dishonesty, fraud, deceit, or misrepresentation;***
- ☑ Conduct ***prejudicial to administration of justice;***
- ☑ ***Violation of some specific state statutes.***

2. Sanctions

a. Typical Examples of Possible Sanction

(1) Disbarment

Disbarment is a ***revocation*** of the lawyer's license to practice, although in most states, a disbarred lawyer who has been rehabilitated may apply to the state bar for readmission (*see infra*, p. 24).

(2) Suspension from Practice

Suspension is a ***temporary revocation*** of the right to practice. After the period of suspension has passed, the lawyer can return to practice. [*See **In re*** **Mackay,** 416 P.2d 823 (Alaska 1964)]

(3) Reprimand or Admonition

For less serious offenses, a state may impose a public reprimand or private admonition.

b. Factors Affecting Sanctions

The sanctions imposed in a given case depend upon all of the circumstances. Aside from the ***seriousness of the offense*** itself, factors that might affect the appropriate penalty include the ***lawyer's mental state*** at the time of the offense, the ***injury*** caused by the offense, any ***aggravating or mitigating factors***, and any ***evidence of rehabilitation.*** [ABA Standards for Imposing Lawyer Sanctions]

(1) **Mental Illness or Chronic Alcoholism**

Mental illness and chronic alcoholism are usually seen as affecting the culpability of a lawyer. Sanctions in such cases are often limited to ***suspending*** the lawyer from practice pending proof of recovery. [*See, e.g.*, **Matter of Walker,** 254 N.W.2d 452 (S.D. 1977); **Petition of Johnson,** 322 N.W.2d 616 (Minn. 1982)]

(2) **Use as a Basis for Anticipatory Suspension**

Alcoholism and mental illness are not only mitigating factors in discipline cases, but may also be a ***basis for suspension*** of a lawyer ***before*** wrongdoing. Although such a sanction has serious consequences, many states use summary procedures to suspend an impaired lawyer before clients' cases are neglected or their interests damaged. [*See* ABA Model Rule for Lawyer Disciplinary Enforcement 23]

EXAM TIP GILBERT

Note the possible effects a lawyer's ***alcoholism or mental illness*** may have on a disciplinary sanction. A court may consider the lawyer's alcoholism or mental illness a ***mitigating factor*** that calls for a lighter sentence (*e.g.*, suspension instead of disbarment). On the other hand, a court also may regard the lawyer's alcoholism or mental illness as a danger to his clients' interests that is a ***ground for anticipatory action.***

3. Stages in Disciplinary Proceedings

a. Complaint to State Bar

Disciplinary proceedings against a lawyer are initiated by lodging a complaint with the state disciplinary authorities. While most complaints come from aggrieved clients, they may also be made by fellow lawyers, judges, or any other person with knowledge of the alleged misconduct.

(1) **Privileged Against Claim of Defamation**

Courts have stressed that the ability to complain about misconduct is a "safety valve" for the public and is vital to public assurance that the bar does not shelter lawyers engaging in such activities. For this reason, the filing of a complaint with the state bar may not be the basis on which the lawyer may later claim defamation. [**Weber v. Cueto,** 568 N.E.2d 513 (Ill. 1991)]

(2) **Distinguish—Federal Civil Rights Action to Enjoin Proceedings**

In a few cases, lawyers have been allowed to file suit under section 1983 of the Federal Civil Rights Act (which allows suit to enjoin a deprivation of federal constitutional rights by state or local officials) where the lawyer alleges that the disciplinary action was instituted in bad faith to harass and punish the lawyer because of his controversial clients, unpopular positions, etc. [**Taylor v. Kentucky State Bar,** 424 F.2d 478 (6th Cir. 1970)]

b. Screening of Complaint by State Bar

As a general rule, complaints are referred initially to a local grievance or administrative committee of the state bar. Where the charges result from lawyer-client misunderstandings, an appropriate discussion with the client at this point usually resolves the matter, often without involving the lawyer at all.

(1) Explanation by Lawyer

If the charge presents a prima facie case of misconduct, however, the lawyer may be asked to submit an explanation to the committee (either personally or in writing). After further investigation, the grievance committee may find the charges unwarranted and dismiss the complaint.

(2) Dismissal Not Reviewable

Since disciplinary proceedings are a matter of internal regulation within the bar, the complaining party has ***no right of review*** once a charge is dismissed by the committee, nor may the party subsequently refile a complaint on the same facts.

c. Hearing Before Grievance Committee

Complaints not disposed of by a preliminary investigation are generally scheduled for a nonpublic hearing before a committee composed of lawyers.

(1) Case Prosecuted by Independent Official

An attorney from the state disciplinary agency is usually appointed to prepare the evidence against the lawyer and present it at the hearing.

(2) Lawyer's Resignation Generally Not Permitted

A lawyer under disciplinary charges will generally ***not*** be permitted to resign, at least not without admitting the offenses in detail. Otherwise, if the lawyer later files a petition for reinstatement (*see infra*, p. 24), there would be no clear findings as to what the lawyer had done.

(3) Lawyer's Right to Procedural Due Process

The accused lawyer is entitled to procedural due process, which means a fair and impartial hearing.

(a) Due Process Required

The following rights are guaranteed by law:

- (i) The right to ***be heard*** and to ***introduce evidence***;
- (ii) The right to ***counsel***;
- (iii) The right to ***cross-examine*** adverse witnesses; and
- (iv) The right to ***fair notice***, which also means that the hearing must be ***limited to charges made in the complaint*** [***In re*** **Ruffalo,** 390 U.S. 544 (1968)].

[*See, e.g.*, Cal. Bus. & Prof. Code § 6085; **Giddens v. State Bar,** 28 Cal. 3d 730 (1981)]

(b) But Not All Due Process of a Criminal Case

A disciplinary hearing is ***not*** treated as a ***criminal proceeding*** and does not provide all of the due process protections required in a criminal case. The lawyer has no right to state-provided counsel, for example.

(c) **No Jury Right**

There is usually also ***no right to a jury trial*** in a disciplinary proceeding.

(d) **Privilege Against Self-Incrimination Applies**

The lawyer has a constitutional right under the Fifth Amendment to refuse to answer questions in disciplinary proceedings concerning the lawyer's professional conduct, and ***no disciplinary action can be taken against the lawyer based solely on such claim of privilege.*** [**Spevack v. Klein,** 385 U.S. 511 (1967)]

(4) **Burden of Proof**

The burden of proof is ***on the party presenting the charge*** (*i.e.*, the state disciplinary agency). Most states permit only ***legally sufficient evidence*** to be considered (*e.g.*, inadmissible hearsay is excluded), and require proof ***exceeding a preponderance of the evidence*** (though allowing something less than proof beyond a reasonable doubt). [**State v. Neilssen,** 136 N.W.2d 355 (Neb. 1965)]

d. **Decision by Grievance Committee**

After the hearing, the grievance committee (or hearing panel) enters its decision—either dismissing the charges against the lawyer or recommending appropriate sanctions.

e. **Review and Determination by Highest State Court**

All the early phases of the disciplinary process are only seen as preparing the case for action by the state's highest court. That is who granted the lawyer the right to practice in the first place, and it is typically the only body that can take away the right. The court's review is limited to the record below, but the court is ***not bound*** by the state bar's findings of fact. The court may independently assess the evidence and pass on its sufficiency. Furthermore, the court may impose a greater or lesser sanction than that proposed by the state bar. [**Selznick v. State Bar,** 16 Cal. 3d 704 (1976)]

EXAM TIP GILBERT

Although the ***burden of proof in a disciplinary hearing*** initially is on the ***party prosecuting*** the charge (*i.e.*, the state disciplinary agency), typically the ***burden shifts when a lawyer challenges the decision*** of the grievance committee. The burden is then on the lawyer to show that the recommended discipline decision was erroneous or unlawful.

---

f. **Reinstatement**

A lawyer suspended for a *fixed* period is deemed ***reinstated at the expiration of the period*** without any formal petition or order. Where a lawyer has been disbarred or suspended from practice for an ***indefinite*** period, the court may subsequently reinstate the lawyer by an ***appropriate order.*** The lawyer must petition the court for reinstatement and must present supporting evidence to convince the court of present fitness to practice law. [***In re*** **Hiss,** 333 N.E.2d 429 (Mass. 1975)]

4. Obligation to Disclose Misconduct by Other Lawyers

The enforcement of professional rules requires assistance from its members. Thus, a lawyer is under an *affirmative duty* to disclose conduct by other lawyers that the lawyer believes to be a violation of the rules of professional conduct. Such disclosure must be made to the tribunal or authority empowered to act upon such violation. [Model Rule 8.3(a)] A lawyer also has a duty to report a judge's violation of rules of judicial conduct. [Model Rule 8.3(b)]

a. Scope of Obligation

Under the Model Rules, a lawyer is required to report misconduct that "***raises a substantial question***" as to the other lawyer's "***honesty, trustworthiness, or fitness as a lawyer.***" That is far fewer than every violation of the Rules of Professional Conduct, but likely more than most lawyers may be comfortable reporting. [Model Rule 8.3(a)]

EXAM TIP GILBERT

Keep in mind that the ***duty to report*** professional violations ***even applies*** to violations discovered during activities and conversations ***unrelated to the practice of law.*** Thus, if two lawyers are complaining to each other about tax increases, and one of the lawyers admits that he underreports his income, the other lawyer has a duty to report the violation.

---

b. Exception for Confidential Knowledge

(1) Client May Prohibit Disclosure

A lawyer may not disclose knowledge of misconduct by fellow lawyers where knowledge of such conduct is protected by the professional duty of confidentiality (Model Rule 1.6). Thus, if the lawyer's client refuses to permit the lawyer to disclose misconduct by the client's former lawyer, for example, the lawyer may not disclose it. [Model Rule 8.3(c)]

(2) Lawyer's Partners

The fact that a lawyer is a partner or associate of another lawyer *does not create any obligation* between them that would excuse either from the duty to disclose misconduct by the other. [**Attorney Grievance Commission v. Kahn,** 431 A.2d 1336 (Md. 1981)]

(3) Information Gained in Lawyer Assistance Program

Most states have created Lawyer Assistance Programs ("LAP") designed to counsel and support the recovery of lawyers who have a problem with drugs or alcohol. Information learned in the course of such a program is treated as if it were ***privileged*** and need ***not*** be reported to disciplinary authorities. [Model Rule 8.3(c)]

5. Effect of Disbarment or Suspension in Other Jurisdictions

A lawyer is subject to sanction in every state in which he is licensed, regardless of where the misconduct occurred, but disciplinary action in one state does not automatically affect a lawyer's standing in other jurisdictions. [Model Rule 8.5(a)]

a. Other States

Typically, the disciplinary action in one state will be accepted as ***conclusive proof of the misconduct*** alleged, but ***not of the sanctions*** warranted by such misconduct. [**Matter of Iulo,** 766 A.2d 335 (Pa. 2001)]

b. Federal Courts

A federal court in the same state is ***not obliged*** to sanction a lawyer simply because a state has done so. The federal system is ***entirely separate,*** and therefore each federal court in which the lawyer has been admitted to practice must evaluate the lawyer's conduct. However, a federal court is likely to impose the same sanction unless the lawyer can show by clear and convincing evidence that it should not do so. [***In re*** **Hoare,** 155 F.3d 937 (8th Cir. 1998); ***In re*** **Kramer,** 282 F.3d 721 (9th Cir. 2002)]

E. Malpractice Action to Compensate an Injured Client

1. Introduction

While the state versions of the ABA Model Rules were written for enforcement through professional discipline, the standards they set forth are applied in other settings as well. The most common such setting is a case for professional malpractice.

COMPARISON OF DISCIPLINARY ACTION AND MALPRACTICE SUIT GILBERT

	DISCIPLINARY ACTION	MALPRACTICE SUIT
FORUM	• Disciplinary tribunal	• Civil court
ADVERSARY	• State bar prosecutor	• Injured plaintiff
PURPOSE	• Protect the public from future misconduct	• Compensate injured plaintiff

2. Relevance of Rules of Professional Conduct in a Malpractice Case

Most states in which the issue has arisen have held that disciplinary proceedings may not grant ***private remedies*** and that the purposes of disciplinary proceedings and malpractice actions differ. Because lawyers are expected to conform to the state's rules of professional conduct in order to avoid professional discipline, however, the question naturally arises whether a breach of those rules constitutes a breach of the standard of care in a malpractice case.

a. Traditional View

The traditional view was a resounding "no." Professional rules are a "just basis for a lawyer's self-assessment or for sanctioning a lawyer," but not a basis for civil liability. [1983 Model Rules, Scope § 18]

b. Current View

However, in real life, courts accept testimony about the professional rules as a guide in determining what is expected of lawyers in particular situations. Thus, even though breach of such a rule is still not negligence per se, courts consider an ethics violation as relevant evidence that a lawyer's conduct was below the appropriate standard of conduct. The Model Rules now acknowledge that reality. [2002 Model Rules, Scope § 20; Restatement § 52(2)]

3. Negligence—Most Common Basis for Malpractice Action

Although the plaintiff in a legal malpractice case may invoke a variety of legal theories, the most common theory is the tort of ***negligence.*** Under this theory, the plaintiff must establish the usual elements of any negligence case: (i) a ***duty of due care***, (ii) ***breach*** of that duty, (iii) legal ***causation***, and (iv) ***damages.***

a. To Whom the Duty of Due Care Is Owed

Ordinarily, a lawyer is liable for malpractice ***only to the lawyer's client.*** However, there are important ***exceptions*** to that general principle:

(1) Prospective Client

A person consulting the lawyer for the purpose of becoming a client is not yet a client and may never become one (*e.g.*, because the lawyer has a conflict of interest). However, the lawyer ***may be guilty of malpractice*** to such a prospective client if the lawyer: (i) ***misuses confidential information*** of the prospective client, (ii) ***fails to protect property*** entrusted to the lawyer by the prospective client, or (iii) ***fails to use reasonable care*** in giving the prospective client legal advice [*e.g.*, saying "you don't have a good case" and causing the prospective client not to get further legal advice). [Model Rule 1.18, comment 9; Restatement §§ 15, 51(1)]

(2) Person Lawyer Invites to Rely on Lawyer's Help

A lawyer may also be liable for malpractice if the lawyer invites a nonclient to rely on the lawyer's legal opinion (*e.g.*, advises the nonclient about the meaning of contract terms). [**Greycas v. Proud,** 826 F.2d 1560 (7th Cir. 1987); Restatement § 51(2)]

(3) Person the Client Expressly Intended to Benefit

If a lawyer is employed by the client to render services ***intended to benefit an identified third person*** (*e.g.*, draft a will to leave money to particular persons), the lawyer may be liable to the ***intended beneficiary***, if the work is done negligently and the gift is not successfully made. [**Lucas v. Hamm,** 56 Cal.2d 583 (1961); Restatement § 51(3)]

(4) Person to Whom a Trustee-Client Owes Duties

A lawyer representing a trustee or similar fiduciary may be held liable for ***malpractice*** to the ***beneficiaries*** to whom the trustee-client owes duties if the lawyer ***knowingly assists*** the trustee-client in the ***breach of a fiduciary duty.*** The lawyer may also be liable for malpractice if he does not try to prevent a breach of fiduciary duty by the trustee-client and preventing the breach would not significantly impair representation of the trustee. *But notc:* Inaction is ***not malpractice*** if thc ***breach of duty is not clear*** or if action would ***violate the lawyer's duty to the trustee-client.*** [**Fickett v. Superior Court,** 558 P.2d 988 (Ariz. 1976); Restatement § 51(4)]

b. Standard of Care: Test for Breach—"Competence and Diligence Normally Exercised by Lawyers in Similar Circumstances"

The level of competency demanded of a lawyer in malpractice cases is usually stated as the "***skill, prudence, and diligence***" possessed by lawyers of ***ordinary skill and capacity*** who perform ***similar services.*** [**Lucas v. Hamm,** 56 Cal. 2d 583 (1961); *see* Restatement § 52, comment g]

(1) Minimum Duty Owed

At a minimum, the lawyer is held to the standard of care exercised by lawyers generally, regardless of whether the lawyer personally possesses such skills.

(2) Higher Standard of Care Owed by Specialists

If a lawyer ***has greater competence***, she is ***bound to exercise it***; *i.e.*, lawyers who hold themselves out as specialists in a particular field (*e.g.*, tax, litigation, probate) will be held to the ***standard of care*** customarily exercised by ***fellow specialists,*** rather than merely that required of other members of the legal community generally. [**Wright v. Williams,** 47 Cal. App. 3d 802 (1975)]

(3) Appointed Counsel

Appointed counsel also owes a duty of due care to her client and may be held liable to a client for malpractice. [**Ferry v. Ackerman,** 444 U.S. 193 (1979)]

(4) Application

(a) Knowledge and Research Ability

As part of the general standard of care, a lawyer is expected to possess knowledge of those "***plain and elementary principles*** of law which are commonly known by well-informed attorneys" and to ***discover*** those additional rules of law which, even though not commonly known, may readily be found ***by standard research techniques.*** [**Smith v. Lewis,** 13 Cal. 3d 349 (1975)]

1) Ignorance of New Laws No Defense

Thus, it is ordinarily ***no defense*** to a malpractice suit that the lawyer was ***unaware*** of recent changes in statutes or case law which affected the correctness of her advice.

2) Factual Investigation

A lawyer is also obliged to make a reasonable investigation of the facts of the case. [**Woodruff v. Tomlin,** 616 F.2d 924 (6th Cir. 1980)]

3) Further Research Required

A lawyer has an ***affirmative duty to investigate*** upon receiving information that should reasonably put the lawyer on notice that further research or action is required. [*See, e.g.*, **Owen v. Neely,** 471 S.W.2d 705 (Ky. 1971)—notice of defect in title]

4) Foreign Law

Normally, lawyers are expected to be familiar with rules of law and procedure in ***their own states.*** However, where in the exercise of reasonable care they should realize that the case involves an issue that must be decided under the law of some other state or country, lawyers ***may*** be under a duty to become familiar with appropriate ***foreign law*** (or associate competent counsel with such familiarity).

(b) No Liability for Errors in Judgment

Lawyers are not, however, liable for every mistake they make in practice. They do not guarantee the soundness of their opinions or the validity of instruments they are engaged to draft. If the action or decision involved is one as to which there is ***reasonable doubt*** by well-informed lawyers, judgmental errors by a lawyer are ***not malpractice.*** [**Biomet Inc. v. Finnegan Henderson LLP,** 967 A.2d 662 (D.C. 2009)]

EXAM TIP GILBERT

If a lawyer's mistake caused his client to lose a case, ***do not automatically assume*** that the lawyer committed ***malpractice.*** Look to see if the lawyer exercised ***due care.*** For example, if a lawyer decided not to take the pretrial deposition of a witness because it appeared that the witness's testimony was unimportant, but it later became evident that the witness's testimony could have helped the client, the lawyer did not necessarily commit malpractice if his decision was reasonable when made and the lawyer otherwise acted with due care.

c. Causation—Harm to Client Must Be Shown

Failure to meet the general standard of care constitutes negligence, but traditionally there is ***no malpractice liability unless harm*** to the client has proximately resulted therefrom. Thus, the client typically must show that ***"but for"*** the lawyer's errors or omissions, the client would have avoided the complained of loss. [Restatement § 53 and comment a; **Winskunas v. Birnbaum,** 23 F.3d 1264 (7th Cir. 1994)]

(1) "Case Within a Case"

In litigation matters, this has meant that the client ***must in effect prove two cases:*** (i) that the ***lawyer was negligent*** in handling the matter, and (ii) ***that*** the ***client would otherwise have won*** the lawsuit. This has often been a very difficult burden for the client—particularly where the case involved disputed facts or close liability issues.

(a) Distinguish—Disciplinary Action

Disciplinary sanctions can be invoked regardless of the "but for" test. Thus, a lawyer could be disciplined for incompetence that does not result in client loss. [*See* Model Rule 1.1]

(2) "Substantial Factor" Test

In an effort to reduce the burden on a malpractice plaintiff, some courts have demanded only that the lawyer's conduct have been a "substantial factor" in the client's loss, *i.e.*, that the client need not prove with certainty that the client would have won the underlying case. [*See, e.g.*, **Conklin v. Hannock Weisman,** 678 A.2d 1060 (N.J. 1996)]

EXAM TIP GILBERT

Remember this important difference between proving a violation of professional conduct and proving malpractice—although a lawyer is subject to ***professional discipline*** for misconduct ***even if harm to someone is not shown***, in a suit for ***malpractice***, the plaintiff must prove that the lawyer's conduct was the cause of the plaintiff's injury. This means that the injury would not have happened ***but for*** the lawyer's negligence.

d. Damages

The plaintiff in a professional negligence case must prove damages—*e.g.*, the money paid out to discharge an adverse judgment, or the value of a lost cause of action. The plaintiff can recover for direct losses and also for losses that are indirect but foreseeable. [Restatement § 53]

e. Liability for Acts of Others

The standard of care may render lawyers liable not only for their own acts, but also for the acts of others:

(1) Co-Counsel

Where several lawyers have been employed to represent a client concurrently, ***each*** owes the duty of care stated above. Ordinarily, ***delegation of responsibility*** among counsel *does not* ***excuse*** one lawyer from malpractice liability for errors or omissions of the others, unless the client agrees to the division of responsibilities.

(2) Partners

Consistent with general partnership law, malpractice by a partner in a law firm generally renders ***all other partners equally liable unless*** the negligent partner had ***no actual or apparent authority*** to act on behalf of the firm in the matter.

(a) But Note—Increased Use of Limited Liability Partnerships

In an effort to change the automatic imputation of liability to all law partners, many states have now adopted statutes that permit creation of limited liability partnerships ("LLP") or limited liability companies ("LLC") that expressly limit liability to the negligent partner and the entity itself, thus immunizing other partners from personal liability.

(3) Employees

A lawyer is generally liable on a theory of ***respondeat superior*** for losses caused to a client by negligent acts of the lawyer's employees or subordinates (*e.g.*, an administrative assistant or clerk carelessly loses a file, throws out a will, or destroys crucial evidence without which the client loses the case).

(4) Referring Lawyer

In addition, a lawyer who refers a client to another lawyer whose negligence causes the client loss ***may be held liable*** for the other lawyer's negligence if the first lawyer made the referral ***without reasonable care*** (*i.e.*, without checking into the lawyer's reputation and skill to whom referred).

4. Other Theories for Malpractice Liability

In addition to the negligence theory for lawyer malpractice, other theories may be available:

a. Intentional Tort

A lawyer may be liable to the client for intentional torts such as fraud, misrepresentation, or misuse of funds.

b. Breach of Contract

The lawyer-client relationship is ultimately based on a contract between the lawyer and client, and sometimes clients prefer to sue for breach of that contract in addition to, or instead of, suing under a tort theory. [Restatement § 55]

(1) Different Statute of Limitations

In many states, the statute of limitations on contract actions is longer than that available for tort claims.

(2) Extra Promises by Lawyer

In other cases, the lawyer may have made particular claims of expertise or willingness to devote extra people to a matter, or may have otherwise assumed duties greater than those that would have been required under the usual standard of care under tort law.

c. Breach of Fiduciary Duty

Increasingly, clients are filing suit alleging that their lawyer breached a fiduciary duty owed to the client; *e.g.*, the lawyer misused confidential information or took the case while burdened by a conflict of interest. [Restatement § 49]

(1) Remedy of Fee Forfeiture

The principal significance of a breach of fiduciary duty claim is that courts have increasingly been willing to sanction lawyers by partially or completely denying them the right to collect fees for the representation, regardless of whether the plaintiff can prove any actual damages. Fee forfeiture is not automatic, and the amount of forfeiture ordinarily is a matter for the court, not the jury. [*See, e.g.*, Restatement § 37; **Burrow v. Arce,** 997 S.W.2d 229 (Tex. 1999)]

THEORIES OF MALPRACTICE GILBERT

A PLAINTIFF MAY INVOKE THE FOLLOWING THEORIES OF MALPRACTICE:

- ☑ ***Negligence***;
- ☑ ***Intentional tort*** (*e.g.*, fraud, misrepresentation, misuse of funds);
- ☑ ***Breach of contract***;
- ☑ ***Breach of fiduciary duty.***

5. Attempts to Limit Malpractice Liability

a. Model Rules Approach

Under the Model Rules, a lawyer may not contract with a client to prospectively limit the lawyer's liability for malpractice ***unless the client is separately represented*** in making the agreement. [Model Rule 1.8(h)(1); Restatement § 54(2), (4)]

b. Settling a Malpractice Claim

A lawyer may not settle a claim for malpractice with an unrepresented client or former client without giving that person ***written notice*** that seeking ***independent counsel*** is desirable and giving the person ***reasonable opportunity to consult such counsel.*** [Model Rule 1.8(h)(2); Restatement § 54(3)]

c. Reimbursement of Client

A lawyer who has breached a duty to his client with monetary effect ***cannot escape professional discipline*** by reimbursing the client for any loss. Thus, even if the lawyer pays the client back for any damage he caused, he is still subject to discipline.

F. Other Potential Consequences of Violating Lawyer Standards

While professional discipline and malpractice are the most common sources of remedies for lawyer conduct, they are not the only ones. Here are a few more. [*See* Restatement § 6]

1. Punishment of the Lawyer for Contempt

Although not often thought of as a device for keeping lawyers "ethical," the power of a court to punish a lawyer for contempt is one of the most direct and effective techniques for enforcing professional standards. Indeed, the contempt sanction may be the only practical way to ***enforce proper standards of courtroom conduct.*** [Restatement § 6, comment g]

2. Disqualification of the Lawyer from Representing a Client

a. Remedy for Conflict of Interest

As you will see in Chapter IV of this Summary, when a lawyer represents a client against the lawyer's former client in the same or a substantially related matter, courts commonly "disqualify" the lawyer from doing so. In effect, the courts enjoin the lawyer from continuing to represent the client. There may also be a possible suit for malpractice, but disqualification is the normal avenue for relief. [Restatement § 6, comment i]

b. Remedy Where Evidence Is Wrongfully Obtained by the Lawyer

Likewise, when a lawyer wrongfully obtains privileged evidence of the opposing client that would give him an advantage as a case goes forward, the lawyer may not only be required to return it but may be disqualified from representing his own client any longer in the matter.

3. Dismissal of the Claim or Defense of a Litigant Represented by the Lawyer

For a particularly serious violation of professional standards, the lawyer's client's claim or defense might be dismissed. The lawyer's client will be initially forced to bear the burden of the lawyer's conduct, but the client will have a potential malpractice remedy to shift the burden back to the lawyer. [Restatement § 6, comment k]

4. Relief for a Client from a Criminal Conviction or Sentence

a. Difficult to Get Malpractice Remedy Against a Criminal Lawyer

Courts often have been reluctant to let a convicted criminal defendant sue his lawyer for malpractice. In part, that reflects judicial concern that lawyers would be reluctant to take criminal cases if every defendant who got convicted could sue them, but courts also say a criminal defendant should not profit financially from the fact another lawyer might have gotten him an acquittal or a reduced sentence.

b. But May Get Relief Based on a Finding of Ineffective Assistance of Counsel

Some cases have set aside a criminal conviction because of incompetence of counsel where the errors of defense counsel were so shocking that they deprived the accused of the constitutional right to ***effective assistance of counsel.*** A defendant must show that counsel's acts or omissions "were outside the wide range of professionally competent assistance," and they must have caused ***"actual prejudice,"*** not just some "conceivable effect" on the outcome. [*See* **Strickland v. Washington,** 466 U.S. 668 (1984)]

5. Criminal Prosecution of the Lawyer

Unfortunately, sometimes lawyers cross the line from their criminal client's advocate to becoming a co-conspirator. When that happens, the lawyer may be criminally prosecuted as well as the client. [Restatement § 8]

Chapter Two

The Relationship Between Client and Lawyer

Chapter Two

CONTENTS	PAGE

Chapter Approach

This chapter provides an overview of a lawyer-client relationship from its beginning to its end.

1. We begin with how the relationship is formed and the duties a lawyer owes even to prospective clients.
2. We move to respective authority of client and lawyer and review the fiduciary duties a lawyer owes each client.
3. Next comes the lawyer's right to charge a reasonable fee and the client's duty to pay it.
4. The chapter closes with how the lawyer-client relationship ends and what duties extend beyond that time.

A. Introduction

1. In General

The relationship between client and lawyer is best understood as based on a contract between them. Some of the terms of that contract are implied by custom and professional rules, but with a few important exceptions, the terms may be varied by agreement between client and lawyer.

2. The Lawyer as Agent

It is also often helpful to see a lawyer as an agent of the client and thus subject to standards imposed by the law of agency. Like any other agent, a lawyer stands in a fiduciary relationship to a client. Indeed, many of the traditional duties owed by a lawyer to a client are derived from fiduciary standards. Fiduciary duties do not change the contractual character of their relationship, but they mean that departures from the customary contract are likely to be closely scrutinized for fairness.

3. Principal Rules Considered

The sources of most of the principles in this chapter are Restatement §§ 14–46 and Model Rules 1.1–1.5, 1.14–1.16 and 1.18.

B. Forming the Lawyer-Client Relationship

1. When a Lawyer-Client Relationship Is Formed

A lawyer-client relationship can be formed in three ways:

a. By Consent

Typically, a lawyer-client relationship is formed when a prospective client indicates a wish to retain the lawyer and the lawyer indicates consent to represent the client. [Restatement § 14(1)(a)]

b. Client's Reasonable Belief

A lawyer-client relationship can also be created when a prospective client indicates a wish to retain the lawyer, the lawyer does not indicate a lack of consent, and the prospective client reasonably believes the lawyer has agreed to the relationship. [Restatement § 14(l)(b)]

e.g. **Example:** In **Togstad v. Vesely, Otto, Miller & Keefe,** 291 N.W.2d 686 (Minn. 1980), a woman whose husband was left paralyzed after a medical procedure consulted with a lawyer about whether to bring a medical malpractice suit. After interviewing the woman, the lawyer told her that she probably did not have a case but that he would discuss it with another attorney. The woman believed that a lawyer-client relationship had been established, but the lawyer did not contact her after the initial interview. When the woman consulted another lawyer one year later, the statute of limitations for medical malpractice had already run. The court found that there was sufficient evidence to establish the existence of a lawyer-client relationship with the first lawyer and awarded malpractice damages to the plaintiffs.

EXAM TIP GILBERT

Remember that a lawyer's consent to represent a prospective client is implied if the lawyer fails to ***clearly decline*** representation and the prospective client ***reasonably relies*** on the representation. The reasonableness of the reliance depends on the circumstances and is a question of fact.

---

c. Court Appointment

A lawyer-client relationship can also be created when a court appoints a lawyer to represent the client. [Restatement § 14(2)]

2. No Obligation to Accept Every Case

Unlike English barristers (who traditionally must accept all cases within their areas of experience upon tender of a proper fee), American lawyers traditionally need not take every matter presented to them. But tradition says that each lawyer should see that people can get legal representation when needed.

a. State Standards

Some state regulations assert a positive ***duty*** for lawyers to represent "the causes of the defenseless or the oppressed," the breach of which could theoretically result in professional discipline. [*See, e.g.,* Cal. Bus. & Prof. Code §§ 6068(h), 6103]

b. Non-Discrimination Obligation

One long-open question has been whether a lawyer may refuse to accept a client because of the person's race, gender or some other characteristic traditionally protected in civil rights legislation. With few exceptions, courts have given lawyers plenary authority to decide whom they will or will not represent, *e.g.*, decide to represent only female victims of spousal abuse. In August 2016, however, the ABA adopted a new Model Rule 8.4(g), discussed *infra,* Chapter V of this Summary, that arguably limits a lawyer's discretion.to "discriminate" in their selection of clients. Only time will tell what the effect of the new rule will be as states decide whether and how to incorporate it into their state rules of professional conduct.

3. Duties to a Prospective Client

Between the time a person discusses the possibility of forming a lawyer-client relationship with a lawyer and the time the relationship is formed (or not formed), the lawyer owes duties to the person who at that time is called a "prospective client." [Model Rule 1.18(a); Restatement § 15]

a. Duty to Protect Confidential Information

A lawyer must protect confidential information revealed by a prospective client as fully as that revealed by a client. [Model Rule 1.18(b); Restatement § 15(l)(a); and *see infra,* Chapter III of this Summary]

(1) Lawyer Who Acquires "Significantly Harmful" Information

As a way of protecting a prospective client's confidential information if no lawyer-client relationship is formed, a lawyer who had discussions with the prospective client that could be "significantly harmful" to that person in the matter is ***prohibited from representing any client*** whose interests are **"*materially adverse*"** to interests of the prospective client in the "same or a substantially related matter." [Model Rule 1.18(c); Restatement § 15(2); *compare* Model Rule 1.9(a)]

(2) Informed Consent Can Waive This Prohibition

The bar to a lawyer's participation in a matter because of receipt of significantly harmful confidential information does not apply if both the prospective client and any affected current clients give informed consent, confirmed in writing. [Model Rule 1.18(d)(1); Restatement § 15(2)(b)] For definitions of "informed consent" and "confirmed in writing," *see* Model Rules 1.0(b) and (e), and Chapter IV of this Summary, *infra*, at p. 77.

(3) Screening Can Allow the Lawyer's Firm to Participate in the Matter

Many reasons explain the failure ultimately to form a lawyer-client relationship. At the time of the initial discussion, for example, the lawyer may not know that the adverse party in the matter is a client of the firm. In such cases, if the lawyer who talked to the prospective client "took reasonable measures to avoid exposure to more disqualifying information than was reasonably necessary to determine whether to represent the prospective client," and if that lawyer is (1) "timely screened from any participation in the matter," (2) "apportioned no part of the fee therefrom," and (3) "written notice is promptly given to the prospective client," the firm may represent a party adverse to the prospective client in the matter. [Model Rule 1.18(d)(2); Restatement § 15(2)(a)]

b. Duty to Protect Prospective Client's Property

If a prospective client entrusts documents or other property to the lawyer before a lawyer-client relationship is formed (*e.g.,* for the lawyer to use to understand what the representation would be about), the lawyer must guard the property in the same manner required for property entrusted by a client. [Model Rule 1.15(a); Restatement § 15(l)(b); *and see infra*, p. 47]

c. Duty to Give Competent Legal Advice

A lawyer does not have to give a prospective client any legal advice at all, but if the lawyer negligently gives the prospective client inaccurate information about the law or the prospective client's need for legal services, the lawyer may be liable for professional malpractice. [Restatement §§ 15(l)(c) and 51(1)].

EXAM TIP GILBERT

Keep in mind that the lawyer's duties to "clients" begin before the attorney-client relationship is established—***even if the lawyer is never hired*** to represent the person. At the very least, the lawyer must protect the prospective client's confidential information and property, and if the lawyer chooses to give legal advice, it must be competent.

4. Duty to Reject Certain Cases

The Model Rules specify two situations in which the lawyer ***must refuse*** employment:

a. Where Representation Would Violate a Disciplinary Standard or Other Law

If representation of a client would force the lawyer to violate applicable rules of professional conduct or other law (*e.g.,* it would violate a prohibition against a conflict of interest), the lawyer must decline the case. [Model Rule 1.16(a)(1)]

b. Where Lawyer's Physical or Mental Condition Is Materially Impaired

If the lawyer's physical or mental condition would materially impair the lawyer's ability to represent the client, the lawyer must decline the case. [Model Rule 1.16(a)(2)]

5. Agreeing on Scope and Objectives of Representation

a. Lawyer Must Document the Scope of the Engagement with the Client

The lawyer must communicate to the client the agreed-upon scope of the representation, "preferably in writing," before or within a reasonable time after beginning the representation. Because in any later litigation, the scope of the representation may be an issue, a written agreement is advisable. [Model Rule 1.5(b)]

(1) Definition of Scope and Objectives of Representation

Consistent with the contractual nature of the lawyer's relationship with a client, the scope and objectives of a given representation may be limited by agreement between lawyer and client. [Model Rule 1.2(a) and comments 6, 7, 8]

(2) Limitation of Representation to Particular Subjects

A lawyer and client may agree that the lawyer will undertake to address some, but not all, legal needs of the client. For example, the lawyer may undertake to incorporate the client's business, but not to give the client income tax advice. [Model Rule 1.2(c); Restatement § 19, comment c]

(3) Limitation on Legal Remedies to Be Pursued in Representation

A lawyer and client may similarly agree that the lawyer will seek to resolve a matter short of litigation or will not pursue remedies against particular persons.

b. Informed Consent of Client Required to Limit Scope or Objectives of Representation

The client must give informed consent to limitations on the scope and objectives of representation, and one of a lawyer's roles is to ensure that the client understands the advantages and risks associated with any limitations on the representation. [Model Rule 1.2(c)]

c. Even Informed Consent Cannot Waive Limitations on Representation That Are Unreasonable Under the Circumstances

All limits on the scope of representation are subject to the requirement that they be "reasonable under the circumstances." Thus, even client consent is insufficient to limit a lawyer's duty to provide competent representation, to avoid putting the lawyer's interest ahead of the client's own, and not to limit the lawyer's ability to represent clients in the future. [Model Rule 1.2(c), comments 7, 8; Rule 5.6]

C. Spheres of Authority of Lawyer and Client

1. In General

The fact that a lawyer is retained to represent the client does ***not*** mean that the lawyer assumes complete control over the case. The client remains the party in interest and, with some exceptions, must be allowed to make decisions about the case. [Model Rule 1.2(a)]

2. Matters Within Client's Exclusive Authority

The decision on matters that will substantially affect the client's rights must be made by the client. When such matters arise, the lawyer has a duty to advise the client on particular courses of action, but the decision itself ***rests with the client.*** [Model Rule 1.2(a); Restatement § 22]

a. Settlement or Compromise of a Civil Action

The client must agree to any settlement or compromise of a civil action. *A fortiori,* the client also has the sole power to authorize dismissal or otherwise to end a case on its merits. [Model Rule 1.2(a); Restatement § 22(1)]

(1) Duty to Inform Client of Settlement Offer

Because the right to settle is the client's, the lawyer must convey all settlement offers to the client unless the client has already specified what offers would be unacceptable or validly granted the lawyer authority to make settlement decisions. [Model Rule 1.2(a); 1.4 and comment 2; Restatement § 20, comment d, and § 22, comment c]

(2) Effect of Unauthorized Settlement or Compromise

While a client can give a lawyer actual authority to conclude a settlement on the client's behalf, a lawyer does not inherently have apparent authority to do so. A client can disclaim a settlement that is unauthorized. [Restatement § 27, comment d; **Luethke v. Suhr,** 650 N.W.2d 220 (Neb. 2002)]

(3) Ratification by Client

If the lawyer agrees to a compromise or settlement without authority to do so, the client may still ***ratify*** it. Ratification will be found if the client claims the benefits of the agreement. [Restatement § 21(4) and comment f, and § 26(3) and comment e; **Daniel v. Scott,** 455 So. 2d 30 (Ala. 1984)]

(4) Client May Dismiss at Any Time

The client may dismiss a case at any time regardless of the lawyer's wish to proceed, but the client's dismissal of the case or direct settlement with the opposing party may entitle the lawyer to whatever fee was provided for in the retainer agreement in event of settlement.

b. Important Decisions in Criminal Cases

Only the lawyer's criminal defense client may decide:

(1) ***what plea to enter;***

(2) whether to ***waive jury trial;*** and

(3) whether to ***testify.***

A lawyer may and should counsel the client about such decisions, but the ***lawyer must accept*** and implement what the client decides as to each. [Model Rule 1.2(a); Restatement § 22(1)]

c. Whether to Appeal

In addition, a lawyer must leave to the client the decision whether to appeal an adverse decision in a civil or criminal case. [Restatement § 22(1)]

EXAM TIP GILBERT

A lawyer must promptly convey any offer to ***settle*** a civil case, or offer of a ***plea bargain*** in a criminal case, to his ***client,*** unless the ***client*** has previously instructed the lawyer that an offer on those terms is acceptable or unacceptable. Even if a settlement offer is unreasonably low, the lawyer must convey it to the client before rejecting it, or the lawyer will be subject to discipline.

3. Matters Within Lawyer's Authority

While decisions about the objectives or "ends" of a representation are the client's to make, the "means" are more often within the authority of the lawyer. Even as to means, however, a lawyer must "consult" with the client, and some questions of means, such as those affecting cost and the impact on third parties, are often left to the client. [Model Rule 1.2(a), comments 1, 2; Restatement §§ 21 and 23]

a. Matters Required by Law

Regardless of a client's instructions, a lawyer has authority to comply with all requirements of law or court orders. The lawyer also has authority to refuse to follow a client direction that the lawyer reasonably believes to be illegal. This authority may not be waived by contract. [Restatement § 23]

b. Procedural Matters

With respect to most procedural matters during a judicial proceeding, the client has little expertise and therefore the lawyer is "impliedly authorized" to act in the client's interest. [Model Rule 1.2(a); Restatement § 21]

c. "Judicial Admissions"

Admissions of fact made by a lawyer in the pleadings or in the course of narrowing the issues for trial (*e.g.,* at the pretrial conference) are deemed "judicial admissions." As such, they are ***conclusive*** and bind the client, unless the court permits them to be amended or withdrawn. (*See* Evidence Summary.) If the court refuses such relief, the client's only remedy would be a ***malpractice*** action against the lawyer for any harm or loss resulting from the admission.

DECISION AUTHORITY—EXAMPLES GILBERT

DECISIONS TO BE MADE BY CLIENT (DECISIONS AFFECTING MERITS)	DECISIONS TO BE MADE BY LAWYER (PROCEDURAL TACTICS)
Acceptance or rejection of settlement offers	Choice of motions to file
Plea to be entered in a criminal case	Scope of discovery to take
Waiver of jury trial in a criminal case	Questions to ask in direct and cross-examinations
Whether to testify in a criminal case	What evidence to introduce

4. Special Problems in Representing Clients with "Diminished Capacity"

Lawyers sometimes represent clients with "diminished capacity," *i.e.,* those whose "ability to make adequately considered decisions" is impaired, typically by youth or old age. Insofar as possible, the lawyer must maintain a ***normal relationship*** with such clients, including ***consulting with them about major decisions.*** [Model Rule 1.14(a); Restatement § 24(1)]

a. Lawyer's Standard if Client Unable to Make Decisions

If a client is unable to make some decisions because of diminished capacity, the lawyer must "pursue the lawyer's reasonable view of the client's objectives and interests as the client would define them if able to make adequately considered decisions on the matter." [Restatement § 24(2)]

b. Consultation with Family or Others

Where helpful in determining the client's likely wishes and needs, the lawyer may consult with family members, caregivers and others who act as informal guardians of the client. These consultations do not violate the lawyer's normal obligation not to discuss confidential client information outside the professional relationship. [Model Rule 1.14(b) & (c) and comments 3 & 8; Restatement § 24, comments c & d]

c. Appointment of Guardian

If the lawyer concludes that the client "cannot adequately act in the client's own interest," the lawyer may take "reasonably necessary protective action," including consulting with family members and others who can protect the client. If necessary, the lawyer may seek appointment of a legal guardian to act for the client. Thereafter, the lawyer must treat the guardian's decisions as those of the client unless the guardian violates legal duties to the client. [Model Rule 1.14(b); Restatement § 24(3) & (4)]

d. Taking Emergency Action on Behalf of a Non-Client

A lawyer is authorized to take legal action to protect the "health, safety or a financial interest of a *non-client* with seriously diminished capacity" against "imminent and irreparable harm." The lawyer must have a good faith belief the person is unrepresented and should only act to prevent the immediate harm. The lawyer will owe the same duties to such a person as are owed to clients who retain the lawyer. The lawyer should tell any court and other counsel the emergency nature of the relationship, and the lawyer normally should not charge a fee for the work. [Model Rule 1.14, comments 9 & 10]

EXAM TIP GILBERT

It is important to note that just because a client is under a disability, it does not mean that the attorney can ignore the client's wishes. The Model Rules ***require*** the attorney to ***maintain a normal relationship*** as much as possible and to ***consult*** with the client about major decisions. Obviously if the client is unable to make decisions (*e.g.,* is in a coma), the lawyer or a guardian would have to make the decisions, but if the client has at least some capacity, he should be advised and consulted, and should assist in making decisions of which he is capable.

D. Formal Duties That Lawyers Owe to Clients

1. Introduction

Legal ethics has traditionally broken out categories of duties that lawyers owe to clients. Most are derived from principles that apply to fiduciaries generally, and this part of the Summary discusses the duties one by one. But overarching all of them, a lawyer's obligation to a client is to act in a manner reasonably calculated to advance the client's lawful objectives as defined by the client. [Restatement § 16(1)]

2. Duty of Competence

The duty to represent a client competently has at least four components: **(i)** the ***legal knowledge,*** (ii) the ***skill,*** (iii) the necessary **thoroughness,** and (iv) the ***preparation*** required to perform the services. These are the four elements of the duty of competence, which is the first principle of the Model Rules. [Model Rule 1.1]

a. Ability to Represent Client

The first two elements of competence, required legal knowledge and skill, describe the lawyer's basic ability to perform the work required. To determine that requires looking at the complexity of the matter, the lawyer's training and experience, and whether the work is usually done by specialists. [Model Rule 1.1, comment 1; Restatement § 52(1), comment b]

(1) Where Lawyer Reasonably Expects to Become Competent

A lawyer ***may*** accept such employment if that lawyer in good faith expects to be able to become qualified to perform the necessary services. The lawyer must undertake whatever work or study is required to attain proficiency in the matter. [Model Rule 1.1, comments 2 & 4]

(2) Association with Competent Counsel

When a lawyer faces a problem outside that lawyer's own area of competence, the lawyer may associate with a lawyer who is already proficient in the area. Association of co-counsel, of course, requires the client's consent. [Model Rule 1.1, comments 6 & 7]

EXAM TIP GILBERT

A fairly common exam question involves a newly admitted attorney who has just put out her shingle when a client with a lucrative case walks in the door. The new attorney really wants to take the case because she has student loans to pay, mouths to feed, etc., but she knows she isn't competent to handle it. Recall that the general rule is ***no competency, no case,*** but the new attorney has two options: (i) ***find a qualified lawyer with whom to associate*** (with the client's consent); or (ii) figure out a way to ***become proficient quickly.*** If she reasonably believes she can do one of those two things, she may ethically take the case.

---

(3) Emergency Matters

Situations can arise in which a client consults a lawyer when there is no time for the lawyer to attain the required knowledge and skill before acting, but the client cannot find or does not want to consult another lawyer. Lawyers who act in such circumstances will not be subject to professional discipline and probably not liable for malpractice, but they should limit their work to that "reasonably necessary in the circumstances." [Model Rule 1.1, comment 3; Restatement § 52(1), comments b & d]

EXAM TIP GILBERT

Keep in mind that in an emergency (*e.g.,* the dreaded call in the middle of the night from a real estate client who has been arrested for battery), a lawyer ***may assist*** a client even if the lawyer lacks competence in that particular area. However, the assistance cannot exceed what is ***reasonably necessary to meet the emergency.***

---

b. Duty of Care in Representing a Client

Even where the lawyer is capable of performing required services for the client, or where competent counsel is associated, the services must be performed with "thoroughness and preparation reasonably necessary for the representation." [Model Rule 1.1; *see also,* Restatement § 52(1), comment c]

(1) Standard Depends on Circumstances

Lawyers' services are costly and are borne by the client, so the attention and preparation the lawyer must put into a case varies with how much is at stake for the client. [Model Rule 1.1, comment 5]

(2) Malpractice Liability

While it is possible for an attorney who has incompetently represented a client to be subject to professional discipline, by far the most common remedy is a suit for professional malpractice against the lawyer. [Restatement § 52(1); *see infra*, p. 26 *et seq.*]

3. Duty of Diligence

The Model Rules also require a lawyer to act with ***reasonable diligence and promptness*** in representing a client. [Model Rule 1.3] The Model Rules note that "no professional shortcoming is more widely resented than procrastination." [Model Rule 1.3, comment 3]

a. Not Precluded from Agreeing to Postponement

A requirement of diligence might seem to require resolving matters quickly, but the Model Rules make clear that a lawyer is not required to use "offensive tactics" and may show everyone in the legal process "courtesy and respect." [Model Rule 1.3, comment 1] For example, a lawyer may agree to "a reasonable request for a postponement that will not prejudice the lawyer's client." [Model Rule 1.3, comment 3]

b. Relation to the Duty of Zealous Representation

There is a long tradition of saying that a lawyer must "zealously" represent a client. In fact, Model Rule 1.3, comment 1, uses the word "zeal" but does not define it, and the Restatement says that "zealousness" is captured by the duties of "competence" and "diligence." [Restatement § 16, comment d]

c. Lawyer Need Not Adopt Client's Viewpoint Personally

Whatever "zealousness" the law requires of lawyers, it never obligates a lawyer personally to adopt a client's viewpoints. Thus, a lawyer may represent a person or position the public consider odious, and indeed should do so if necessary to not deny representation to such persons or positions. [Model Rule 1.2(b) and comment 5]

d. Requirement to Carry a Matter Through to Its Conclusion

The duty of diligence requires a lawyer to pursue a matter on the client's behalf until a matter is concluded or the representation otherwise ends. The lawyer should "clarify" whether the representation continues, preferably in writing, and must "consult" with the client about who will handle an appeal, if any. [Model Rule 1.3, comment 4]

e. Sole Practitioner's Duty to Have a Transition Plan

While not described as a formal requirement, each sole practitioner "may" be required to have a plan for what happens in case of the lawyer's death or disability. Another lawyer should be designated to review the lawyer's files, notify clients of the situation, and take any "immediate" action required on the clients' behalf. [Rule 1.3, comment 5]

4. Duty of Communication

The ABA Model Rules also require a lawyer to "explain a matter" to the client "to the extent reasonably necessary to permit the client to make informed decisions" about the representation. [Model Rule 1.4(b)]

a. Specific Requirements

The communication requirement demands that the lawyer:

(i) Let the client know promptly about ***circumstances*** as to which the ***client's informed consent is needed;***

(ii) Reasonably ***consult*** with the client ***about the means*** to use to accomplish the client's objectives;

(iii) ***Keep each client informed*** about the status of the client's matters;

(iv) ***Comply promptly with reasonable client requests for information;*** and

(v) Be sure the client understands any ***relevant limitations on the lawyer's conduct*** imposed by the rules of professional conduct.

[Model Rule 1.4(a)]

b. Right to Withhold Certain Information

If disclosure of certain information would be likely to be "imprudent" (*e.g.,* where the information is a diagnosis that the client is mentally ill), such disclosure may be "delayed." However, the lawyer may not withhold information to serve the lawyer's own or someone else's interest or convenience. [Model Rule 1.4, comment 7]

5. Duty of Confidentiality

The duty of confidentiality is such a central obligation of a lawyer that it is considered in detail in Chapter III of this Summary. (*See infra*, p. 62 *et seq.*)

6. Duty of Loyalty

The duty of loyalty—*i.e.,* the duty to avoid conflicts of interest—is of such importance that it too merits a full chapter. It is described in detail in Chapter IV of this Summary. (*See infra*, p. 78 *et seq.*)

7. Duties with Regard to Client Property

As another part of the broad fiduciary duties owed each client, a lawyer must keep the funds and property of clients ***safe and entirely separate*** from the lawyer's own assets. These rules may seem hyper-technical, but because their violation is often characterized as ***"stealing"*** from a client, it is one of the most-often enforced and tested parts of the law governing lawyers. [Model Rule 1.15; Restatement §§ 44(1) & 46(1); Cal. Rule 4–100]

a. Separate Bank Account

All funds belonging to the client that are received by the lawyer must be deposited in one or more ***separately identified*** bank accounts (usually called "trust accounts" or "clients' funds accounts"). The lawyer may use a single trust account to hold money of many clients, but a careful accounting must be made of the funds of each client. [Model Rule 1.15(a) and comment 1; Restatement § 44(1) and comment d]

(1) No Commingling

In general, the lawyer must not deposit any personal funds in these bank accounts, although a lawyer may deposit small amounts into the trust account to pay the ***bank charges*** thereon. [Model Rule 1.15(b)]

(2) Location of Accounts

Absent client consent, the accounts must be maintained in the state where the lawyer's office is located. [Model Rule 1.15(a)]

(3) Fees and Expenses Advanced by Client

The lawyer must deposit monies advanced by the client to cover future ***fees and expenses*** into the trust account. [Model Rule 1.15(c); Restatement § 44(1) and comment f; Cal. Rule 4–100]

b. Withdrawals from Joint Funds

A lawyer who receives money that belongs in part to the client and in part to the lawyer (*e.g.,* a settlement in a contingent fee case) must deposit the ***entire*** sum in the client's trust account.

(1) Undisputed Fee

If the lawyer's portion is undisputed and the amount is fixed, the lawyer ***must withdraw it as soon as possible*** (to prevent commingling with clients' funds) and promptly turn the client's share over to the client. [Model Rule 1.15(d); Restatement § 44(1) and comment f; Cal. Rule 4–100]

(2) Disputed Funds

But if the client disputes the lawyer's right to receive all or any portion of the funds, the disputed portion may ***not be withdrawn*** until the controversy is resolved. [Model Rule 1.15(d) and comment 3; Restatement § 44(2) and comment h]

(3) Funds Potentially Belonging to a Third Party

A lawyer holds the client's funds in a fiduciary capacity and cannot distribute them except as authorized by the client or ordered by a court. Thus, without authorization, the lawyer cannot disburse funds even if the lawyer personally concludes that the client owes the money involved to a third party (*e.g.,* the client's doctor or other creditors). [Model Rule 1.15(e) and comment 4; Restatement § 44(2) and comment g]

c. Duties Regarding Custody of Clients' Property (Other than Funds)

As a fiduciary, the lawyer must identify and label securities and other property of the client upon receipt thereof, and must deposit such property at once in a ***safe deposit box or other suitable storage facility.*** [Model Rule 1.15(a); Restatement §§ 45 & 46]

EXAM TIP GILBERT

Note that there are two requirements regarding client property: (i) the property must be kept ***safe***, and (ii) it must be kept ***separate.*** For exam purposes, the safety requirement is fairly easy—the lawyer has to store the property in a safe place—for money, that's in the bank and for other property, in a safe deposit box or other safe place—so that it doesn't get stolen, destroyed, etc. It also means the lawyer can't use the property or borrow against it.

A more likely exam topic will involve keeping the property separate from the lawyer's property. Recall that although the lawyer can commingle several ***clients'*** funds in a trust account, he ***cannot put any of his own money*** in there except to pay the bank fees. Also, if the lawyer receives a settlement check or other payment to the client from which his fee is to be paid, he can take his fee out of the fund only if there is no dispute about rights to the money in the account. If there is a dispute, the lawyer cannot withdraw the disputed amount until the issue is resolved.

CHECKLIST OF LAWYER'S DUTIES TO CLIENT GILBERT

A LAWYER OWES THE FOLLOWING DUTIES TO THE CLIENT:

- ☑ Duty of ***competence***—act with knowledge, skill, thoroughness, and preparation;
- ☑ Duty of ***diligence***—pursue the matter with zeal and promptness;
- ☑ Duty of ***communication***—keep client informed;
- ☑ Duty of ***confidentiality***—not reveal client information;
- ☑ Duty of ***loyalty***—avoid conflicts of interest;
- ☑ Duties with regard to ***client property***—keep safe and separate from lawyer's own assets.

E. Particular Issues Surrounding Fees for Legal Services

1. Introduction

a. Client Obligations to Lawyers

While lawyers have several important obligations to clients, the converse is not true. The Model Rules are silent on the client's obligations (because the Model Rules are written to regulate lawyers, not clients), and the Restatement identifies only (i) a duty to indemnify the lawyer for liability to which the client exposed the lawyer without the lawyer's fault, and (ii) the duty to fulfill any contractual obligations to the lawyer (*e.g.*, an agreement to tell the lawyer the truth and to turn over all relevant documents). [Restatement § 17]

b. Special Rules Regulating Legal Fees

That leaves the most important client obligation, the duty to pay the lawyer's fee. Both the Model Rules and the Restatement address this issue primarily in terms of limits on what a lawyer may charge and restrictions on what the lawyer's fee agreement may provide.

2. Timing and Content of the Fee Agreement

When the lawyer has not regularly represented a client, the lawyer must communicate the basis or rate of the fee to the client, preferably in writing, ***before or within a reasonable time*** after commencing the representation. [Model Rule 1.5(b); Restatement § 38(1)]

a. Required Subjects to Be Agreed

Three matters must be specified in the fee agreement:

(1) Amount or Basis of the Fee

The amount of the fee or the basis for its calculation (*e.g.,* hourly rate of the lawyer, contingent fee) must be set out.

(2) Scope of Work

The agreement must specify what the lawyer will be expected to do for the client to earn the fee (*see supra*, p. 39).

(3) Expenses

An estimate of costs likely to be incurred and charged to the client.

[Model Rule 1.5(b); Restatement § 38(1)]

b. Written Agreement Preferable

A fee agreement, unless for a contingent fee, is enforceable ***whether oral or written.*** Technically, under the Model Rules, it need only be "communicated to the client" and the client's silence will be deemed consent. However, good practice dictates that the agreement be in writing and signed by both parties. [Model Rule 1.5(b); Restatement § 38; for contingent fees, *see infra,* p. 50]

c. Ambiguities Construed from Position of the Client

Because the lawyer initiates the fee agreement and is presumed capable of saying things clearly, in the event of a fee dispute, the contract will be construed "as a reasonable person in the circumstances of the client would have construed it." [Restatement § 18(2), comment h]

d. Where Fee Agreement Entered into After Representation Begins

If no fee arrangement is made at the outset of the representation, the burden will be on the lawyer to show that the substance of any contract made later, and the circumstances of its formation, were fair and reasonable to the client. [Restatement § 18(l)(a)]

3. Requirement that Fees Be No More than Reasonable

Courts may refuse to enforce a fee agreement against a client and may impose professional discipline upon a lawyer if the fees charged are found to be "unreasonable." [Model Rule 1.5(a); Restatement § 34] The corresponding terms in other lawyer codes are "clearly excessive" [ABA Model Code of Professional Responsibility, DR 2–106(A)], or "unconscionable" [Cal. Rule 4–200].

a. Determining "Reasonableness"

The "reasonableness" of a fee agreement depends upon ***all relevant circumstances.*** In this respect, the interests of both clients and lawyers must be considered; *i.e.,* excessive fees would deter the use of legal services, while inadequate compensation might undermine effective representation [Restatement § 34, comment b]

b. Relevant Factors

The following factors have regularly been cited as keys to the determination of reasonableness, although they are not the only ones that a court may consider:

(i) The ***time and labor*** required, the ***novelty and difficulty*** of the issues, and the ***skill*** needed to perform the legal services;

(ii) The likelihood, if apparent to the client, that taking the case will mean the lawyer will be ***precluded from other employment,***

(iii) The ***fee customarily charged*** for the services in the locality;

(iv) The ***amount involved*** and the ***results obtained;***

(v) ***Time limitations imposed*** by the client or the circumstances;

(vi) The ***nature and length of the attorney-client relationship;***

(vii) The ***experience, reputation, and ability*** of the lawyer; and

(viii) Whether the fee is ***fixed or contingent.***

[Model Rule 1.5(a); Restatement § 34, comment c]

c. Fee Arbitration

Several states allow clients who are dissatisfied with their bills for legal services to have them reviewed by an arbitrator. Most such plans are voluntary, but lawyers are exhorted to submit to arbitration. [Model Rule 1.5, comment 9]

4. Special Issues Relating to Contingent Fee Agreements

Contingent fees depend upon success in the case; *i.e.,* by agreement, the lawyer is to receive a percentage of whatever the client recovers at trial or by settlement—and nothing if the client loses. [Restatement § 35]

a. Propriety of Contingent Fee Agreements

In this country, the problem of contingent fees has been resolved in favor of permitting their use, subject to regulation designed to prevent abuses. [*See* Model Rule 1.5(c); Restatement § 35]

(1) Factors Supporting Use of Contingent Fees

Contingent fees have the advantage of enabling poor clients with meritorious claims to enforce them without compromising for a small fraction of their total value. It is also urged that such arrangements help to support and encourage a body of independent lawyers ready to challenge wrongs done to their clients from any source.

(2) Specific Regulatory Requirements

In addition to the requirements for any fee agreement, the Model Rules state that a contingent fee agreement must:

(i) ***Be in writing*** and the writing must be ***signed by the client;***

(ii) ***State the method by which the fee is to be determined***, including the lawyer's percentages in the event of settlement, trial, or appeal;

(iii) ***Identify expenses to be deducted*** from the recovery and whether they are before or after the lawyer's percentage is calculated; and

(iv) ***Be followed up with a written statement*** accounting for disposition of the recovery.

[Model Rule 1.5(c)]

(3) Reasonableness Requirement

A contingent fee may be higher than a fixed or hourly fee because of the increased risk the lawyer assumes. However, contingent fees are subject to the reasonableness requirement applicable to all fees. [Model Rule 1.5(a)(8); Restatement § 35, comment c]

EXAM TIP GILBERT

If faced with a question involving a contingent fee, keep in mind that the amount of a contingent fee must be ***reasonable at the time the contingent fee agreement is made*** and is at least subject to review if the case involves significantly less work than expected. Further, a contingent fee agreement must be in writing and signed by the client, unlike a non-contingent fee which is only "communicated to the client" and only "preferably in writing."

(4) Maximum Limits on Contingency Fees

In a few states, ***court rules*** fix maximum percentages that may be charged by lawyers under contingent fee contracts. (Usually, the maximum declines as the size of the recovery increases—*e.g.*, 50% of the first $1,000, 40% of the next $2,000, 30% of the next $5,000, etc.) Such schedules have been upheld against attacks that they constitute unconstitutional interference with lawyers' freedom to contract. [**American Trial Lawyers Association v. New Jersey Supreme Court,** 316 A.2d 19, *aff'd,* 330 A.2d 350 (N.J. 1974)]

b. Kinds of Cases in Which Contingent Fees Are Prohibited

(1) Domestic Relations Cases

Because of the sensitive family relationships involved in domestic relations proceedings, and the wish to encourage compromise, contingent fee arrangements are prohibited in most domestic relations cases (divorce, custody, etc.). [Restatement § 35(1)(b)]

(a) Model Rules

The Model Rules specifically prohibit a lawyer from accepting a fee ***"contingent upon obtaining a divorce, alimony, property settlement, or support."*** The rationale is that the contingent fee might interfere with the possibility of reconciliation. [Model Rule 1.5(d)(1); Restatement § 35(1)(b) and comment g]

(b) Distinguish—Post-Divorce Matters

Once a divorce has been ***granted,*** and the current proceedings involve only collection of a debt (*e.g.,* past due alimony), some courts permit contingent fee arrangements. [Model Rule 1.5(d)(1) and comment 6; Restatement § 35, comment g]

(2) Criminal Cases

A lawyer is prohibited from taking a criminal case on a contingent fee.

(a) Criminal Defense

A lawyer may not represent a criminal defendant on a contingent fee basis. The rationale sometimes given for this rule is that legal services in such cases do not yield the client a fund or property with which to pay the fee, but the better argument is that such a fee might discourage the lawyer from encouraging the client to accept an otherwise desirable plea agreement that might lower what the lawyer received. [Model Rule 1.5(d)(2); Restatement § 35(1)(a) and comment (f)(i)]

(b) Criminal Prosecution

Likewise, a lawyer may not prosecute a case on a contingent fee basis because it might interfere with a prosecutor's duty to do justice even if it involves dismissing a case. [Restatement § 35, comment f(ii); **People *ex rel.* Clancy v. Superior Court,** 39 Cal. 3d 740 (1985)]

5. Fee in the Absence of a Valid Fee Contract

If a lawyer and client have not agreed on a fee, or the fee agreement is invalid, the lawyer is entitled to recover the ***reasonable value*** of services rendered. [Restatement § 39]

6. Minimum Fee Schedules

In the past, some state and local bar associations published schedules of minimum fees for various kinds of legal services. In some instances, the fees in the schedules were offered merely as a "suggestion" of the "going rate" for particular services, but in other instances, lawyers were threatened with discipline if they regularly undercut the fees stated in the schedules.

a. Violation of Antitrust Laws

In **Goldfarb v. Virginia State Bar,** 421 U.S. 773 (1975), the United States Supreme Court held that a fee schedule that had the ***effect*** of creating uniform fees for legal work connected with interstate commerce was illegal as price fixing under section 1 of the Sherman Act.

b. Fees A Matter of Private Contract or Legal Decree

The result of *Goldfarb* is that specific fees are no longer a matter for bar association determination or review. Fees are either the product of private negotiation between lawyer and client, as discussed above, or they are established by court order or controlling legislation, as discussed below.

7. Legislative Regulation of Fees

Congress and some state legislatures have set ***maximum*** fees for certain types of legal services. Typical examples include legal services rendered in connection with probate of a decedent's estate, guardianships, workers' compensation claims, Social Security claims, and representation of indigents in criminal proceedings. In general, state courts adhere rigorously to these legislative ceilings on fees, and disciplinary action may be taken against lawyers who attempt to avoid the limitation.

a. Effect on Right to Counsel

The impact of these limits can be severe. For example, Congress limits lawyers in Prison Litigation Reform Act cases to 150% of actual damages recovered. Thus, where a prisoner won the case but recovered only $1 in nominal damages, his lawyer's fee was capped at $1.50. [**Bovin v. Black,** 225 F.3d 36 (1st Cir. 2000)]

b. "Ordinary" vs. "Extraordinary" Services

Some statutes are drafted to mitigate the above problem by specifying a ceiling only for the lawyer's "ordinary" services in handling the case. Such statutes empower the tribunal hearing the claim to award ***additional*** reasonable fees for "extraordinary" services. [**Bias v. Oklahoma,** 568 P.2d 1269 (Okla. 1977)]

8. Setting Fees in Class Actions, Derivative Suits, and Certain Civil Rights Actions

In cases involving multiple plaintiffs or fees paid by the losing party, the rules often provide for judicially established attorneys' fees.

a. Lodestar Approach

Under the most common approach now used, the court establishes a "lodestar," *i.e.*, the number of hours reasonably expended multiplied by the lawyer's reasonable hourly rate. [**Hensley v. Eckerhart,** 461 U.S. 424 (1983)] The lodestar amount is presumed to be a reasonable fee. [**Pennsylvania v. Delaware Valley Citizens' Council for Clean Air,** 478 U.S. 546 (1986)]

(1) Prevailing Rates

The reasonableness of the lawyer's rate is determined by comparing it to the prevailing market rate in the community. Thus, even if the actual lawyer works for a labor union or is otherwise actually paid less that those rates, she is entitled to the market rate. [**Raney v. Federal Bureau of Prisons,** 222 F.3d 927 (Fed. Cir. 2000)]

(2) Proportionality Not Required

Also, the attorney's fee may be substantially in excess of the amount the plaintiff recovered if necessary to reward the lawyer for efforts on the plaintiff's behalf. [**City of Riverside v. Rivera,** 477 U.S. 561 (1986)]

b. Common Fund Method

In cases where the lawyer recovers a substantial sum for the plaintiff or class, many courts now award the lawyer a percentage of the recovery, as if there had been a contingent fee agreement. [**Vizcaino v. Microsoft Corp.,** 290 F.3d 1043 (9th Cir. 2002)]

c. Negotiating Attorney's Fees as Part of Overall Settlement

A difficult conflict of interest can arise if the defendant offers to make a generous settlement in favor of the plaintiff class but conditions it on the plaintiff's lawyer taking a less than reasonable fee. The Supreme Court has held that accepting such a settlement may be part of a lawyer's duty, so many lawyers now negotiate a fee agreement with the class in advance. The lawyer will be paid out of a court award of fees if it is equal to the agreed amount, but out of the clients' award if not. [**Evans v. Jeff D.,** 475 U.S. 717 (1986); **Venegas v. Mitchell,** 495 U.S. 82 (1990)]

9. Protecting Lawyer's Right to Compensation

a. Fee Collection in General

In collecting a fee from a client, a lawyer may not use legally prohibited methods, harass the client, or reveal the client's confidential information. If there is a dispute about the fee owed, the lawyer has the burden of proof about the services rendered and their value. [Restatement § 41 & 42]

b. Retaining (Possessory) Lien

In many states (but not California), a lawyer has, by statute or judicial decision, a ***possessory lien*** on property, documents, and funds belonging to the client that come into the lawyer's possession by reason of the employment. The basic value of the retaining lien lies in the ***inconvenience*** that the client or the client's successors experience in being denied access to the property. Ordinarily, a retaining lien ***cannot*** be sued upon by the lawyer (although it can be asserted as a ***defense*** to a suit by the client demanding return of his property).

(1) Documents Prepared by the Lawyer

A lawyer ordinarily need not turn over documents prepared by the lawyer and not yet paid for by the client *(e.g.,* a will or contract drafted for the client). [Restatement § 43(1)]

(2) Limited to Property Acquired as Attorney

With respect to other property of the client that the lawyer holds, a retaining lien attaches ***only*** to property that comes into the lawyer's possession in the lawyer's capacity ***as attorney*** for the client. Hence the lien does ***not*** apply to documents or other materials received by a lawyer while acting as trustee, escrow holder, director, etc., for the client.

(3) Note—Retaining Lien on Needed Files Void

Even if there is a written agreement by which the lawyer has a retaining lien on a client's papers and files as security for the fees, such lien will ***not*** be upheld as applied to files the client needs to pursue an active case.

c. Charging (Nonpossessory) Lien

In many states, in addition to the retaining lien, a lawyer has, by statute or judicial decision, a "charging lien." This lien gives the lawyer the right to have ***any fund or recovery*** obtained for the client serve as security for the attorney's fees and disbursements in that matter. For example, a lawyer who prosecutes a contingent fee case to judgment is recognized as having a lien on the judgment for the amount of the contingent fee and expenses. [Restatement § 43(2)]

(1) Charging Lien Created by Contract

In some states, including California, the common law charging lien is ***not*** recognized. In those states, however, the lawyer and client may, by ***express*** agreement, create a lien on the client's prospective recovery to secure the attorney's fees and expenses. In general, the express lien is subject to the same rules and limitations as the common law lien.

(2) Advantages over Retaining Lien

The major advantage of the charging lien over the retaining lien is that the charging lien can be ***affirmatively enforced.*** If the client fails or refuses to pay the agreed fee, the lawyer can file a legal action to foreclose the lien on the client's judgment (or whatever fund or recovery has been obtained).

(3) Limitations on Charging Liens

At the same time, the charging lien is subject to limitations:

(a) Limited to Fees in Particular Case

The lien is limited to the fees and costs incurred by the client in connection with the particular action in which the judgment or settlement is obtained. It does ***not*** secure other fees owed by the same client on other matters. [Restatement § 43(2)(c)]

(a) No Lien for Fees in Defense

In addition, a lawyer does not have a charging lien on property involved in litigation where the lawyer merely ***defeats*** a claim against the client. The lien applies only where there is some recovery or affirmative relief.

(4) Time at Which Charging Lien Attaches

Most states permit the lawyer to assert a charging lien against the client's interest only when a judgment or settlement is obtained. However, provided the lawyer gives the defendant ***notice*** of the contingent fee interest and the lien is held to attach to the ***cause of action*** (*see supra*, p. 55), the client may not defeat a charging lien by settling the claim ***directly*** with the defendant. Furthermore, a number of states have ***expanded*** the scope of charging liens and permit them to attach at earlier stages in the proceeding, thus preventing the client from settling the case without paying the lawyer.

(a) No Right to Continue Case

The lien merely assists the lawyer in recovering her fee. Even if the client settles the claim directly with the defendant, the settlement itself is ***effective.*** The lawyer has ***no right to continue the case to judgment*** (in hopes of getting a larger recovery and hence a bigger fee). [Model Rule 1.2(a); Restatement § 43(2)(d)]

COMPARISON OF ATTORNEYS' LIENS	
RETAINING LIEN	**CHARGING LIEN**
• ***Possessory lien***—client property, documents, and funds that come into the lawyer's possession in the lawyer's capacity as attorney for the client	• ***Nonpossessory lien***—any fund or recovery obtained for the client in that matter
• ***General lien*** for the balance the client owes to the lawyer	• ***Specific lien*** covering only the lawyer's services in the action in which the recovery was obtained
• ***Not affirmatively enforceable*** in court	• ***Can be affirmatively enforced***
• Lien on needed files is ***void***	• Can be created ***by express agreement*** if not recognized by state statute

F. Terminating the Lawyer-Client Relationship

1. Introduction

The attorney-client relationship typically concludes when a matter is resolved and the lawyer has performed all necessary legal services. [Model Rule 1.3, comment 4; Model Rule 1.16, comment 1] However, either the lawyer or the client may also seek to terminate the relationship ***before*** completion of the matter.

2. Withdrawal by Lawyer

Once a lawyer undertakes to represent a client, the lawyer may not simply terminate their relationship at will. A lawyer's decision to withdraw should be made only on the basis of "compelling circumstances," and the lawyer should make all "reasonably practicable" efforts to minimize possible adverse effects on the client. [Model Rule 1.16(d); Restatement §§ 32 & 33]

a. Duty to Withdraw

Under certain circumstances, the lawyer has an *obligation* to withdraw from employment.

(1) Employment Violates Rules of Professional Conduct

A lawyer has a duty to withdraw from a representation when she knows (or should know) that continued employment will result in violation of a standard of professional conduct, *e.g.*, where the lawyer would be involved in assisting the client to commit a crime or fraud. [Model Rule 1.16(a)(1); Restatement § 32(2)(a)]

(2) Personal Inability to Continue Employment

Likewise, the lawyer must withdraw if the lawyer's mental or physical condition materially impairs the lawyer's ability to provide effective representation. [Model Rule 1.16(a)(2); Restatement § 32(2)(b)]

(3) Discharge by Client

The lawyer must withdraw if discharged by the client, even if the lawyer believes the client's reasons for the discharge are unjustified and foolish. [Model Rule 1.16(a)(3); Restatement § 32(2)(c); *and see* below]

b. Permissive Withdrawal

Where withdrawal is ***not required,*** the lawyer is under a general duty to continue the employment to its natural conclusion. However, there are specific exceptions that ***permit*** a lawyer to withdraw from a matter.

(1) No Material Adverse Effect on Client

A lawyer may withdraw, even over the client's objection, if the withdrawal can be accomplished without material adverse effect on the client. It is not clear, however, if there will ever be such a finding where a client firmly objects to withdrawal. [Model Rule 1.16(b)(1); Restatement § 32(3)(a)]

(2) Client Involves Lawyer in Illegal Conduct

The lawyer may also withdraw if the client has employed, plans to employ, or persists in employing the lawyer in what the lawyer "*reasonably believes*" *is* criminal or fraudulent conduct. [Model Rule 1.16(b)(2), (3); Restatement § 32(3)(d), (e)]

(3) Repugnant Demands by Client

A lawyer may withdraw if the client insists on taking action that the lawyer "considers ***repugnant*** or with which the lawyer has a ***fundamental disagreement.***" [Model Rule 1.16(b)(4); Restatement § 32(3)(f)]

(4) Client Fails to Fulfill Obligation to the Lawyer

The lawyer may withdraw if the client fails to pay the required fee or fails to comply with some other obligation to the lawyer, but the lawyer must give reasonable warning that withdrawal will follow unless the obligation is met. [Model Rule 1.16(b)(5); Restatement § 32(3)(g)]

(5) Relationship Unreasonably Difficult

A lawyer may withdraw if the client has rendered the obligation "unreasonably difficult" for financial or other reasons (*e.g.,* client will not cooperate with attorney). [Model Rule 1.16(b)(6); Restatement $32(3)(h)]

(6) Consent of Client

A lawyer may withdraw when the client ***gives informed consent*** to the termination of employment. [Restatement § 32(3)(c).

(7) Other Good Cause for Withdrawal

Finally, a lawyer may withdraw when other good cause for withdrawal exists. [Model Rule 1.16(b)(7); Restatement $32(3)(i)]

WITHDRAWAL BY ATTORNEY GILBERT

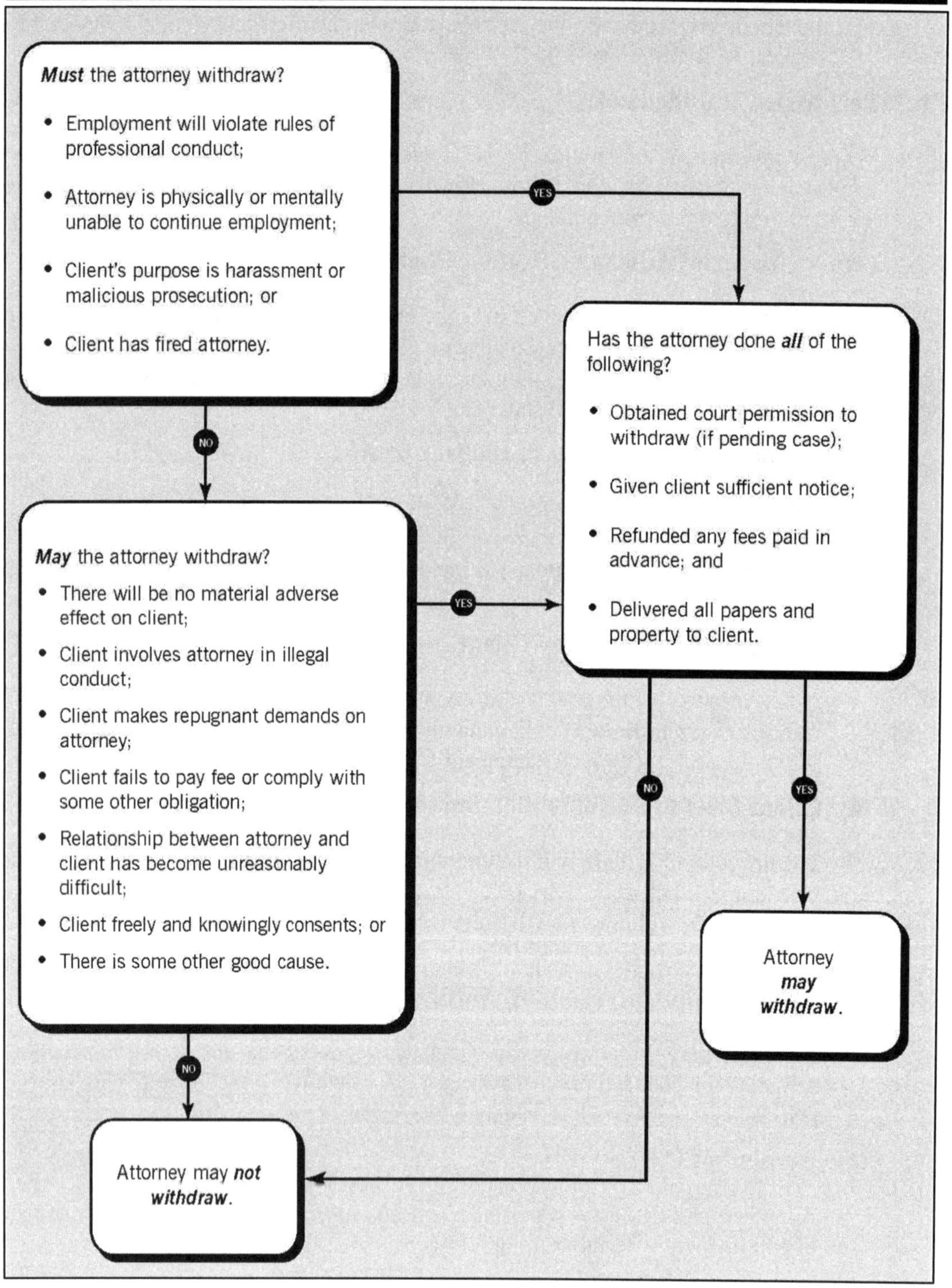

c. General Obligations of Lawyer in Withdrawing from Employment

Whether withdrawal is mandatory or permissive, the lawyer has a duty to ***safeguard the rights and interests*** of the client. [Restatement § 33(1)]

(1) Approval of Court in Litigation Matters

When a matter is pending before a court or other tribunal, the lawyer may have to obtain ***permission from the court*** to withdraw. [Model Rule 1.16(c); Restatement § 32(5)]

(2) Notice to Client

The lawyer may not withdraw until the client has been given sufficient notice so that other counsel can be retained. [Model Rule 1.16(d)]

(3) Refund of Unearned Attorney's Fees

Upon withdrawal from employment, the lawyer must ***refund*** any fees the client paid in advance which the lawyer has not earned. [Model Rule 1.16(d)]

(4) Delivery of Clients' Materials

The lawyer must also promptly return to the client ***all papers and property*** to which the client is entitled. [Model Rule 1.16(d)]

3. Discharge by Client

Unlike the limitations on a lawyer's freedom to withdraw from employment, the right of a client to terminate the attorney-client relationship is ***virtually unconditional.*** Termination may come ***at any time, with or without just cause.*** [Model Rule 1.16(a)(3); Restatement § 32(1)]

a. Provision for "Irrevocability" Invalid

It follows that any provision in a retainer agreement that purports to make the lawyer's employment irrevocable is ***void.*** [**Richette v. Solomon,** 187 A.2d 910 (Pa. 1963)]

b. Judicial Refusal to Allow Discharge in Exceptional Cases

In some instances, courts may ***refuse*** to permit the discharge of a lawyer because it would disrupt a trial. For example, where a client seeks to discharge a lawyer during trial in order to make a "flaming" personal address to the jury, the court may refuse to honor such a request. [**Dennis v. United States,** 183 F.2d 201 (2d Cir. 1950); Restatement § 32(5)]

EXAM TIP GILBERT

Keep in mind that although the general rule is that a client may fire his lawyer at any time with or without cause, most courts require the court's permission for a substitution of attorneys ***after a lawsuit has been filed.*** Courts usually grant the necessary permission, but permission may be denied if a substitution of attorneys would cause ***undue delay or disruption.*** A lawyer must also obtain permission of the court to withdraw from a matter that is pending before the court, but if permission is denied, the lawyer ***must continue*** the representation even if there is good cause for withdrawal.

---

c. Continuing Fiduciary Duty of Lawyer

The fact that a lawyer is discharged without cause does ***not*** relieve the lawyer of fiduciary obligations to the client. As in the case of withdrawal, the lawyer is still prohibited from revealing confidential information or from representing conflicting interests [Restatement § 33(2); *see infra*, p. 62 *et seq.*]

d. Liability of Client Under Fee Contract

While the client is free to discharge the lawyer for any reason, the client may still be ***contractually*** liable in the event the client terminates the relationship ***without cause.*** [Restatement § 40]

(1) Fixed Fee

If a fixed fee agreement was involved (a set amount for the particular case or transaction), the lawyer may be entitled to recover on a quantum meruit basis for the work done but may not recover more than the amount set in the agreement.

(2) Nonrefundable Retainer Fee Ineffective

A lawyer typically may not avoid the consequences of discharge by charging a "nonrefundable retainer." Such agreements provide that once the lawyer has taken the case, even if the lawyer is later terminated, the client owes the entire fee. Because such agreements limit the right to terminate the lawyer and are likely to constitute an unreasonably excessive fee, they are usually unenforceable and a basis for sanctioning the lawyer. [***In re*** **Cooperman,** 83 N.Y.2d 465 (1994)]

(3) Contingent Fee—Measure of Recovery

There is a split of authority as to the proper measure of recovery where the case was being handled on a contingent fee basis.

(a) Recovery of Full Contingent Share

Some courts hold that the discharged lawyer is entitled to the ***full share*** of any recovery ultimately obtained by the client, particularly if the lawyer was discharged on the eve of the verdict after rendering all services. [**Dombey v. Detroit Toledo & Ironton Railroad,** 351 F.2d 121 (6th Cir. 1965)]

(b) Recovery of Reasonable Value of Services

The more common view is that the contingent fee contract is ***not enforceable*** where the client discharges the lawyer, because to enforce the contract would significantly deter clients from exercising ***their essential right to change lawyers.*** These courts permit the discharged lawyer to recover only the ***reasonable value of services actually rendered.*** [**Fracasse v. Brent,** 6 Cal. 3d 784 (1972); Restatement § 40(2)]

(c) Recovery Requirement

Under either approach, however, the lawyer usually gets ***nothing*** unless and until the client ***recovers*** on the claim, either by settlement or judgment. [*See* **Plaza Shoe Store v. Hermel,** 636 S.W.2d 53 (Mo. 1982)]

Chapter Three

Duty to Protect Confidential Information of the Client

CONTENTS PAGE

Chapter Approach

A general rule of agency law says that no agent may use or reveal confidential information of the principal without the principal's consent. [Restatement (Third) Agency §805(2)]. This rule is especially important in the practice of law, given the sensitivity of issues with which lawyers often deal and the importance of getting the client to give the lawyer truthful information necessary for effective representation.

Protection of confidential client information is often seen as the most important single obligation of a lawyer, and the principles in this Chapter underlie many of the rules found elsewhere in this Summary, such as those in Chapter IV on conflicts of interest, Chapter V on obligations to third parties, and Chapter VI on ethics in litigation.

This chapter considers the three most important doctrines that govern a lawyer's dealing with confidential client information—the ***attorney-client privilege,*** the ***work product doctrine,*** and the ***professional duty of confidentiality.***

The sources of most of the principles in this chapter are Restatement §§ 59–93 and Model Rule 1.6. The elements of all three doctrines are regularly tested on the MPRE.

A. Introduction

1. The Three Key Legal Doctrines Distinguished

Three related but quite different doctrines govern a lawyers dealing with confidential client information:

a. ***The attorney-client privilege,*** is a rule of ***evidence*** that protects certain information from disclosure ***even*** in ***judicial proceedings;***

b. ***The work product doctrine,*** is a rule of civil procedure that protects information from disclosure, primarily in ***pre-trial discovery;*** and

c. ***The professional duty of confidentiality,*** is a rule of ***legal ethics*** requiring that a lawyer not disclose the much larger body of information learned by the lawyer that is "relating to the representation" of a client.

2. Focus in Model Rules and in Restatement

The attorney-client privilege and work product doctrine are judicial creations that are primarily applied to cases where one party seeks to compel disclosure of information during discovery or trial. As applied to any given matter, both privileged and work product information is ***also protected by the professional duty of confidentiality*** because it is related to the representation. The Restatement is the best source for analysis of both the attorney-client privilege and work product doctrine. [Restatement §§ 68–93] The Model Rules join the Restatement to address the professional duty to protect confidential information, whether or not privileged. [Model Rule 1.6; Restatement §§ 59–67]

EXAM TIP GILBERT

Learn the differences between the attorney-client privilege, the work product doctrine and the professional duty of confidentiality. Each is fair game for testing in legal ethics courses and on the MPRE. The ***attorney-client privilege*** applies to ***communications*** between ***privileged persons***, in a ***confidential*** setting, while seeking or providing ***legal advice.*** The ***work product*** doctrine covers only material ***prepared by a lawyer*** in ***preparation for litigation.*** Facts in both categories are ***immune from compelled discovery or testimony***. The ***professional duty of confidentiality*** protects all ***information related to the representation,*** however and whenever learned, against ***voluntary*** disclosure by the lawyer, but a court with jurisdiction of a matter may ***require*** a lawyer to ***disclose*** relevant ***unprivileged*** information otherwise protected by this duty of confidentiality

B. Attorney-Client Privilege

1. Introduction

The ***legal*** privilege against compelled disclosure governs whether a lawyer or client may be required by legal process to disclose what a client has revealed to the lawyer in confidence and what advice the lawyer has given the client. The privilege is based on the need to ensure that every person may freely and fully confide in his lawyer so as to be adequately represented. [**Upjohn Co. v. United States,** 449 U.S. 383 (1981)]

2. Subject of the Privilege

The privilege is discussed in detail in the Evidence Summary. Briefly, however, four basic elements are necessary for the attorney-client privilege to apply:

(i) There must have been a ***communication***;

(ii) The communication must be between someone who was (or wanted to be) a client to an ***attorney acting as such at the time;***

(iii) The communications must be made ***in confidence*** (without strangers present); and

(iv) The communications must be made ***for the purpose of obtaining legal assistance.***

[Restatement § 68]

a. Requirement of a Communication—The Problem of Physical Evidence

The privilege applies only to ***"communications"*** from the client; *i.e.,* information transmitted orally or in writing from the client to the attorney and from the attorney to the client. It also covers information passed to or from certain agents of either the attorney or the client. It does ***not*** protect incriminating documents or physical evidence turned over to the lawyer by the client, or evidence discovered by the lawyer on his own while investigating the case (*e.g.*, the murder weapon or the stolen property). [**Morrell v. State,** 575 P.2d 1200 (Alaska 1978); Restatement § 119; *see infra*, p. 73]

EXAM TIP GILBERT

Watch for an exam question in which the client turns documents or other evidence over to the attorney. An item does ***not*** become privileged merely because it was given to an attorney. The privilege extends only to ***communications.*** Thus, if the item would be discoverable in the client's hands, it is equally discoverable in the attorney's hands.

b. Requirement that Communication Be Made "in Confidence"

The usual communication between lawyer and client takes place in the lawyer's office with the door closed. If the communication takes place under less than confidential circumstances, the entire privilege may be lost.

(1) Third Party in a Position to Overhear

The presence of a third party may destroy the privilege. If the client's statement is made when it is clearly possible for someone other than the lawyer or lawyer's employee to hear it, the statement is ***not*** privileged. [**People v. Harris,** 57 N.Y.2d 335 (1982)]

e.g. **Example:** Shortly after being arrested, Harris wanted to talk to a lawyer. The call was placed and a police officer showed Harris to the phone. Another person was already in that room, and before the police officer could leave, Harris told the lawyer, "Oh, my God, I think I've killed [victim]." The court held that this statement was not privileged because it was made in the presence of third parties, whose presence was known to the defendant.

EXAM TIP GILBERT

An exam question in this area will often have a client make a statement in the presence of other people. Check to see exactly who these people are. If they are (i) ***agents of the attorney*** (*e.g.,* a secretary or law clerk) ***or the client*** (*e.g.,* an accountant to help explain his books or a minor's parents) or (ii) someone there ***to further the attorney-client relationship*** (*e.g.,* a translator or investigator), the privilege is ***not*** lost. But if a conversation occurs in front of friends at a party or in the middle of the lawyer's crowded waiting room, it is not privileged.

(a) Distinguish—Eavesdroppers

In the past, the presence of an unsuspected eavesdropper was sometimes held to destroy the confidentiality of a communication. Under modern evidence law, that is no longer true; an eavesdropper can be prohibited from testifying about a confidential communication.

(2) Waiver by Subsequent Disclosure

The privilege may later be lost if the client does not treat the communication as confidential, such as where the client discloses the lawyer's opinion in the course of business negotiations with a third party. [**Jonathan Corp. v. Prime Computers, Inc.,** 114 F.R.D. 693 (E.D. Va. 1987)]

EXAM TIP GILBERT

Keep in mind that the attorney-client privilege exists for the benefit of the client, not for the benefit of the lawyer. Therefore, the ***client is the "holder" of the privilege*** and is the one who can claim or waive the privilege. However, if the client has not waived the privilege, and if someone tries to obtain privileged information when the client is not present, the lawyer must assert the privilege on the client's behalf.

3. Special Cases to Which the Privilege Applies

a. Corporation or Government as "Client"

The privilege against disclosure of confidential communications extends to ***corporate and government*** clients as well as to personal clients. [**Radiant Burners v. American Gas Association,** 320 F.2d 314 (7th Cir. 1963); **Upjohn Co. v. United States,** 449 U.S. 383 (1981); Restatement §§ 73, 74]

(1) Privilege Applicable to All Legal Counsel

The attorney-client privilege of corporations applies to confidences made both to in-house counsel and to independent attorneys retained by the corporation.

(2) Not Available to Avoid Legitimate Discovery

However, like a personal client, a corporation may not use the attorney-client privilege as a means of avoiding discovery. Thus, where the corporation simply "funnels" papers and files to its lawyers, the privilege does not apply. [**Radiant Burners v. American Gas Association,** *supra*]

(3) No Privilege for Nonlegal Communications

As with individual clients, the professional relationship necessary to invoke the privilege does not exist when a corporate client seeks ***business or personal*** advice as opposed to legal assistance. [Restatement § 73(3)]

(a) Distinguish—"Mixed" Communications

Nevertheless, the privilege is ***not*** lost simply because relevant nonlegal advice is contained in communications that involve legal advice. Otherwise, the corporate client would be under an impossible burden in deciding what it could or could not disclose to its lawyers. [**Satcom International Group PLC v. Orbcomm International Partners, LP.,** 1999 WL 76847 (S.D.N.Y. 1999)]

(4) No Individual Privilege for Personal Confidences of Corporate or Government Officials

The lawyer for a corporation or the government is normally ***not*** the personal lawyer for corporate or government officials, even if the officials think otherwise. Thus, a corporate officer's confession of wrongdoing to the corporate lawyer might be privileged in a case where the ***corporation*** is the defendant, but *not* where the officer is tried ***as an individual.*** [***In re*** **Lindsey,** 158 F.3d 1263 (D.C. Cir. 1998)—White House counsel talking to President about possible personal criminal liability]

b. Information Shared by Co-Clients or Clients with a Common Interest

If two or more clients are represented by the same lawyer, or have separate lawyers but a common interest in a matter, they and their lawyers may share the information each provides in the course of preparing their common case without losing the privilege. [**Eisenberg v. Gagnon,** 766 F.2d 770 (3d Cir. 1985); Restatement §§ 75, 76]

(1) Privileged Against Third Parties

Any of the clients may assert the privilege against the government or any other third party who attempts to compel disclosure of the communication. [**Hunydee v. United States,** 355 F.2d 183 (9th Cir. 1965)]

(2) Not Privileged in Later Dispute Among Clients

However, if the clients later have a falling-out, each may use the disclosure of the others against them in the subsequent litigation. [**Ohio-Sealy Mattress Manufacturing Co. v. Kaplan,** 90 F.R.D. 21 (N.D. Ill. 1980)]

4. Exceptions to the Attorney-Client Privilege

a. Consent by Client

When the client ***consents*** to the disclosure of privileged information, the privilege no longer protects such information. [Restatement § 78(1)]

b. Disclosure of Future Crime or Fraud

The attorney-client privilege ***does not cover*** a communication in which the client seeks the services of a lawyer to further the planning or commission of a ***future crime or fraud.*** [Restatement § 82; Cal. Evid. Code § 956]

e.g. **Example:** Client asks Lawyer to help her prepare false documents to defraud X. Client's request is not covered by the privilege; both Client and Lawyer could be compelled to testify about the request.

(1) Distinguish—Past Crime or Fraud

The attorney-client privilege ***does protect*** confidential communications in which the client reveals the ***previous*** commission of a crime or other unlawful act.

(2) Distinguish—Crime or Fraud Prevented

If the lawyer tells the client that the planned conduct is illegal and the client abandons the plan, information about the original communication remains privileged. [Restatement § 82(a)]

c. Disclosure for Lawyer Self-Protection or to Collect a Fee

A lawyer may also reveal sufficient privileged information to defend himself, his associates, or his employees against charges *of* ***negligence or misconduct,*** or to collect a fee owed to the lawyer. [Restatement § 83; **Meyerhofer v. Empire Fire & Marine Insurance Co.,** 497 F.2d 1190 (2d Cir. 1974)]

CHECKLIST OF EXCEPTIONS TO ATTORNEY-CLIENT PRIVILEGE GILBERT

A COURT *MAY* COMPEL DISCLOSURE OF THE FOLLOWING CLIENT INFORMATION:

- ☑ In a later dispute among ***co-clients,*** information that had been shared by them in their common case;
- ☑ Information for which disclosure is expressly or impliedly ***authorized by the client*** (*e.g.,* by revealing it or not treating it as confidential);
- ☑ Information relevant to a ***dispute involving attorney fees or the attorney's conduct*** (*e.g.,* malpractice case, misconduct charges);
- ☑ Communication seeking lawyer's help in committing a ***future crime or fraud.***

5. Responsibilities of Lawyer in Asserting the Attorney-Client Privilege

a. Duty to Assert Privilege

A lawyer has a duty "to advise the client of the attorney-client privilege and timely to assert the privilege unless it is waived by the client." [Restatement § 78]

b. Response to Wrongful Order to Disclose

A court should not require a lawyer to disclose privileged information. To do so would render the privilege meaningless. Nevertheless, sometimes courts do order disclosure of privileged information, and the question arises as to what the lawyer should do.

(1) Resist at All Costs

Some courts hold that an ***attorney must refuse to disclose*** information believed to be privileged ***regardless of the personal consequences.*** For example, it has been suggested that a lawyer ordered to testify under threat of a citation for contempt should ***go to jail*** rather than disclose confidential information without the consent of the client. [Cal. Bus. & Prof. Code § 6068(e); **People v. Kor,** 129 Cal. App. 2d 436 (1954)—lawyer should accept punishment and "take his chances on release by a higher court"]

(2) Comply with Court Order

However, the ABA seems to impose a ***less rigorous duty*** upon the lawyer in this situation. The Model Rules say that a lawyer ***may*** reveal the confidences and secrets of a client when "required by . . . ***court order.***" [Model Rule 1.6(b)(6)]

(3) Preferred Approach

Where the propriety of the court's disclosure order is questionable, the best solution for the lawyer would seem to be to ***assert all nonfrivolous claims on behalf of confidentiality*** and then, if the client so directs, respectfully allow himself to be placed in contempt by the trial court so as to get the matter tested on appeal. If the order is sustained on appeal, then the lawyer should disclose it. [*See* Model Rule 1.6, comment 13]

6. Waiver by Disclosure or Failure to Object

It is important to assert the attorney-client privilege because a failure to do so, or a voluntary disclosure of the privileged information, causes the privilege to be ***lost forever.*** [Restatement §§ 78, 79]

a. Subject Matter Waiver

Another reason the issue of waiver is so important for lawyers and clients is that waiver of the privilege with respect to one item may be held to be a waiver with respect to ***all*** items dealing with the ***same*** subject matter. [***In re*** **Sealed Case,** 877 F.2d 976 (D.C. Cir. 1989); Restatement § 79, comment f]

b. Inadvertent Disclosure

In discovery, it sometimes happens that a lawyer inadvertently turns over more material than is required, and among the documents is privileged material. If the lawyer has taken reasonable measures to prevent that from happening and seeks to reclaim the material within a short time, courts often excuse the inadvertence and deem the privilege not waived. [Restatement § 79, comment h; *compare* Model Rule 4.4(b)—duty to notify opponent of receipt of inadvertently disclosed material]

c. Waiver by Putting Communication in Issue

Another way to waive the privilege is to assert the fact of the communication by way of claim or defense (*e.g.,* a claim of acting on advice of counsel waives the privileged character of the lawyer's opinion). [Restatement § 80]

7. After Client's Death

The attorney-client privilege has been held to continue even after the death of the client out of concern that fear of later revelation might discourage candor from the client. However, some courts have allowed a lawyer to reveal privileged information to verify to whom the client meant to leave a gift under a will. [**Swidler & Berlin v. United States,** 524 U.S. 399 (1998); Restatement § 81]

C. Work Product Doctrine

1. What Qualifies as Work Product

The work product doctrine protects information with the following characteristics against discovery:

(i) ***tangible material*** (or its **intangible equivalent** in unwritten or oral form);

(ii) ***not*** itself constituting part of the ***underlying facts***; and

(iii) ***prepared by a lawyer for litigation*** then in progress or in reasonable anticipation of future litigation.

[Restatement § 87(1); **Hickman v. Taylor,** 329 U.S. 495 (1947); Federal Rules of Civil Procedure, Rule 23(b)(3)]

a. Rationale

Discovery is intended to require disclosure of available facts, but we expect lawyers not to exploit their opponent's hard work. And if material is readily available to all parties, each is required to obtain it themselves rather than free-riding on the work of others.

b. Tangible Material

Disclosure of photographs, notes, memoranda, expert reports, and the like, likely would all qualify as work product. Basic facts are not themselves work product, but a lawyer's memorandum about the significance of even publicly available material would be protected against disclosure. Restatement § 87, comments f, g]

c. Litigation

The work product doctrine generally applies to any adversarial proceeding, whether in state or federal court, before an arbitration tribunal, or as part of an administrative proceeding. [Restatement § 87, comment h]

2. Relation Between the Work Product Doctrine and the Attorney-Client Privilege

Both principles create significant confidential information that a lawyer must protect. The work product doctrine differs from the attorney-client privilege in at least three ways:

a. Work Product Not Limited to Confidential Communications Between Lawyer and Client

The attorney-client privilege is more limited in origin; it is limited to confidential communications between lawyers and clients or their agents. Work product, on the other hand, can come initially from many sources and only its relevance to litigation makes it protected against disclosure.

b. Privilege Not Limited to Materials Created in Anticipation of Litigation

While work product is a litigation-focused doctrine, the attorney-client privilege can relate to confidential information about any lawful purpose, *e.g.*, planning a corporate merger or drafting a client's will.

c. Privilege Protection Is Absolute; Work Product Protection Is Conditional

If a communication is protected by the attorney-client privilege, a court will not order its disclosure even to protect an important third party interest such as helping a person seek relief from his conviction. [**State v. Macumber,** 544 P.2d 1084 (Ariz. 1976)] A court may order "ordinary" work product disclosed, however, if it finds the adverse party:

(i) has a substantial need for the material in order to prepare for trial; and

(ii) is unable **without undue hardship** to obtain the substantial equivalent of the material by other means. [Restatement § 88]

3. Differences Between the Treatment of Ordinary and Opinion Work Product

a. Definition of Opinion Work Product

Opinion work product consists of the lawyer's opinions and mental impressions; all other work product is "ordinary" and subject to disclosure under the conditions just described. [Restatement § 87(2)]

b. Limits on Compelled Disclosure of Opinion Work Product

A court will order disclosure of opinion work product only if:

(i) the client waives the work product protection;

(ii) the client or lawyer uses the work product in a hearing, such as to refresh the memory of a witness;

or (iii) ***extraordinary circumstances*** justify disclosure.

The "extraordinary circumstances" test is intended to offer less that the absolute protection given to privileged material but a much higher protection that that given ordinary work product. [Restatement § 89]

4. The Crime-Fraud Exception

Like the attorney-client privilege, work product protection does not apply to materials prepared to assist a client get assistance to engage in a crime or fraud that the client later commits, or to aid a third person to do so. [Restatement § 93]

D. The Professional Duty of Confidentiality

1. Professional Duty of Confidentiality Broader than Attorney-Client Privilege or Work Product

The Model Rules require a lawyer not to disclose ***any*** information "relating to the representation of a client," no matter from whom learned or under what circumstances. The duty of nondisclosure thus covers considerably more information than is protected by the attorney-client privilege or the work product doctrine. [Model Rule 1.6(a)]

a. Effect of Information Becoming Generally Known

Taken literally, the concept of "information relating to the representation" could include even information widely reported in press accounts or otherwise no longer secret. The Restatement excludes "generally known" information from its definition of what is confidential; Model Rule 1.6 does not. [Restatement § 59; Model Rule 1.6(a)]

b. Affirmative Duty to Protect Confidential Information

A lawyer's duty with respect to confidential information is not passive; the lawyer must "make reasonable efforts to prevent" any "inadvertent or unauthorized disclosure of it." For example, in dealing with electronic media, the lawyer must assess and invoke measures reasonably necessary to avoid being intercepted. [Model Rule 1.6(c) and comments 18 & 19; Restatement § 60(1)(b)]

PROTECTION OF CLIENT'S INFORMATION

SOURCE OF PROTECTION	SCOPE	EXAMPLES
ATTORNEY-CLIENT PRIVILEGE	• Only ***communications*** between client and attorney are covered	Conversation between attorney and client
	• Must be ***confidential*** (no client third party present)	Letters between attorney and client
	• Protected against ***compelled testimony***	Question at a deposition or trial
WORK PRODUCT	• Materials prepared by or for lawyer in ***anticipation of litigation***	List of questions lawyer plans to ask an opposing witness
	• Protected against discovery or other forced disclosure absent "substantial need" or "extraordinary circumstances"	Not required to show the other side absent judicial finding that is substantial need
DUTY OF CONFIDENTIALITY	• ***Any information*** relating to representation is covered	Relevant preexisting documents and things (but ***not*** fruits or instrumentalities of crime)
	• Protected from ***voluntary disclosure*** and from ***use harmful to client***	Revealing on Facebook or in way that embarrasses the client

2. Differences Between Privileged and Confidential Material—Illustrations

a. Identity of Client

In most cases, the identity of a client is ***not*** itself a "communication" and hence is generally not privileged. But the fact that the client had consulted a lawyer is "related to the representation" and must be kept confidential.

(1) Identity Privileged Where It Might Incriminate Client

It has been held that the government may not compel a lawyer to disclose the name of the client on whose behalf the lawyer was acting in paying a large sum of unreported income taxes, because the ability to consult a lawyer would be impaired by such disclosure. Compelling the lawyer to disclose the client's identity would tend to ***incriminate*** the client for nonpayment of the taxes. [**Baird v. Koerner,** 279 F.2d 623 (9th Cir. 1960)]

(2) Identity Need Not Always Be Kept Confidential

Typically, a lawyer has "implied authority" to say whom she represents in order to "carry out the representation." Otherwise, a court or opposing counsel could not know on whose behalf she appeared. [Model Rule 1.6(a)] But sometimes even such a disclosure could be harmful to the client. A lawyer reporting information regarding political corruption and graft to an investigating commission, for example, should withhold the informant's identity to protect the client's safety. [***In re*** **Kaplan,** 8 N.Y.2d 214 (1960)]

b. Whereabouts of Client

(1) Whereabouts as Privileged

Absent other circumstances, a lawyer is ***privileged*** not to disclose a client's address if supplied by the client in confidence and for the ***purpose*** of allowing the lawyer to ***communicate*** with the client. [***Ex parte*** **Schneider,** 294 S.W. 736 (Mo. 1927)]

(2) Whereabouts as Confidential

Whether or not the client's address is privileged, again the lawyer must treat it as confidential if disclosure could harm or embarrass the client.

(3) Compelled Disclosure Where Violation of Court Order

When a lawyer applies for a court order on behalf of a client, the lawyer impliedly represents to the court that the client will abide by the terms and conditions of the order. Therefore, as an officer of the court, the lawyer ***must*** advise the court of the client's whereabouts (*i.e.,* there is neither privilege nor confidentiality) if the lawyer learns that the ***client has violated*** the order ***and*** cannot persuade the client to cease the violation. [**Dike v. Dike,** 448 P.2d 490 (Wash. 1968)—lawyer must disclose address of client who took child away after receiving visitation rights from the court]

c. Fee Arrangements with Client

(1) Generally Not Privileged

Information regarding the fees paid or owed by a client to a lawyer is generally *not* protected by the attorney-client privilege. [**United States v. Haddad,** 527 F.2d 537 (6th Cir. 1975)]

(2) Confidentiality Applies

While fee information is usually not legally privileged, it relates to the representation and thus is confidential. A lawyer is ***not ethically free to disclose the client's fee arrangements*** without client consent or pursuant to court order (*e.g.*, in discovery).

d. Effect of Strangers' Presence

While the attorney-client ***privilege does not apply*** to communications made in the presence of third parties (and thus not "in confidence"), the professional ***duty of confidentiality applies*** even to information learned from third parties or where third parties were present.

e.g. **Example:** Information about a client's net worth is disclosed by the client's banker in the presence of a friend of the client. The lawyer is required to treat it as within the professional obligation of confidentiality.

e. No Difference as to Physical Evidence

Neither the attorney-client privilege nor the duty to preserve client secrets requires or permits a lawyer to take possession of or help secrete fruits or instrumentalities of a ***crime.***

(1) Duty to Turn Over to Police

When the lawyer takes possession of physical evidence, she ***must*** turn it over to the police even if it thereby incriminates the client, although it may be kept long enough to run necessary tests on the evidence. [**State v. Olwell,** 394 P.2d 681 (Wash. 1964); Restatement § 119]

(2) Mere Information Handled Differently

If the lawyer merely knows the whereabouts of physical evidence but has not taken possession of it, the information is protected by the ethical duty of confidentiality. [**People v. Belge,** 83 Misc. 2d 186 (1975)]

3. Period During Which Duty and Privilege Apply

Neither the privilege nor the duty of confidentiality is limited to the time of a lawyer's employment.

a. Before Employment

Confidential information disclosed to a lawyer by a potential client in discussions ***preliminary*** to any actual employment is protected by the attorney-client privilege ***and*** the ethical obligation of confidentiality. This is true even if no agreement is reached regarding representation or if the lawyer refuses to take the case (*i.e.,* even if no "client" relationship developed). [Model Rule 1.18(b); Restatement §§ 15(l)(a), 70; *and see supra*, p. 38]

(1) Rationale

This encourages potential clients to discuss the facts of their cases freely when they first consult a lawyer without concern that the lawyer may later testify against them or use information so obtained in representing an adversary. Furthermore, it helps the lawyer get all the facts needed to decide whether to take the case. [**Taylor v. Sheldon,** 173 N.E.2d 892 (Ohio 1961)]

(2) May Affect Right to Accept Employment from Opposing Side

Where preliminary discussions disclose confidential information, the lawyer will thereafter be prevented from representing the opposing side (although the lawyer's firm might not be prevented). [Model Rule 1.18(c); Restatement § 15(2); *and see infra*, p. 94]

b. After Employment Ceases

The duty to preserve confidential information also ***continues after*** the lawyer is no longer employed by the client. [Model Rules 1.6(a)]

EXAM TIP GILBERT

Sometimes the facts of an exam question will indicate that the representation is over (*e.g.,* the client fired the attorney, the trial is over and there is no appeal, or even that the client died). Or the question may show that the representation never really began (*e.g.,* the client consulted the attorney but never hired her). Don't let these facts lead you astray; remember that the attorney-client privilege and duty of confidentiality ***start even before the actual representation begins*** and ***continue after it is over*** if the doctrinal elements are otherwise satisfied.

4. Permitted Disclosures Within Law Firm

Unless the client specifies otherwise, a lawyer may properly discuss the client's affairs with partners or associates, as this conforms to ordinary law firm procedures in which members usually work together in representing a client. Furthermore, the lawyer may make such disclosures to secretaries, investigators, and other employees of the firm as are reasonably required. [Model Rule 1.6(a); Restatement § 61]

a. Disclosure to Outside Personnel

The lawyer may even give limited information from her files to persons outside the law firm for ***bookkeeping, accounting,*** or other legitimate purposes, provided the client does not object. [Model Rule 1.6(a); Restatement § 61]

b. Duty to Safeguard in General

However, as part of the duty to protect the information, the lawyer owes a duty to use reasonable care to prevent employees and associates from disclosing confidential information obtained from a client. Specifically, the lawyer is charged with ***selecting and training*** responsible persons and with ***supervising their access*** to clients' files. [Model Rules 5.1, 5.3(a); Restatement § 60(1)(b)]

5. Prohibition of Use of Confidential Information for Lawyer's Benefit

It is a standard principle of agency law that an agent must not use confidential information for the agent's own gain, even if that use would not be adverse to the interest of the principal.

a. Model Rules Position

The Model Rules prohibit a lawyer's personal use of confidential client information only when it would be ***detrimental*** to the interest of the client. [Model Rule 1.8(b)]

b. Restatement Distinction

The Restatement acknowledges the Model Rules position but notes that, under agency law, the lawyer would be obliged to turn over to the client any profit made using the client's information. Thus, the Model Rules apply for purposes of lawyer discipline, but not as a matter of financial liability. [Restatement § 60(2)]

6. Exceptions to the Duty of Confidentiality

Some exceptions to the duty to protect a client's secrets are identical to exceptions to the attorney-client privilege (*e.g.,* client consent and sharing of one co-client's information with another co-client). [Model Rule 1.6(b); Restatement §§ 61 & 62] The following additional exceptions are described as discretionary, not mandatory, and a lawyer is said to be neither subject to discipline nor financial liability for a decision to make or not make the disclosure.

a. Information "Impliedly Authorized" to Carry out the Representation

This is the exception that allows the lawyer to accomplish anything for a client that involves dealing with others. Given how broadly confidential information is defined, this provision is essential to let the lawyer talk to the other side or enter an appearance before the court. The scope of the exception is largely defined by what disclosures would be in the client's interest. [Model Rule 1.6(a) and comment 5; Restatement § 61]

b. To Prevent Reasonably Certain Death or Substantial Bodily Harm

The Model Rules also permit disclosure of information that the ***client does not want disclosed*** when the lawyer reasonably believes disclosure is necessary to prevent ***reasonably certain death or substantial bodily harm.*** The lawyer may reveal an act even if the client is not the one likely to commit it, even if the likely death or injury is not "imminent," and whether or not the act is a crime. [Model Rule 1.6(b)(1); Restatement § 66(1)]

e.g. **Example:** A lawyer learns that the client's brother's business has polluted the local water supply in a way that will cause the premature death of 50 people over the next 10 years. The lawyer's client does not want to expose his brother's act. Even though the offender was not the client and the deaths may not occur soon, the lawyer may disclose the increased risk to public health.

c. Revelation of Future Crime or Fraud

Both the Restatement and the Model Rules also provide that a lawyer may reveal client information to prevent, mitigate, or rectify [i] ***substantial*** financial injury that has not yet occurred, that is [ii] ***reasonably certain*** to result from a client's past or future crime or fraud, if [iii] ***the lawyer's*** services were used in committing the crime or fraud. The "lawyer's services" element was inserted to persuade lawyers that this authority to disclose is another way to protect lawyers against the consequences of representing a dishonest client. [Model Rule 1.6(b)(2) & (3); Restatement § 67; *and see infra*, p. 108]

d. Securing Advice About Compliance with Professional Standards

This is the "even lawyers need a lawyer" principle. A lawyer may reveal confidential client information to another lawyer in an effort to get advice about the first lawyer's professional duties. [Model Rule 1.6(b)(4)]

e. Lawyer Self-Protection or to Collect a Fee

A lawyer may reveal sufficient confidential information to defend himself, his associates, or his employees against charges of ***negligence or misconduct,*** or to collect a fee owed to the lawyer. Ordinarily, however, a lawyer may not use this principle to reveal client information to answer social media criticism. [Model Rule 1.6(b)(5); Restatement § 64]

f. Court-Compelled Disclosure

By definition, a court will not compel a lawyer to disclose information protected by the attorney-client privilege even if it is highly relevant to the resolution of a contested issue in a case. A lawyer should make all reasonably available objections to disclosure, but relevant unprivileged information subject to the lawyer's duty of confidentiality ***may be compelled*** to be disclosed in a deposition or at trial. [Model Rule 1.6(b)(6); Restatement § 63; **Fellerman v. Bradley,** 493 A.2d 1239 (N.J. 1985)]

g. To Detect Conflicts of Interest Arising from Change of Employment

A special problem of concern to lawyers seeking to change firms or firms considering a merger is knowing who the other lawyer or firm represents or represented and thus how many conflicts of interest the possible change might create. Lawyers are permitted to disclose the names of their clients and the nature of their cases to address such conflict issues, even if the information would be otherwise confidential, unless the disclosure would "compromise the attorney-client privilege or otherwise prejudice the client." [Model Rule 1.6(b)(7)]

CHECKLIST OF EXCEPTIONS TO THE DUTY OF CONFIDENTIALITY — GILBERT
A LAWYER MAY REVEAL THE FOLLOWING CLIENT INFORMATION:
☑ Information for which disclosure is expressly or impliedly ***authorized by client;***
☑ Information necessary to prevent ***reasonably certain death or substantial bodily harm;***
☑ Information revealing intent to commit future ***crime or fraud reasonably certain to result in substantial financial harm if lawyer's services used*** (or to prevent, mitigate, or rectify financial harm if client has ***already*** acted);
☑ Information necessary for the lawyer ***to obtain legal ethics advice;***
☑ Information relevant to a ***dispute involving attorney fees or the attorney's conduct*** (e.g., malpractice case, misconduct charges);
☑ Information ***compelled by court*** or other governmental tribunal;
☑ Information relevant to ***potential conflicts of interest*** created by a possible change in employment or law firm merger.

Chapter Four

Duty of Unimpaired Loyalty—Conflicts of Interest

CONTENTS PAGE

Chapter Approach

In addition to the duties of competence, diligence, communication, and confidentiality, a lawyer owes a client a duty of unimpaired loyalty. Thus, the lawyer may not represent a client when the lawyer has a conflict of interest, unless the client gives informed consent.

The four major kinds of conflicts of interest discussed in this chapter are:

1. Conflicts between the interests of ***two or more clients that the lawyer is representing at the same time.*** Such conflicts especially arise in litigation matters but can also come up in nonlitigation situations.
2. Conflicts between the ***lawyer's personal interest and the interest of the client*** (*e.g.,* the lawyer enters into a business transaction with the client, receives a gift from the client, etc.).
3. Conflicts between the ***client's interest and that of a third party to whom the lawyer owes obligations.*** Here we look for facts such as a third party paying the lawyer's fee, *e.g.,* a lawyer paid by an insurance company to represent its policyholder.
4. Conflicts between the lawyer's ***duties to a current client and*** the lawyer's ***continuing duties to a former client.***
5. The chapter then looks at ***imputation***, the principle that when a lawyer is disqualified due to a conflict of interest, others associated with the lawyer will usually also be disqualified.
6. The chapter closes by examining how each of these principles applies to current and former government lawyers.

The sources of most of the principles in this chapter are Restatement §§ 121–135 and Model Rules 1.7–1.13.

A. Introduction

1. Basic Standard for Identifying a Conflict of Interest

The Restatement and ABA Model Rules provide overall standards for determining when a lawyer has a conflict of interest. The specific kinds of conflicts discussed in this chapter are derived from these basic principles.

a. Restatement—Substantial Risk of Material and Adverse Effect on Representation

The Restatement defines a conflict of interest as when "there is a ***substantial risk*** that the lawyer's representation of the client would be ***materially and adversely affected***" by one of the four kinds of issues discussed in this chapter. [Restatement § 121]

b. Model Rules—Significant Risk of Material Limitation on Representation

The Model Rules state the rule as a prohibition of a lawyer's representation when there if a "significant risk" that the representation "will be ***materially limited***" by the lawyer's other interests or responsibilities. [Model Rule 1.7(a)]

c. Same Test Used Throughout the Representation

The significance of these largely identical tests is that they turn on the ***current risk*** that a lawyer's work on behalf of a client will be impaired. The law once distinguished between "potential" conflicts that were not disqualifying and "actual" conflicts that required corrective action. Both authoritative tests today instead look at how great the ***current risk*** is that the lawyer's loyalty may be impaired, whether now or later.

2. Representation in Spite of a Conflict

a. Definition of Informed Consent—Basic Test

In most conflict situations, the key issue will be whether a client has given informed consent to proceeding in spite of the conflict. Both the Restatement and the Model Rules say that consent is informed when the client or former client has "***reasonably adequate information*** about the ***material risks*** of such representation." [Restatement § 122(1); Model Rule 1.7(b)(4)]

b. Informed Consent Must Be Confirmed in Writing

The Model Rules also require that the client's consent have been "confirmed in writing," *i.e.*, that the lawyer at least recorded the client's consent in a writing that the lawyer promptly sent to the client. [Model Rule 1.7(b)(4); Model Rule 1.0(e)—informed consent, and Model Rule 1.0(b)—confirmed in writing.]

c. Decision of Client Determinative

If a client decides (for whatever reason) that the conflict is undesirable, the lawyer must defer to that opinion and withdraw, despite the lawyer's own belief that the representation could be handled properly.

EXAM TIP GILBERT

Always keep in mind that "informed" consent means just that—that the client has ***sufficient information*** about the risks and the alternatives to make her decision. If the client does not have important information, the consent is ***invalid***.

d. Nonconsentable Conflicts

Although the client's informed consent can waive most conflicts of interest, some conflicts cannot be waived:

(1) Representing Opposing Parties in Same Litigation

Cases in which the lawyer represents both sides in the same case are deemed not subject to client consent, even if informed clients want to give that consent. In part, this is because a lawyer on both sides of a case would confuse the court and jury, regardless of the clients' preferences. [Model Rule 1.7(b)(3); Restatement § 122(2)(b)]

(2) Inability to Give Adequate Representation to Each Client

A second kind of conflict not subject to consent conflict arises when a reasonable lawyer would conclude that ***competent and diligent representation*** could ***not*** be afforded each client. Such a situation might exist, *e.g.,* if the lawyer's clients are bidding against each other for the same piece of property and the lawyer cannot benefit one client other than at the expense of the other. [Model Rule 1.7(b)(1); Restatement § 122(2)(c); **Baldasarre v. Butler,** 625 A.2d 458 (N.J. 1993)]

(3) Representation Prohibited by Law

In a few circumstances (*e.g.,* some cases involving government entity clients or minors or clients facing the death penalty), state law renders the conflict not waivable by client consent. [Model Rule 1.7(b)(2); Restatement § 122(2)(a)]

3. Consequences of Failing to Deal Properly with a Conflict of Interest

a. Disqualification

Most commonly, especially in cases where a client or former client seeks to prevent a lawyer from representing someone else, the courts will "disqualify" the lawyer who has a conflict of interest from further participation in a matter. This remedy is basically an injunction against violation of the conflicts rules, and it may be invoked in addition to any other sanctions. [Restatement § 6(8)]

b. Discipline

If the lawyer does not obtain consent, or if disclosure to the clients was less than candid, the lawyer is subject to professional discipline. [Model Rule 1.7; Cal. Rule 3–310]

c. Malpractice Liability

In addition, a lawyer who undertakes multiple representation without making full disclosure runs a risk of civil liability to a client who suffers a loss caused by such lack of disclosure. [**Crest Investment Trust, Inc. v. Comstock,** 327 A.2d 891 (Md. 1974)]

d. Fee Forfeiture

Further, courts in conflict of interest case are increasingly forcing lawyers to forfeit all or part of their fees in a matter as a sanction for the breach of fiduciary duty in doing work despite a conflict of interest, whether or not the client suffers actual damage. [Restatement § 37; **Hendry v. Pelland,** 73 F.3d 397 (D.C. Cir. 1996)]

B. Concurrent Representation of Clients with Conflicting Interests

1. Introduction

The lawyer's obligation to exercise independent professional judgment on behalf of ***each*** client can be severely tested where the interests of more than one of a lawyer's client are at stake in a given matter. Problems arise whenever a lawyer seeks to represent ***two or more*** clients with ***differing*** interests in an outcome.

2. General Standards

What Model Rule 1.7 calls a ***"concurrent conflict of interest"*** exists in three basic situations:

a. Directly Adverse Representation in the Same Case

The most obvious, but relatively unusual, situation is one in which the lawyer finds herself representing both the plaintiff and defendant in the same case. More often, it arises when one defendant represented by the lawyer becomes a third-party plaintiff suing another of the defendants the lawyer represents in the matter. Typically, any relief the lawyer gets for one of the clients would be at the expense of the other. [Model Rule 1.7(a)(1)]

b. Directly Adverse Representation in Unrelated Cases

This more common situation arises when the client the lawyer is representing in the current matter opposes a client the lawyer represents in some other, wholly unrelated matter. Again, on behalf of one client, another may suffer injury, but, at least in the particular matter, the other client will be represented by counsel not similarly burdened by a conflict, so both clients should get vigorous representation. The key concern making this a conflict is the sense that the lawyer is being disloyalty to the client being opposed.

c. Representation Materially Limited by Obligations to Another Client

Cases falling under this standard do not involve matters in which the two clients are opposing parties. Rather, here the action taken on behalf of Client A will have a significant impact on Client B that might limit the lawyer's willingness to pursue the interest of Client A fully and effectively. For example, Clients A & B might both be making claims against a defendant who lacks the funds to pay both of the claims completely. To a lawyer representing them both, a dollar obtained for Client A would tend to mean a dollar less for B, so arguably neither client would receive the individualized loyalty to which each client is entitled. [Model Rule 1.7(a)(2)]

3. Lawyer's Obligation in Such Situations

When any of the above three situations arise, the lawyer must ***decline*** or ***withdraw*** from the representation(s), unless informed consent of each affected client is possible and obtained. [Model Rule 1.7; Restatement § 122]

4. Application of Standards to Common Situations—Litigation Matters

The likelihood of impaired judgment and prejudice to the client is greatest when the lawyer seeks to represent several clients in the same litigation.

a. Criminal Proceedings—Constitutional Considerations

The problem of differing interests frequently arises when a lawyer is appointed to represent several indigent defendants in the same criminal proceeding. If the defendants' interests are in fact divergent, there is more than an ethical problem. Each accused is ***constitutionally*** entitled to the assistance of his own counsel, and it is the ***duty of the court*** to appoint separate counsel whenever differing interests appear. [**Holloway v. Arkansas,** 435 U.S. 475 (1978); **Cuyler v. Sullivan,** 446 U.S. 335 (1980); Restatement § 129]

(1) Accusations by One Client Against Another

If one defendant accuses a co-defendant of committing the crime, their interests are clearly adverse, and representation of both by the same appointed counsel is unconstitutional. This is true regardless of whether the accusing defendant denies guilt or admits it. [**White v. United States,** 396 F.2d 822 (5th Cir. 1968); **Commonwealth v. Westbrook,** 400 A.2d 160 (Pa. 1979)]

(2) Differences in Strength of Case

Common representation may also be unconstitutional where the defenses available to one client defendant are stronger or different than those available to the others. The defendant with the stronger case may be prejudiced by failure of the shared lawyer to establish or emphasize his unique defenses, and vice versa. [**Campbell v. United States,** 352 F.2d 359 (D.C. Cir. 1965)]

(3) Privately Retained Counsel

If the two defendants are not indigent and have jointly retained ***private*** counsel, it is their shared counsel's duty to advise them of any potential conflict of interest. On appeal, the test of their joint counsel's representation will be whether it amounted to actual prejudice.

b. Civil Litigation

Several persons injured in the same incident may seek to retain a single lawyer to represent them in jointly litigating their respective claims. Such claimants may have potentially differing interests which could make multiple representation improper, absent informed consent. Like the criminal defendants just discussed, they may accuse each other or have claims of varying strength. [Restatement § 128]

(1) Consent May Not Be Possible

As discussed on p. 79, if one of several plaintiffs is ***also*** named as a cross-defendant (*e.g.,* plaintiffs A and B sue D; D cross-complains against A claiming that A was jointly liable in causing injury to B), a lawyer ***cannot*** represent the co-plaintiffs, even with client consent. The lawyer would in effect be representing both sides in an adversary action, where interests must necessarily differ.

e.g. **Example:** A lawyer typically may not represent ***both driver and passenger*** in a negligence action against a common defendant, at least if the passenger contends that the accident resulted from the concurrent negligence of the *driver* and the defendant. If the lawyer asserts the driver's negligence on behalf of the passenger, he will prejudice the interest of the driver who is also his client. [**Jedwabny v. Philadelphia Transportation Co.,** 135 A.2d 252 (Pa. 1957)]

(2) Consent Not Possible if Client Consent Cannot Be Fully Informed

Sometimes, a lawyer may learn facts from one co-client that that client will not let the lawyer disclose to other co-clients. If the information would be necessary to make each client's consent fully informed, the lawyer will not be able to proceed in the face of the conflict of interest.

c. Divorce Proceedings

If a state's divorce proceedings require a judicial hearing in which the spouses will be designated as opposing parties in litigation, the conflict is nonconsentable even if the spouses prefer to use a single lawyer.

(1) No Fault Dissolution

Even where such proceedings are no longer adversary in nature (*e.g.,* many states' dissolution proceeding which eliminates any determination of fault), differing interests over subjects like ***property and child custody*** create a conflict and make separate representation essential in most cases.

(2) Distinguish—Prelitigation Matters

A lawyer sometimes may ***counsel*** spouses who are contemplating a separation or dissolution as to their mutual rights and obligations, but only after ***full disclosure*** of the conflicting interests and with the ***informed consent*** of both spouses, confirmed in writing.

(3) Document Preparation

Again, if informed consent is obtained, a lawyer ordinarily may prepare a written agreement providing for division of property, support, and child custody, which the parties acting ***pro se*** can then submit to the court in an *uncontested* proceeding. [**Klemm v. Superior Court,** 75 Cal. App. 3d 893 (1977)]

d. Liquidation and Reorganization Proceedings

Regardless of whether individual bankruptcies or major corporate receiverships are involved, liquidation and reorganization proceedings usually involve diverse and conflicting interests which make only some multiple representations proper.

(1) Basic Categories of Parties

There are usually three main classes of parties to such proceedings: ***creditors, stockholders, and management groups,*** each with its own particular interests. And within each class there may also exist various subclasses whose interests are similarly divergent (*e.g.,* secured and unsecured creditors, preferred and common stockholders).

(2) Joint Representation Strictly Scrutinized

Courts have insisted upon the unimpaired loyalty of lawyers who represent parties to such proceedings. Sometimes a lawyer may be permitted to represent several small claimants in a given group simply because none could afford to hire a lawyer otherwise, but a lawyer for "junior" claimants (*e.g.,* general creditors or common stockholders) typically may *not* also represent "senior" claimants (*e.g.,* bondholders or preferred stockholders). [**Woods v. City National Bank,** 312 U.S. 262 (1941); ***In re* Iannochino,** 242 F.3d 36 (1st Cir. 2001)]

e. Representing Two Clients with Inconsistent Legal Positions in Two Unrelated Cases

Absent informed consent from both clients, confirmed in writing, a lawyer must not represent two clients in separate, unrelated matters when they have inconsistent legal positions if there is a substantial risk that the representation of one client will be materially limited by the lawyer's responsibilities to the other client.

Example: Lawyer represents two clients in different cases that are pending in different tribunals. On behalf of Client One, Lawyer needs to argue that a certain statute is unconstitutional. On behalf of Client Two, Lawyer needs to argue that the same statute is constitutional. Aside from that legal issue, the cases are unrelated. However, Client One's case will be heard next week in the intermediate appellate court that hears cases from Judicial District Six. Client Two's case will be tried seven months from now in a trial court in Judicial District Six. Thus, the appellate court's decision in Client One's case is likely to become the controlling precedent in Client Two's case. This presents a substantial risk that Lawyer's representation of one client will be materially limited by her responsibilities to the other client. Therefore, Lawyer must fully disclose the situation to both clients and seek their informed, written consent. If either or both clients will not consent, Lawyer must seek the court's permission to withdraw from one or both cases. [*See* Model Rule 1.7, comment 24]

f. Lump Sum Settlement for Several Clients

A lawyer who, with informed consent, represents more than one client in litigation may face divergent interests when a lump sum settlement is offered by the other side. Here, again, the lawyer must carefully preserve independent judgment and loyalty to *each* client.

(1) Consent of Each Client After Full Disclosure

To prevent conflicting interests, *each client must consent* to the aggregate settlement after being advised of: (i) the *existence and nature of all claims* involved in the proposed settlement, (ii) the *total amount* of the settlement, and (iii) the *participation of each person* in the settlement. [Model Rule 1.8(g); Restatement § 128]

(2) Application to Criminal Defendants

The Model Rules extend the requirement of informed consent to situations where a lawyer represents multiple criminal defendants considering nolo contendere or guilty pleas that might have an impact on the other defendants. [Model Rule 1.8(g)]

5. Representing Opposing Clients in Unrelated Matters

The prohibition on representing opposing sides in adversary proceedings applies even where the adversary proceedings are unrelated. Absent both clients' informed consent, a lawyer employed by a client to provide legal services in a lawsuit may ***not*** simultaneously agree to represent another party in a different lawsuit against that same client. [Model Rule 1.7(a)(1); Restatement § 128(2); **Grievance Committee v. Rottner,** 203 A.2d 82 (Conn. 1964)]

(1) Avoiding Appearance of Divided Loyalty

No actual effect on the lawyer's effective representation is necessary. The prohibition is designed to maintain ***public confidence in the bar*** by assuring existing clients that they will have the ***undivided loyalty*** of their lawyers throughout the duration of employment. [**Jeffrey v. Pounds,** 67 Cal. App. 3d 6 (1977)]

(2) Application to Members of a Corporate Family

A lawyer prohibited from filing suit against a client may also be prohibited from maintaining an action against a parent, subsidiary, or sibling corporation of that client. Corporate family relationships are too varied to state a bright-line rule forbidding such suits, but the lawyer must ask whether: (i) the corporations are in effect ***one entity;*** (ii) the lawyer has agreed to treat the corporate family as a ***single client***; or (iii) the lawyer's obligations to one of the entities will *impair* pursuit of the claim against the other. [Model Rule 1.7, comment 34; ABA Opn. 95–390]

6. Application of the Standards to Nonlitigation Matters

a. Real Estate Transactions

A lawyer for the seller of real property has a conflict representing the buyer without the informed consent of both clients, confirmed in writing. Indeed, some major real estate deals may be so contentious and complex that the conflict may not be consentable at all. [**Baldasarre v. Butler,** 625 A.2d 458 (N.J. 1993)]

b. Borrower and Lender

The same problems may arise where a lawyer purports to represent both borrower and lender on a mortgage or other security. Again, such representation is improper without full disclosure to both sides of the potential conflicts and the parties' informed consent. [***In re* Greenberg,** 121 A.2d 520 (N.J. 1956)]

7. Special Problems of Corporate Counsel

The lawyer for a corporation or other complex organization faces a situation in which the interests of *stockholders, officers, directors, and employees* of the corporation are to some degree inherently in conflict. The lawyer may not be able to serve each totally in a given situation.

a. Entity Theory of Representation

The ABA Model Rules take the traditional view that the *corporate entity is the client,* and its own interests are to be favored over those of any constituent part. As a result, corporate counsel normally has only one client—the corporation itself. [Model Rule 1.13(a); Restatement § 131 and comment b]

b. Representing Both the Corporation and One or More Constituents

A lawyer representing the corporation may also represent one or more of its individual constituents (*e.g.,* represent the corporation and the driver of its truck that allegedly hit the plaintiff). However, such situations must be treated as the lawyer would treat any other conflict of interest and each client must give informed consent, confirmed in writing. [Model Rule 1.13(g); Restatement § 131, comment e]

c. Organizational Constituent Acts Contrary to the Interest of the Entity

Challenging issues can arise when a seemingly authorized official acts contrary to the interest of the lawyer's organizational client, *e.g.,* causes the entity to violate the law. How a lawyer may or must respond to such issues is discussed in Chapter V of this Summary at pp. 106–108.

EXAM TIP GILBERT

Keep in mind that the lawyer must act in the best interests of the ***organization*** and not any particular officer, employee, or other person associated with the organization. Beware of exam questions where a lawyer is asked to act in the interests of the corporation's president or other official when that ***conflicts with the best interests of the organization.***

C. Personal Interests That May Affect Lawyer's Judgment

1. Introduction

Another basic kind of conflict of interest arises when a lawyer would profit at the client's expense. For example, if the lawyer owns a significant financial interest in the party the client wants to sue, the lawyer would benefit personally if the client did not prevail. Thus, absent informed consent, it is improper for a lawyer to purchase or otherwise knowingly have a property or financial interest adverse to the client. [Restatement § 125, comment c; Model Rule 1.7(a)(2)] Model Rule 1.8 and Restatement §§ 125—127 address other interests that may adversely affect a lawyer's professional judgment.

2. Business or Financial Transactions with Client

When a lawyer enters into a business transaction with a client, courts see a danger that the lawyer may breach the fiduciary duty to avoid ***overreaching or undue influence.*** Thus, *e.g.,* where the lawyer invests in the client's business, the courts examine such transactions with great care. [Model Rule 1.8(a); Restatement § 126; **Committee on Professional Ethics v. Mershon,** 316 N.W.2d 895 (Iowa 1982)]

a. Presumption of Undue Influence

Even apart from the ethics rules, courts generally hold that a lawyer who enters into a business transaction with a client must overcome a presumption of overreaching or undue influence by ***affirmative evidence*** to the contrary. Failure to present such evidence is grounds for *setting aside the transaction,* regardless of the legal sufficiency of the consideration. [**Benson v. State Bar,** 13 Cal. 3d 581 (1975)]

b. Model Rules Approach

The Model Rules define specific circumstances that must exist to permit any business transaction between lawyer and client, other than a standard commercial transaction, *e.g.,* one in which the lawyer buys a dinner at the client's restaurant. The Model Rules requirements are:

(i) ***The terms must be fair and reasonable*** and have been ***transmitted in writing*** to the client in an ***understandable*** form;

(ii) ***The client must be advised in writing*** that it would be desirable to ***get independent counsel*** and given reasonable opportunity to do so; and

(iii) ***The client must consent in writing*** to the terms of the transaction and the lawyer's role in it, including whether the client expects the lawyer to protect the client's interest.

[Model Rule 1.8(a); Cal. Rule 3–300; Restatement § 126; *and see* ***In re*** **Brown,** 559 P.2d 884 (Or. 1977)]

c. Related Issue

Likewise, a lawyer ***may not purchase property*** (directly or through any intermediary) at a probate, foreclosure, or judicial sale in an action in which the lawyer or any member of her law firm appears as attorney for a party, or in which the lawyer is acting as executor, trustee, etc. Again, the potential for overreaching disqualifies the lawyer as a purchaser. [*See* Model Rule 1.8(b); Cal. Rule 4–300]

3. Gifts or Bequests to Lawyer

A related issue of undue influence or overreaching is raised when a lawyer or his relative receives a substantial gift or bequest from a client who is unrelated to the lawyer. In this context, "relative" includes a spouse, child, parent, grandparent, grandchild, and other persons with whom the lawyer has a close, familial relationship. [Model Rule 1.8(c)]

a. No Solicitation of Substantial Gift

It is improper under ***any*** circumstances for a lawyer to ***ask*** that any ***substantial*** gift be made to the lawyer or for the lawyer's benefit. [Model Rule 1.8(c); Restatement § 127]

e.g. **Example:** Lawyer is an alumnus of Port Arthur School of Law. The school asked Lawyer to represent it in defense of a pending case. In the midst of the work, Lawyer told the school's dean that his daughter would love to attend the school, but that she did not want to pay the high tuition. The dean arranged for Lawyer's daughter to be admitted on a full scholarship. Lawyer is subject to discipline for soliciting a substantial gift from the school to his daughter.

b. Token Gifts Permitted

A lawyer may accept a small gift from a client (*e.g.,* an appropriate holiday present or a small token of appreciation). [Model Rule 1.8, comment 6; Restatement § 127(2)(c) and comment g]

c. Beneficiary Under an Instrument

A lawyer must insist that ***any instrument*** (typically a will) giving the lawyer a substantial gift be prepared by a different lawyer. [Model Rule 1.8(c); Restatement § 127(1); **State v. Horan,** 123 N.W.2d 488 (Wis. 1963)]

(1) Presumption of Undue Influence

Apart from the ethical issue, a probate court may presume undue influence if a gift under a will is made to the lawyer who drafted the will; *i.e.,* the lawyer may not be entitled to receive the gift unless she can produce ***independent evidence*** showing that the testator chose to make the gift freely and independently. (*See* Wills Summary.)

(2) Exception—Drafting Wills for Personal Friends or Relatives

Most courts ***do*** permit a lawyer to prepare wills for the lawyer's family, friends, or relatives even though the will names the lawyer (or members of the lawyer's family) a beneficiary, ***provided*** that there is no hint of overreaching and that the bequest is reasonable under the circumstances. [*See* Model Rule 1.8(c); Restatement § 127(2)(a); **State v. Collentine,** 159 N.W.2d 50 (Wis. 1968)]

d. Executor, Trustee, Counsel

Along the same lines, a lawyer may seek to have a client name her executor, trustee, or counsel in an instrument, although the lawyer must go through the process of informed consent if the fees potentially involved may cause the lawyer not to be independent in the advice she gives the client. [Model Rule 1.8, comment 8; **State v. Gulbankian,** 196 N.W.2d 733 (Wis. 1972)]

EXAM TIP GILBERT

Sometimes an exam question will present a longtime client who wants to leave the lawyer something in her will in appreciation of assistance over the years, or a client who wants to name the lawyer executor because she trusts the lawyer to handle the estate. Remember that ***neither*** the gift nor the appointment ***is automatically prohibited,*** but that the lawyer should advise the client to hire an ***independent attorney*** (not the lawyer's partner) to draft the will. If the client refuses to seek independent counsel, you need to analyze the facts to determine whether there is an ethical problem. Facts such as the client having had a long and ongoing relationship with the lawyer, having been a friend or family member, or the reasonableness of the gift or appointment, all tend to show there was not over-reaching by the lawyer. But circumstances such as a large gift to the lawyer, the lawyer suggesting the gift, etc., point to a prohibited conflict of interest. (And remember, in addition to the ethics rules, probate law may provide for a rebuttable presumption of undue influence in these cases.)

4. Publication Rights Concerning Subject Matter of Employment

Prior to the conclusion of all aspects of a case, a lawyer generally may not acquire publication rights from the client as to the subject matter of the lawyer's employment. [Model Rule 1.8(d); Restatement § 36(3)] This prohibition is based on the possibility that the ownership of such rights might have an adverse effect on the lawyer's exercise of independent professional judgment. For example, great media interest in a sensational case might influence the lawyer, consciously or unconsciously, to conduct the case in a manner that would enhance the value of the publication rights but prejudice the client's position.

e.g. **Example:** In a notorious California criminal case, an attorney and his client entered into a fee agreement that provided that, in return for his legal services, the attorney was granted the exclusive literary and dramatic rights to the client's life story, including the account of the trial. The court held that the attorney's financial stake in the literary contract motivated him to take a position adverse to his client and created a prejudicial conflict of interests. [**People v. Corona,** 80 Cal. App. 3d 684 (1978)]

cf. **Compare:** In another California case involving a similar fee agreement, although the defendant was willing to waive the potential conflict of interests, the trial judge disqualified his attorneys. The California Supreme Court found that the defendant had competently and knowingly waived the conflict and that the disqualification denied the defendant his right to counsel of his choice. [**Maxwell v. Superior Court,** 30 Cal. 3d 606 (1982)]

5. Prohibition on Acquiring Interest in Subject Matter of Employment

A slightly different problem is presented when the lawyer has or acquires an interest in the claim or property that is the subject matter of litigation being conducted for the client. Thus, a lawyer conducting patent litigation for a client may not become part owner of the patent. [Model Rule 1.8(i); Restatement § 125]

a. Rationale

It is sometimes said that this prohibition is to eliminate the lawyer's incentive to stir up litigation. A better rationale is that if the lawyer is personally interested in the litigation, the lawyer might be tempted to give less weight to the client's judgment of an acceptable settlement.

b. Exception—Security for Fees

Both the ABA Code and Model Rules specifically recognize that a lawyer may acquire a financial interest in the subject of litigation to ***calculate and secure fees***, *e.g.,* the lawyer may charge a contingent fee and may enforce an attorney's lien (*see supra*, pp. 50–54).

6. Sexual Relations with a Client

The Model Rules provide that a lawyer may not have a consensual sexual relationship with a client unless that relationship existed "when the client-lawyer relationship commenced." [Model Rule 1.8(j)]

a. Rationale

It may seem intrusive to regulate a client's relationship with someone who also happens to be his lawyer, but the Model Rules identify three justifications for the prohibition:

(i) The sexual relationship is "almost always unequal" and can "use the trust of the client to the client's disadvantage;"

(ii) The lawyer is likely to lose the emotional distance required to advise the client with independent professional judgment; and

(iii) It may be difficult later to distinguish which discussions were intended to be privileged from those that were entirely personal. [Model Rule 1.8, comment 17]

b. Application to Corporate Client Representatives

Although literal sexual relations with a corporation defy imagination, the Model Rules prohibition also applies to a lawyer for an organization's relationships with any "constituent" of the organization who "supervises, directs or regularly consults with that lawyer concerning the organization's legal matters." [Model Rule 1.8, comment 19]

7. Negotiating Employment with Opposing Firm

A problem of increasing importance can arise when a lawyer seeks to take a job with another firm but is currently representing a client in a matter in which that firm has a client on the other side. The issue has not yet become the subject of a specific Model Rule provision.

a. Recommended Action

The Restatement says that when the discussions have become ***concrete*** and the interest in the move is ***mutual,*** the lawyer must tell the client about the situation and seek ***informed consent*** to continue the representation. In the absence of such disclosure, the lawyer must ***end the employment discussions*** until the matter is over. [Restatement § 125, comment d; ABA Opn. 96–400 (1996); **Kala v. Aluminum Smelting & Refining Co.,** 688 N.E. 2d 258 (Ohio 1998); *compare* Model Rule 1.6(b)(7)—limited right to reveal confidential information; Model Rule 1.12(b)—judge's law clerk may negotiate for employment with private firms only after notifying the judge]

b. Law Firm Mergers

The same requirements and procedures should apply when law firm merger discussions reach the concrete and mutual stage. [Restatement § 125, comment d; **Stanley v. Richmond,** 35 Cal. App. 4th 1070 (1995)]

8. Personal Interest Conflicts Addressed Elsewhere

In addition to the personal interest conflicts already discussed, four other kinds of Rule 1.8 conflicts are considered elsewhere in this Summary:

a. **Attempting to limit liability for malpractice,** see Model Rule 1.8(h), at Chapter I, p. 32, *supra.*

b. **Using client information for the lawyer's own benefit,** see Model Rule 1.8(b), at Chapter III, p. 74, *supra*

c. **Financial assistance to a client**, see Model Rule 1.8(e), *infra* at Chapter VI, p. 140.

d. **Aggregating the settlement of claims of multiple clients**, see Model Rule 1.8(g), this Chapter, *supra* at p. 84.

D. Interests of Third Persons Affecting Lawyer-Client Relationship

1. Introduction

The lawyer is under a duty to disregard the desires or interests of any third person that would ***impair the lawyer's independent judgment and loyalty*** to the client. [Model Rule 1.7(b); Restatement § 134] The major situations where this may occur are discussed below.

2. Compensation from Third Parties for Representing Client

A lawyer may not accept any form of compensation from a third person for services to the client unless: (i) the client ***gives informed consent,*** (ii) the third person ***does not interfere with the lawyer's independence*** or the representation of the client, and (iii) the arrangement ***does not compromise the client's confidential information.*** [Model Rule 1.8(f); Restatement § 134(1)]

EXAM TIP GILBERT

A common question in this area sets up a person who needs legal assistance but with someone else ready to pay the legal fees. It might be, for example, a parent paying the child's legal fees or a corporation paying the fees for its officer or employee. Note that this type of situation is ***not automatically prohibited,*** but it should raise a red flag for you. You should check the facts of the question carefully to be sure that the lawyer ***remembers who the client is***—the person with the legal problem, not the person with the checkbook—and that the lawyer's ***independence and loyalty are not affected.*** If it seems that the person paying the fee is able to exert influence on the lawyer (*e.g.,* the parent or the corporation is telling the lawyer how to proceed), then the representation is *not* proper.

3. Employment by Lay Intermediary

Nor may a lawyer accept employment by a corporation or anyone else who would have the ***right to direct or control*** the lawyer's professional judgment in representing other clients.

[Model Rule 5.4(c); Restatement § 134(2)] This principle reinforces the rule, *e.g.,* against a bank employing lawyers to write wills for bank customers.

4. Representing Liability Insurer and Insured

But the most common illustration of third-party interests intersecting with those of a lawyer's client occurs when an insurance policy company provides that the insurance company will indemnify the insured against liability to third persons up to the monetary limits of the policy, and that the company will provide a lawyer (selected and paid by the company) to represent the policyholder in any lawsuit filed against her. These policies typically also provide that the insured agrees to cooperate in defending against claims covered by the policy.

a. Nature of Problem

When a claim is brought against an insured under the liability policy, differing interests may arise. The insured wants the dispute settled without personally incurring liability, whatever the cost may be to the insurance company. On the other hand, the company wishes to pay as little as possible in resolving the case—whether in the form of payment to the opposing party *or* in its costs of litigation.

b. Propriety of Representation

Despite these potential conflicts, the insurance company's providing a lawyer to defend the insured is an essential ingredient of liability insurance, and it is both proper and common for a lawyer selected by the insurance company to represent the policyholder in defending claims brought against it. [Restatement § 134, comment f]

c. Duty of Lawyer to Avoid Conflicting Interest

However, many areas of conflict can arise that the lawyer must avoid, including:

(1) Policy Coverage in Dispute

Insurance policies often cover certain situations (*e.g.,* negligence) but not others (*e.g.,* intentional harm). The insured naturally wishes any liability to be covered under the policy, while the insurer is best served if liability is found to be in the excluded area. [*E.g.,* **Parsons v. Continental National American Group,** 550 P.2d 94 (Ariz. 1976)—defendant admitted facts to lawyer suggesting he intentionally injured the plaintiff]

If a dispute arises between the insured and the insurance company as to whether the claim is covered under the policy, the lawyer has a conflict of interest and may ***not represent both*** the insurer and insured on that issue. (As a practical matter, the insurance company often agrees to defend the action "with a reservation of rights"—meaning that it will defend the claim now without waiving any policy defenses it may later have against the insured for payment of the damage award.)

(2) Settlement Proposals—Policy Limits Cases

The interests of the insurance company and the insured may also conflict where a settlement demand is made by the plaintiff that is ***within or close to the policy limits.***

(a) Obligation of the Insurer

The insurance company must take care to protect the interests of the insured. When a settlement offer close to the policy limits is made, the insurer must evaluate the offer as though its liability exposure was for the whole of plaintiff's claim, not just part of it. If the insurer rejects the offer negligently or in bad faith, it may be liable for ***all*** of a subsequent judgment—even the part above the policy limits.

Example: Plaintiff sued Defendant (insured), claiming personal injury damages of $100,000. Defendant's liability insurance was limited to $10,000. Plaintiff offered to settle the case for $10,000 (policy limits). Naturally, Defendant wanted the insurance company to accept the settlement offer and avoid the risk of a judgment against him personally in excess of the policy limits. On the other hand, the insurance company thought it had nothing to lose and everything to gain by litigating the matter and possibly getting a lower verdict. After the jury awarded Plaintiff $100,000, the court imposed liability on the insurance company in excess of the policy limits for failure to meet its duty to consider Defendant's interest in accepting the proposed settlement. [**Crisci v. Security Insurance Co.,** 66 Cal. 2d 425 (1967)]

(b) Obligation of Lawyer

A lawyer representing both the insurer and insured who is faced with such a settlement offer should advise both clients of the conflict of interest involved. The lawyer is obliged to use all best efforts to ***see that the interests of the insured are protected.*** Lawyers who regard themselves as primarily lawyers for the insurance company, and act accordingly, risk liability to the policyholder.

(3) Collusion or Failure to Cooperate by Insured

In certain instances, especially those involving liability claims against the insured by members of her own family, the policyholder refuses to cooperate fully in defending against the claim, *e.g.*, Son claims he slipped and fell in driveway as result of insured Mother's negligence in failing to remove grease and Mother affirmatively admits her conduct was negligent.

(a) Withdrawing from the Case

If a lawyer suspects collusion or lack of cooperation by the insured, the lawyer may: (i) recommend to the insured that she seek independent counsel, and (ii) withdraw from the proceedings altogether. [Model Rule 1.16(b)(2)]

(b) Duty in Course of Withdrawal

If a suit is pending, however, the lawyer may withdraw only with leave of court and after giving the insured reasonable time to obtain a new lawyer. [Model Rule 1.16(c), (d)]

5. Juvenile Court Proceedings

A lawyer retained by a parent or guardian to defend a child in delinquency or criminal proceedings owes a duty to act as *advocate* for the child. It is the court's function, not the lawyer's, and not the parent or guardian's, to decide whether the child needs punishment, rehabilitation, parental care, or the like.

a. Disclosure and Decisionmaking

As with any other client, the lawyer owes a duty to disclose all relevant considerations and submit important decisions to the child. [*Compare* Model Rule 1.14—decisionmaking by someone with diminished capacity (*see supra*, pp. 42–43)]

b. No Client Responsibility to Parent

Even if the fee is being paid by the parents, the lawyer's obligation is to the child (the client). Thus, for example, absent client consent, the lawyer must refuse to disclose information relating to the representation to the parents, and the attorney-client privilege pertains to the child and not the parents. Likewise, the lawyer must follow the child's decisions as to the case, rather than the parents.

c. Potential Conflicts of Interest with Parents

There may be cases where the parents' interests conflict with those of the child even more fundamentally, *e.g.*, where a child is cited for delinquency because of parental neglect. In such cases, the lawyer may ***not represent both*** the parents and the child.

E. Conflict Between Interests of Current and Former Clients

1. Introduction

a. The Basic Rule

A lawyer "who has formerly represented a client in a matter" may not later "represent another person in the same or a substantially related matter" if the new client's "interests are materially adverse to the interests of the former client" without the former client's "informed consent confirmed in writing." [Model Rule 1.9(a); Restatement § 132]

b. Rationale

This conflict of interest arises because the lawyer owes the former client some continuing duties. At the very least, the lawyer has a continuing duty to ***protect the former client's confidential information.*** The new representation might put performance of that continuing duty at risk, or in some cases, complying with the continuing duty could adversely affect what the lawyer can do on behalf of the current client. At the same time, a lawyer does not owe a former client the same duty of loyalty owed to a current client. Thus, the Restatement warns that turning each particular "engagement into a lifetime commitment would make lawyers reluctant to take new, relatively modest matters." [Restatement § 132, comment b]

c. What Is a Matter?

The most fundamental question in applying the basic rule is defining what constitutes a "matter," but the answer is ambiguous and "depends on the facts of a particular situation or transaction." The most obvious illustration is a litigated case that bears a discrete number, but the concept is clearly broader and includes identifiable transactions, whether or not completed. On the other hand, a "lawyer who recurrently handled a type of problem for a former client is not precluded from later representing another client in a factually distinct problem of that type." [Model Rule 1.9, comment 2; Restatement § 132, comment d(iii)]

d. When a Matter Is at an End: The "Hot Potato" Rule

You remember that a lawyer may not file suit against, or even negotiate a contract across the table from a current client. It thus becomes important to know when a current matter ends and the former client rules take over. That happens when the lawyer is mandatorily required to withdraw from the matter, or when the now-former client has discharged the lawyer. A lawyer may not, however, intentionally terminate the client a current client "like a hot potato" in order to make the less-limiting former client rules effective. [Restatement § 132, comment c; **Packer Intl. v. Varian Associates,** 670 F.Supp. 1363 (N.D. Ohio 1987)]

2. Prohibition on Switching Sides in Same Matter

A lawyer may ***not*** successively represent opposing parties in the ***same*** litigation. Thus, it is obviously ***improper*** and a denial of ***due process*** for a lawyer hired to represent an ***accused in a criminal case*** thereafter to become a prosecutor and represent the state against the accused on the same charge. [Model Rule 1.9(a) and comment 1; Restatement § 132 and comment d(i)]

3. Prohibition on Representation in Substantially Related Matters

The most common bar to a lawyer's later representation applies where the lawyer would be taking a position materially adverse to a former client in a matter that is not the same but is ***substantially related*** to the prior matter. The critical issue in such cases is typically whether there is a "substantial risk" that the lawyer will ***use confidential information*** obtained in the prior representation in a way that would "materially advance the case" against the former client. [Model Rule 1.9(a) and comment 3; Restatement § 132 and comment d(iii)]

a. Prior Work Exposed Lawyer to Relevant Facts

A lawyer who represented a businessperson and learned her detailed financial information may not represent her spouse in a divorce action. [Model Rule 1.9(a), comment 3; Restatement § 132 and comment d(iii)]

b. Cases Involving a Contract the Lawyer Drafted

Similarly, a lawyer who drafted a contract provision for one client may not represent the opposing party to the contract and allege the contract is ambiguous or invalid. In addition to the issue of confidential information, any other rule might give lawyers an incentive to leave terms ambiguous in the hopes of further business. [Model Rule 1.9(a) and comment 1; Restatement § 132 and comment d(ii)]

c. Former Client Now a Witness in Present Case

Because the interest to be protected is that of the former client, even if that client is not a party to the new case, the lawyer will be disqualified if the former client will be an essential witness for the other side and confidential information might be used by the lawyer to impeach the former client. [**United States v. Iorizzo,** 786 F.2d 52 (7th Cir. 1986)]

d. Former Client's Expectation That Information Would Be Held Confidential Is Required

For information to be confidential, there must be some expectation that it will be kept confidential. Thus, where a lawyer had represented two clients in a joint venture and there had been complete sharing of business information, there was no expectation of confidentiality and it was not improper for the lawyer to represent one of the clients in the bankruptcy of the other. [Restatement § 132, comment i; **Allegaert v. Perot,** 565 F.2d 246 (2d Cir. 1977)]

e. **Information That Has Become Generally Known**

Although a lawyer has a very broad duty of confidentiality with respect to information relating to a prior representation, sometimes the passage of time means that the information becomes widely known, readily observable or no longer of significance in the current matter. Courts properly may conclude that protection of such information does not justify treating matters as substantially related. [Model Rule 1.9(c), comment 8; Restatement § 132, comment d(iii)]

f. **Actual Disclosure of Confidential Information Not Required to Resolve Substantial Relationship Issue**

In determining whether or not two matters are substantially related, a court is not required to determine what confidential information might have been disclosed or used against the former client. To make that inquiry would require the former client to disclose that which it had a right to protect. [Model Rule 1.9, comment 2; Restatement § 132, comment d(iii); **T.C. Theatre Corp. v. Warner Bros. Pictures, Inc.,** 113 F. Supp. 265 (S.D.N.Y. 1953)—case in which the "same or substantially related" test was first announced]

4. Consent of Affected Clients Can Waive Conflict

As in the case of other kinds of conflicts of interest, a lawyer may undertake "conflicted" representation if both the current and former client gives ***informed consent,*** confirmed in *writing.* [Model Rule 1.9(a)]

SUMMARY OF CONFLICT OF INTERESTS—EXAMPLES GILBERT
INTERESTS OF CURRENT CLIENTS:
• Clients with ***directly adverse*** interests in ***same case***
• Clients with ***directly adverse*** interests in ***unrelated cases***
• Criminal ***co-defendants***
• ***Co-parties*** in civil litigation
• Multiple clients in ***nonlitigation matters*** (*e.g.*, seller and buyer of real estate)
• ***Current client*** with interest ***adverse to former client in same case***
PERSONAL INTERESTS OF LAWYER:
• ***Financial interests adverse*** to client
• ***Proprietary interest in the subject matter*** of employment
• ***Publication rights in the subject matter*** of client's case
• ***Business or financial transactions*** with client
• ***Gifts or bequests*** to lawyer
• Interest in ***employment with opposing firm***
INTERESTS OF THIRD PERSONS:
• ***Current client*** with interest ***adverse to former client in substantially related matter***
• ***Compensation from third person*** for representing client
• ***Lay employer's right to control*** lawyer's professional judgment in representing clients
• Representation of liability ***insurer and insured***
• Parental interference in ***juvenile court*** proceedings
INTERESTS OF FORMER CLIENTS:
• Lawyer switches sides in the same case
• Confidential information lawyer learned representing former client could be used on behalf of lawyer's new client against the former client in the current case

F. Imputed Disqualification of Affiliated Lawyers

1. General Rule and Personal Interest Exception

In general, the prohibition on representing clients because of a conflict of interests extends to all persons affiliated with the lawyer. Thus, if one lawyer in a practice organization has a conflict of interest, all affiliated lawyers do. [Model Rule 1.10(a); Restatement § 123]

a. Exception for Personal Interest Conflicts

Imputation does not extend to conflicts based on a "personal interest" of the lawyer that "does not present a significant risk of materially limiting the representation of the client" by the rest of the firm." A lawyer with strong political beliefs might not be able to represent some clients effectively, for example, but other lawyers in the firm would be able to do so unaffected by the first lawyer's beliefs. [Model Rule 1.10(a)(1) and comment 2]

b. Application to Personal Interest Conflicts in Model Rule 1.8

The specific personal interest conflicts discussed earlier in this Chapter and based on Model Rule 1.8(a) through (i) are expressly imputed throughout law firms. The prohibition against some ***sexual relationships with a client*** found in Model Rule 1.8(j), however, is expressly ***not imputed***. [Model Rule 1.8(k)].

c. Lawyers Related as Spouses

When one spouse is on one side of a case and the other spouse who works for a different firm is on the other side, there is a danger that each might receive the other's telephone messages or otherwise make inadvertent disclosures and might compromise the interests of clients. Thus, the two related lawyers may not themselves represent clients who are directly adverse unless their clients give informed, written consent. The Model Rules impose the same prohibition in the case of parent-child and sibling relationships, although the assumption about sharing income and telephone calls is often much less likely in such cases. The risks of these effects is considered entirely personal to the lawyers, however, so the firms for which spouses work are not automatically barred from representing opposing interests. [Model Rule 1.7, comment 11; Restatement § 123, comment g]

2. Private Law Firms

The most common application of the general principle of imputation is to persons affiliated as partners, associates, and other lawyers in a private law firm.

a. Offices in Multiple Cities

The rule even applies where one firm has offices in different cities. Thus, if a client is represented by lawyer A in one city, A's partners in another city are disqualified from representing clients in an unrelated suit against A's client. [Model Rule 1.10(a); **Westinghouse Electric Corp. v. Kerr-McGee Corp.,** 580 F.2d 1311 (7th Cir. 1978)]

b. Affiliated Persons or Firms

Even different firms that have been working on a case with a disqualified firm may themselves be disqualified pursuant to this rule. The factual question will be whether the relationship between the firms was *close enough* to warrant concern that prohibited confidential information may have passed between them. [**Fund of Funds, Ltd. v. Arthur Andersen & Co.,** 567 F.2d 225 (2d Cir. 1977)—firm disqualified; **American Can Co. v. Citrus Feed Co.,** 436 F.2d 1125 (5th Cir. 1971)—no disqualification]

c. Persons Other than Lawyers with Disqualifying Information

Similar problems can arise if a law firm hires a nonlawyer, *e.g.,* a secretary or a law student, who had worked for the firm on the other side of a major case, but imputed disqualification is less automatic in such cases. Ordinarily, such persons may be screened (*i.e.,* isolated through the firm's timely imposition of procedures to protect confidential information [Model Rule 1.0(k)]) from participation in the matter. [Model Rule 1.10, comment 4; Restatement § 123, comment f; **Herron v. Jones,** 637 S.W.2d 569 (Ark. 1982)]

d. When Disqualified Person Has Left Law Firm

If a lawyer who would have had a personal conflict of interest has permanently ceased association with a law firm, leaving no records and no person in the firm who would be similarly disqualified, the firm is no longer prohibited from undertaking a representation. [Model Rule 1.10(b); Restatement § 124(1)]

Example: Partner of Law Firm One represents client A in the *A v. B* case. She obtains confidential information from A. Then she leaves Law Firm One to start her own law firm, taking all of A's records with her. If no other lawyer at Law Firm One had access to the confidential information received from A, any lawyer at Law Firm One may represent B in the *A v. B* case.

e. When Person Leaves Disqualified Law Firm

The converse is also true. If a person who would have been vicariously disqualified at a law firm in which one member had a conflict of interest then leaves the law firm without having learned any disqualifying information about the matter, that lawyer will no longer be prohibited from working on the matter at a new firm. [Model Rule 1.9(b)]

3. Other Practice Organizations

The imputed disqualification rule in the Model Rules is stated in terms of a "firm," but that term is defined very broadly to include "lawyers employed in a legal services organization or the legal department of a corporation or other organization." [Model Rule 1.0(c), 1.10(a); Restatement, § 123] However, application to organizations with no common economic interest is less clear.

a. Lawyers Sharing Office Space

When lawyers share office space but otherwise do not work on each other's cases or share revenue from them, imputed disqualification will not be imposed if each lawyer's confidential information is adequately protected. [Restatement § 123, comment e; **United States v. Bell,** 506 F.2d 207 (D.C. Cir. 1974)]

b. Government Legal Offices

In general, government legal offices are treated as a "firm" for purposes of imputation. But the practical effect of potentially making it impossible for an entire government legal office to act has caused courts to be more cautious about disqualifying such offices. [Model Rule 1.0(c), comment 3; 1.11(d), comment 2; Restatement § 123, comment d;

State v. Jones, 429 A.2d 936 (Conn. 1980)—refusal to disqualify entire prosecutor's office]

4. Screening as a Remedy for Imputed Disqualification of a Lateral Hire

For many years, the rule was that a law firm could not avoid imputation by *screening* a disqualified lawyer and thus continue its representation in the case. Courts were concerned that there will be no way to assure that law firms will respect the screens they are required to impose, but the ABA has now changed that rule in a limited but important class of cases.

a. Cases Where Screening Is Permitted

In the case of a conflict arising under Model Rule 1.9(a) or (b), *i.e.*, knowledge of confidential information about the "same or a substantially related matter," where the ***disqualified lawyer moves to another private firm***, that new firm may represent someone adverse to the former client if it "timely screens" the lawyer from any participation in the matter. [Model Rule 1.10(a)(2); Restatement § 124(2)]

b. Nature of the Screening Required

In addition to screening the lawyer from participation in the matter, the lawyer must "be apportioned no part of the fee therefrom," then "written notice" must be "promptly given to any affected former client" to ascertain compliance with the rule, and "certifications of compliance" with the rules must be given to the former client at "reasonable intervals" and "upon termination of the screening procedures." [*Compare* Model Rule 1.0(k), comments 8–10; *see also,* Restatement § 124—limited screening where "no substantial risk" confidential information will have "material adverse effect"]

5. Use of Work Product

If a firm is *disqualified* from acting as counsel in a matter after beginning work, its work product *may be used* by successor counsel, but only to the extent it is not tainted by containing or reflecting use of confidential information. [**First Wisconsin Mortgage Trust v. First Wisconsin Corp.,** 584 F.2d 201 (7th Cir. 1978)]

G. Limitations on Representation by Current and Former Government Lawyers

1. Introduction

Over the years, the ABA has sought to make it relatively easy for lawyers to accept government jobs and later move into private practice. Often the process occurs more than once in a lawyer's career. Thus, when a lawyer leaves or enters government, special conflicts questions are presented. But, as with moves from one private practice setting to another, the rules try to protect both the government and private clients' interests.

In recent years, the ABA has extended similar principles to former judges, arbitrators, mediators and third party neutrals, with the result that Model Rules 1.11 and 1.12 have a lot in common with each other and both contrast in part with Model Rules 1.9 and 1.10's treatment of former client issues.

2. Former Government Lawyer

a. Lawyer Having Personal and Substantial Involvement in a Matter

A former government lawyer may not represent a private client in any ***matter*** in which the lawyer participated ***personally and substantially*** while in government, unless the appropriate government agency consents. [Model Rule 1.11(a); Restatement § 133(1)]

e.g. **Example:** Attorney is the District Attorney of Colma County. She is in charge of 16 deputies working out of five offices spread throughout the county. Her rubber-stamped signature appears on every paper that goes out of the five offices. In theory, she is personally responsible for every detail of every case; in fact, most of Attorney's day is consumed in supervision and administration. The disqualification rule would cover only the relatively few cases in which Attorney did become personally and substantially involved.

(1) "Matter" Defined

The word "matter" means any "judicial. . . . proceeding, application, request for a ruling, . . . contract, claim, controversy, . . . or other particular matter involving a specific party or parties." [Model Rule 1.11(e)] Among the things ***excluded*** from this definition is the drafting of legislation or regulations of ***general*** applicability. [Restatement § 133]

e.g. **Example:** When Lawyer worked for the State Consumer Protection Agency, she was assigned to draft regulations to govern the conduct of on-line salespeople. The regulations she drafted were adopted by the agency. A year later, Lawyer left government service and entered private practice. She was asked to represent American Marketing Company (an on-line sales company) in a dispute with the State Consumer Protection Agency. The essence of the dispute was the proper application of the regulations that Lawyer herself drafted. She could represent American because drafting regulations was not a "matter"; it did not involve specific facts and specific parties.

cf. **Compare:** When serving as Oakville City Attorney, Lawyer drafted a city ordinance for the rezoning of a particular tract of land owned by Developer. The drafting of such an ordinance is a "matter" because it involved one specific situation and one party. Thus, when Lawyer later enters private law practice, she may not work on a case that involves that ordinance. [*See* Restatement § 133]

(2) "Personal and Substantial" Defined

The term ***"personal and substantial"*** also has a narrow meaning. It means that the lawyer worked on the matter ***herself*** and that her work was more than trivial. Personally signing a pleading in a matter, for example, would be personal and substantial involvement if the lawyer read the document and personally approved it.

(3) Imputation to Partners and Associates

As is now true in the case of many lateral transfer private lawyers, a former government lawyer's ***firm*** is ***not*** disqualified if: (i) the tainted lawyer is ***screened from any participation*** in the matter, (ii) the tainted lawyer ***shares no fees*** earned from the case, and (iii) written notice is promptly given to the appropriate government agency. [Model Rule 1.11(b); *and compare* Model Rule 1.10(a)(2)—former private lawyer; Model Rule 1.12(c)—former judge or law clerk]

b. Lawyer Having Confidential Government Information

Even if the lawyer's work on a matter was not personal and substantial while in government, a lawyer may not represent a private client adverse to another private party about whom the lawyer learned confidential government information without the consent of that adverse party. [Model Rule 1.11(c); Restatement § 133(2)]

(1) "Confidential Government Information" Defined

"Confidential government information" is information obtained under government authority and which, at the time the rule is invoked, the government may not disclose or which is otherwise not available to the public, e.g., confidential FBI investigative files. [Model Rule 1.11(c)]

(2) Imputation

Once again, the tainted lawyer's firm may handle the matter if, and only if, the tainted lawyer is adequately screened and notice is given to the lawyer's former agency. [Model Rule 1.11(c)]

c. Lawyer Coming to Government from Private Practice

A lawyer in government service is subject to Model Rules 1.7 (concurrent conflict of interest) and 1.9 (duties to former clients). In addition, the lawyer may not participate in work on any matter in which the lawyer was ***personally and substantially*** involved while in nongovernmental employment (*e.g.,* where the government and former client have the same interest so there is no Rule 1.9 violation), unless the appropriate government agency gives informed consent, confirmed in writing. [Model Rule 1.11(d)(1), (2)(i)]

d. Lawyer Negotiating for Private Employment

A government lawyer may not negotiate for private employment with any person involved in a matter on which the government lawyer is working. [Model Rule 1.11(d)(2)(ii); *compare* Model Rule 1.12(b)—judge or law clerk negotiating employment]

3. Federal Statute Governing Employees Including Lawyers

The Federal Conflict of Interest Act, originally passed in 1963, imposes substantial ***criminal sanctions*** for certain representation of private parties after government service, whether or not the government service was as a lawyer. A lawyer needs to know these rules because, where they are more restrictive than the Model Rules, lawyers must abide by the tougher restrictions.

a. Permanent Bar

A lawyer who has participated ***personally and substantially*** in a ***matter*** while in government service is ***barred forever*** from ***contacting the government about it*** on behalf of a private client. But the former government lawyer ***may personally work*** on the cases back at the firm as long as she ***does not contact*** the government orally or in writing. [18 U.S.C. § 207(a)(1)]

b. Two-Year Bar

A lawyer is barred for ***two years*** from ***contacting the government*** about any matter within the lawyer's ***official responsibility*** while in government, even if the lawyer did no personal work on it at all. [18 U.S.C. § 207(a)(2)]

4. Former Judge, Arbitrator, Mediator or Other Third-Party Neutral

Judges often retire before the end of their career and may even practice or serve as "private judges" after they retire. This makes the ethics of that transition particularly important. Transitioning from work as a government lawyer is the model for judges, not the framework for moving from one private firm to another.

a. Judge Who Has Become a Practicing Lawyer

A judge who retires or resigns and becomes a practicing lawyer may not "represent anyone in a matter" in which the lawyer "participated personally and substantially" as a "judge or other adjudicative officer" or as a "law clerk to such a person" unless all parties to the proceeding give "informed consent, confirmed in writing." [Model Rule 1.12(a) and comment 1]

b. Application to an Arbitrator, Mediator or Other Third-Party Neutral

The same limitations derived from government settings apply to private lawyers acting as arbitrators, mediators or other third-party neutrals, except that an arbitrator who served as a partisan on a multi-member arbitration panel may later represent that party. [Model Rules 1.12(a) & (d) and comments 2 & 3]

c. Negotiating for Employment with a Lawyer for or Party to a Matter

A person serving as a judge, an arbitrator, a mediator or another third-party neutral may not negotiate for employment with any party to or lawyer for a matter in which the person is appearing before that person. A law clerk to a judge may negotiate for employment with a party to a matter in which the clerk is working personally and substantially, but only after the clerk notifies the judge of the negotiations. [Model Rules 1.12(b)]

d. Availability of Screening as a Way to Avoid Disqualification

The disqualification of a lawyer under these rules will not be imputed to the rest of that lawyer's firm if the lawyer is "screened" from any participation in the matter, from any part of the fee in the matter, and notice is "promptly given" to the parties and to any "appropriate tribunal" to assure compliance with the screening requirements. [Model Rules 1.12(c) and comments 4 & 5]

Chapter Five

Lawyer Obligations to Third Persons and the Legal System

CONTENTS PAGE

Chapter Approach

Although the duties of a lawyer to the client are the beginning of any analysis of legal ethics, the law imposes important ***limitations*** on what a lawyer may do on the client's behalf and imposes ***affirmative duties*** to third parties. This Chapter collects several of those important limitations and duties:

1. Giving Candid Advice Without Assisting Illegal Conduct
2. Duties When Representing an Organization
3. Being Honest and Candid in Communicating with Others
4. Contact with an Opposing Party or other Third Person
5. Duty to Avoid Knowing Harassment or Discrimination
6. Encouragement to Provide Pro Bono Service
7. Obligation to Help Improve the Legal System

The sources of most of the principles in this Chapter are Restatement §§ 94–103 and Model Rules 1.2(d), 1.13, 2.1–2.4, 3.9, 4.1–4.3, 6.1–6.5, 8.2 and 8.4(f) & (g).

A. Giving Candid Advice Without Assisting Illegal Conduct

1. Duty to Give Candid Advice

In counseling a client, a lawyer must "exercise independent professional judgment and render candid advice." [Model Rule 2.1]

a. Duty Not to Sugarcoat Reality

A lawyer must give the client ***straightforward*** advice that may involve "unpleasant facts and alternatives that a client may be disinclined to confront." A lawyer should not withhold advice from a client because it may be unpalatable. [Model Rule 2.1, comment 1; Restatement § 94, comment h]

b. Right and Duty to Counsel About Nonlegal Considerations

The Model Rules expressly authorize a lawyer to "refer not only to law" but also to things such as ***"moral, economic, social and political factors"*** that may lead to a wise course of action for the client. Indeed, failure to include such factors may sometimes constitute inadequate advice. [Model Rule 2.1, comment 2; Restatement § 94(3), comment h]

2. Duty Not to Counsel or Assist Illegal or Fraudulent Conduct

At the same time, a lawyer may not counsel or assist the client to engage in conduct that the lawyer knows is illegal or fraudulent. [Model Rule 1.2(d); Restatement § 94(1), (2)] e.g. **Example:** A lawyer who knowingly assists in preparation of a client's ***fraudulent income tax returns*** both violates the criminal law and is subject to professional discipline as a lawyer. [**Committee on Legal Ethics of the West Virginia State Bar v. Hart,** 410 S.E.2d 714 (W. Va. 1991)]

a. Violation of Court Order

Although not directly mentioned in the Model Rules, lawyers are equally prohibited from counseling or assisting a client to violate a court order. [Restatement § 94, comment d; ***In re* Robinson,** 639 A.2d 1384 (Vt. 1994); *compare* Model Rule 8.4(d)—conduct prejudicial to administration of justice]

b. Advice About Enforcement Policy

A lawyer may not counsel a client to engage in an act the lawyer knows to be illegal simply because it is unlikely the client will get caught or be punished. [Restatement § 94, comment f]

c. Right to Refuse to Assist Likely Crime or Fraud

A lawyer may refuse to assist a client in conduct the lawyer reasonably believes to be illegal even if the conduct is arguably legal. [*See, e.g.,* Model Rule 1.16(b)(2)—lawyer's right to withdraw in such a case]

3. Discussing Legal Consequences of Conduct

Lawyers are sometimes asked about conduct that if undertaken would be illegal. In such cases, a lawyer *may discuss* the legal consequences of proposed conduct with a client as long as the lawyer ***does not advocate*** the client's undertaking it or counsel the client on how to avoid detection or escape arrest. [Model Rule 1.2(d); Restatement § 94(2)]

4. Good Faith Testing Bounds of the Law

What a lawyer *may* do is assist a client to commit an act that will, in good faith, test the validity, scope, meaning, or application of the law. [Model Rule 1.2(d); Restatement § 94(2)(a)]

EXAM TIP GILBERT

Be sure that you understand the distinction between providing a legal analysis of a client's questionable conduct and aiding a client in the commission of a crime. A lawyer ***may*** discuss a proposed course of conduct with a client, explain that the conduct would be unlawful, and give an opinion regarding the likely consequences of such conduct. However, the lawyer ***must not*** knowingly advise a client to commit a crime or assist a client in illegal conduct.

B. Special Duties When Representing an Organization

1. Duty to Treat the Entity as the Client

As we saw in Chapter IV, p. 85, an organization is inherently a bundle of often-conflicting interests that has to operate as if it were of one mind. Lawyers who represent organizations deal with that reality by representing "the organization acting through its duly authorized constituents." We call that representing the organizational "entity." [Model Rule 1.13(a) and comment 1; Restatement §§ 96 & 97]

a. Constituent Communications Protected as Confidential for the Organization

Communications from "constituents," *e.g.*, officers, members, employees and others at the organization are the way any lawyer learns most about what issues the organization is facing. The lawyer must treat all such communications as confidential client information of the organization, but not of the persons who made the disclosures. [Model Rule 1.13, comment 2]

b. Same Principle Protects the Communications as Privileged

Similarly, if a communication meets the requirements for attorney-client privilege protection, the holder of the privilege is the organization, not the communicating constituents. Thus, if disclosing the information the lawyer learned from an organization's president would allow authorities to convict the president but protect the organization against prosecution, the lawyer may make the disclosure. [Model Rule 1.13, comment 2]

c. Lawyer's Duty to Clarify Whom the Lawyer Represents

(1) Lawyer May Represent a Constituent Along with the Organization

It is possible for a lawyer to represent both the organization and one or more of its constituents if the requirements of Model Rule 1.7 are met. This might happen when the company truck driver has an accident and both she and the organization are sued. [Model Rule 1.13(g)]

(2) Lawyer's Duty Not to Let Constituent Mistakenly Believe the Lawyer Represents Her

Organizational lawyers often regularly deal with constituents who come to trust and confide in the lawyers. Because of the potentially serious consequences of a constituent's mistaken believing the lawyer represents her along with the organization, the lawyer "shall explain the identity of the client when the lawyer knows or reasonably should know that the organization's interests are adverse" to the constituent's interest. [Model Rule 1.13(f) and comment 10]

2. Representing an Organization When a Constituent Violates Duties to It

a. Lawyer Ordinarily Must Let People with Authority Make Decisions

The way a lawyer's duty to the entity usually operates is that the lawyer lets organizational constituents make decisions within their areas of responsibility. The lawyer may advise about policy choices, but her primary role is to help the entity lawfully carry out those choices. [Model Rule 1.13, comment 3]

b. The Lawyer's Duties Change When a Constituent Seeks to Violates the Law

Special obligations are imposed upon a corporation's lawyer who learns that someone is acting ***illegally*** and in a way that will ***significantly injure*** the corporation.

(1) Basic Obligation—Reporting Up

If a lawyer learns that someone within the organization is violating or intends to [i] ***violate a legal obligation to*** the organization or [ii] commit ***a violation of law that reasonably might be imputed*** to the organization, **and** either [i] or [ii] is ***likely to result in substantial injury*** to the organization, then the lawyer shall proceed as ***reasonably necessary*** in the best interests of the organization.

(2) What the Lawyer Must Do

The conditions just identified presumptively require the lawyer to refer the situation to higher authority in the organization, even ultimately to the highest authority that can act to correct the situation, typically a corporation's board of directors. [Model Rule 1.13(b) and comment 4; Restatement § 96, comments e & f; *compare* 17 CFR §§ 205.3 *et seq.*—Sarbanes-Oxley Act regulations]

(3) Lawyer's Duty to Protect the Organization

The premise of the Model Rule 1.13(b) process is that the organization can correct its own problems. A lawyer should, to the extent practical, "minimize the risk of revealing" the problem to persons who are outside the organization.

c. Lawyer's Authority—Reporting out

After enough cases arose in which organizations seemed to have covered up problems rather than dealt with them, however, the Model Rules now give lawyers permission to disclose ("may reveal") information to those outside the entity who may be in a position to take effective action.

(1) Conditions That Must Be Present and Action the Lawyer May Take

If the lawyer is [i] ***unsuccessful*** in getting the matter resolved by the highest authority in the organization and [ii] the matter is ***clearly a violation of law*** and [iii] ***reasonably certain*** to result in substantial injury to the organization, the lawyer may refer the matter to others outside the organization insofar as the lawyer ***reasonably believes necessary*** to prevent the threatened ***substantial injury***. [Model Rule 1.13(c) and comment 6]

(2) Possible Requirement of Withdrawal

Under some circumstances, to avoid continuing to assist the organization's wrongdoing, the lawyer may be required to withdraw and notify affected persons of the withdrawal. This is what used to be called "noisy withdrawal." [Model Rule 1.13, comment 6; Restatement § 96, comment f; *see also* Model Rule 1.6(b)(2) & (3)]

(3) Exception—Lawyer Hired to Defend Against Charges

The Model Rules expressly ***withhold*** this authority to "report out" in cases where a lawyer was retained to investigate or defend the corporation against the charges that would otherwise be reported. [Model Rule 1.13(d)]

d. Lawyer's Duty to Report Wrongful Discharge

A lawyer who "reasonably believes" that she was discharged or had to resign for taking the steps required by Model Rule 1.13(b) or (c) is ***required*** to "proceed as the lawyer reasonably believes necessary to assure that the organization's highest authority" knows what happened to the lawyer, presumably to cause the organization to change its ways. [Model Rule 1.13(e) and comment 8]

C. Requirement of Honesty in Communications with Non-Clients

1. Basic Obligation of Truthfulness

A lawyer may not knowingly make a ***false statement of material fact or law*** to a third person in the course of representing a client, even if it might seem to serve the client's interest to do so. [Model Rule 4.1(a); Restatement § 98] This obligation is consistent with the lawyer's broad duty to avoid "conduct involving dishonesty, fraud, deceit, or misrepresentation." [Model Rule 8.4(c)]

2. Duty to Come Forward with Information

A lawyer sometimes even has an obligation to correct a ***misapprehension of material fact*** by a third person, but this is not a general obligation of candor. [Model Rule 4.1(b); Restatement § 98(3)]

a. Restatement Provision

The Restatement leaves open what the law requires to be revealed. It says that a lawyer may not "conceal or knowingly fail to reveal that which he is required by law to reveal." [Restatement § 98(3)]

b. Model Rules Requirement

The Model Rules say that a lawyer may not "knowingly fail to disclose a material fact to a third person when disclosure is necessary to avoid assisting a criminal or fraudulent act by a client, unless disclosure is prohibited by Rule 1.6" (the duty to protect confidential client information). [Model Rule 4.1(b); *and see* Model Rule 1.6(b)(2) & (3)—right to disclose to prevent client fraud]

c. Possible Mandatory Disclosure Under Rule 4.1(B)

A possible stealth effect of the 2003 amendment to Rule 1.6 could transform the discretionary character of disclosure under Rule 1.6(b)(2) and (b)(3) into ***mandatory disclosure*** under Model Rule 4.1(b) in cases where the attorney is unable to withdraw or otherwise avoid assisting an illegal act. The latter rule requires disclosure of material facts "necessary to avoid assisting a criminal or fraudulent act by a client, unless disclosure is prohibited by Rule 1.6." Insofar as Rule 1.6(b)(2) and (b)(3) no longer prohibits disclosure, the mandatory character of Rule 4.1(b) seems to apply with full force. [Model Rule 4.1(b)]

3. The Lawyer's Duty in Negotiations

Issues of honesty and affirmative disclosure often arise in the context of negotiations. In general, a lawyer has *no duty* to do the other side's fact research *nor any right* to reveal facts that would undermine the client's position.

a. Puffing and Other Subjective Assertions

It is part of the essence of negotiation that a lawyer may magnify the strength of the client's position, and a reasonable hearer would not take many of a lawyer's statements as literally true. [*See* Model Rule 4.1(a) and comment 2; Restatement § 98, comment c]

e.g. **Example:** In a personal injury negotiation, a lawyer's statement to defense counsel that "any jury would award my client at least a million dollars" would ordinarily constitute permitted puffing, not prohibited dishonesty.

EXAM TIP GILBERT

It is important to remember that although puffing is allowed in negotiations, a lawyer must ***not*** make a false statement of ***material fact.*** The key factor in determining whether a statement contains a material fact is whether the opponent would be ***reasonable in relying*** on the statement. If so, the statement is not mere puffery.

b. Ordinarily No Duty to Correct Misapprehensions Not Involving Act by Lawyer or Client

Furthermore, a lawyer who believes that an opponent is underestimating the strength of its position has no duty to correct that belief unless the lawyer or client has caused the underestimation. [**Brown v. County of Genessee,** 872 F.2d 169 (6th Cir. 1989)—opponent miscalculated amount of her lost pay]

c. Exceptions When Disclosure Is Required

In some cases, a lawyer has been required to disclose information. Although a failure to disclose might not literally assist a fraud, the opponent's lack of knowledge of pertinent facts may be so obvious and important that courts have required disclosure.

e.g. **Example:** A settlement of a case was *set aside* when the plaintiff's lawyer had failed to disclose to the defendant that the plaintiff, for whom damages had been negotiated based on life expectancy, had already died. [**Virzi v. Grand Trunk Warehouse,** 571 F. Supp. 507 (E.D. Mich. 1983)]

e.g. **Example:** A prosecutor was held to have a duty to tell a criminal defendant, prior to accepting a guilty plea, that physical evidence of the defendant's guilt had been accidentally destroyed. [**Fambo v. Smith,** 433 F. Supp. 590 (W.D.N.Y. 1977)]

D. Specially Assumed Duty of Candor—The Lawyer as Evaluator

1. Giving Opinions to Nonclients

A lawyer may be asked by the party on the other side of a transaction to ***certify facts or issues of legal authority*** on which the other party may rely. That might seem odd, but it actually is commonly done in the interest of time and reducing cost, so unless contrary to the interest of the lawyer's client in a given situation, the lawyer may do so. [Model Rule 2.3; Restatement § 95] The certifications may take the form of formal opinion letters (*e.g.,* "the client is validly incorporated"); at other times they take the form of title examinations for property the client wants to sell or mortgage.

a. Model Rule Requirements

The Model Rules call this practice making an "evaluation for use by third persons" and permit it whenever it is "***compatible*** with other aspects of the lawyer's relationship with the client." [Model Rule 2.3(a); *and see* Restatement § 95(1)]

b. Duty of Care in Making Evaluation

Because the evaluation is made with the knowledge that a third party will rely on it, the lawyer will be ***liable to the third party*** for any negligence in determining the facts. [**Greycas, Inc. v. Proud,** 826 F.2d 1560 (7th Cir. 1987)—lawyer certified client's title to farm equipment for a lender without checking public records; in fact, the equipment had all been previously mortgaged to its full value]

c. When Opinion May Adversely Affect Client

Because the lawyer must be accurate and candid in the opinion, if investigation of the facts reveals information that would have to be disclosed which would embarrass or otherwise ***adversely affect*** the client, the lawyer must ***obtain the client's consent*** before going ahead with the opinion. [Model Rule 2.3(b)]

d. Undisclosed Confidential Information Remains Confidential

Facts disclosed in the opinion are, of course, thereafter not privileged. Thus, the client may limit the scope of the evaluation, but the lawyer should describe any material limitation in his report. Any facts learned by the lawyer that are ***not*** required to be disclosed, must continue to be treated by the lawyer as ***confidential*** and are protected by Model Rule 1.6. [Model Rule 2.3(c)]

EXAM TIP GILBERT

Note that Model Rule 2.3 (regarding giving opinions to nonclients) applies when the ***client*** is the person or entity whose affairs are to be evaluated by the lawyer. The Rule does not apply when a client asks his lawyer to evaluate the affairs of the opposing party.

---

2. When Lawyer's Opinion Is to Be Widely Disseminated

Consistent with the above rules, when a lawyer agrees to certify facts to a large number of persons who can be expected to rely on the lawyer, the lawyer has a special obligation to be ***complete, accurate, and candid.***

a. Application—Tax Shelter Opinions

When a lawyer gives a widely disseminated legal opinion about the tax treatment likely to be afforded an investment, the lawyer must candidly disclose and estimate the degree of risk that the IRS will not allow the tax deductions being sought, even if such disclosure will be contrary to the interest of the lawyer's client in maximum sales of the investment. [ABA Opn. 346]

b. Due Diligence Required

A lawyer is not a guarantor of every fact in disclosure materials about a company or transaction, or even those upon which the lawyer relies in rendering an opinion. However, if facts the lawyer learns seem inconsistent, or the lawyer has any other reason to doubt their accuracy, the lawyer has a ***duty to inquire*** to determine what the correct facts are. [ABA Opn. 335]

3. Regular Letters Required by Accountants as Part of Client Audits

A standard part of corporate practice is responding to periodic letters from auditors inquiring about the status of the client's litigation to determine what loss reserves, if any, the client should be required to establish. Responses to these letters are "evaluations" within the meaning of Model Rule 2.3, but the legal and accounting professions have established a "treaty" prescribing certain ground rules for such letters. [Restatement § 95, comment f]

a. Likelihood Client Will Prevail in Pending Cases

Auditors would like lawyers to tell them precisely what the chances are that the client will prevail in pending cases, and lawyers are equally reluctant to do so. In part, that is because litigation is uncertain and, in part, it is because an admission that the client has a 75% chance of losing would have value to the client's opponent. Thus lawyers need only say if the chance the opponent will win is ***probable*** (*i.e.,* extremely high) or ***remote*** (*i.e.,* extremely remote). No estimate need be given of cases that fall between those extremes.

b. Unasserted Possible Claims

A harder issue is presented when the lawyer knows that someone might have a claim against the client but no suit has been filed yet and the potential opponent might go away.

(1) Information Confidential

Such information about client contingent liabilities is clearly ***confidential*** (*see supra*, pp. 70–72), because disclosure might be embarrassing to the client or might even ***cause*** the potential claimants to assert the claims.

(2) Opine Only on Extreme Cases

Under the lawyer-accountant treaty, lawyers need only disclose claims that: (i) are ***probable*** of assertion, (ii) if asserted, the client faces a reasonable possibility of ***losing***, and (iii) are large enough to be ***material.***

E. Contact with an Opposing Party or Other Third Person

1. Person Represented by Counsel

A lawyer who ***knows*** that another person is represented by counsel in a particular matter ***must not communicate*** with that person on any subject of the controversy, unless that person's counsel is present or has given prior consent or the communication is authorized by law or court order. [Model Rule 4.2; Cal. Rule 2–100(A); Restatement § 99(1)]

a. Scope of Prohibition

Note that Model Rule 4.2 prohibits contact with ***any*** person represented by counsel, not just an adverse party. Thus, the rule covers individuals before a suit or charge is actually filed, as well as people such as victims in a criminal case or witnesses who may have counsel in the matter.

(1) Improper Intent Not Required

If the lawyer knows that someone has counsel in the matter, it is improper for the lawyer to even respond to contact initiated by the represented person, except to suggest that the person could have his attorney contact the lawyer. [Model Rule 4.2, comment 3; ***In re*** **News America Publishing, Inc.,** 974 S.W.2d 97 (Tex. 1998)]

(2) Represented Persons May Meet

Represented persons may communicate without their lawyers and even settle the matter on their own. A lawyer may help prepare the client for such a meeting. [Restatement § 99(2), comment k]

b. Application of the Rule to Corporations and Other Organizations

When the "person" protected by Rule 4.2 is an impersonal organization, the lawyer is only barred from talking to some of the individuals who work for the organization:

(1) Individuals Treated as Part of the Organizational "Person"

Persons to whom opposing counsel may not speak are: (i) those who have authority to settle the matter for the organization, (ii) those who regularly talk with the organization's counsel about the matter, and (iii) those whose conduct or statements in the matter may be imputed to the organization for purposes of liability. [Model Rule 4.2, comment 7; Restatement § 100]

(2) Special Rule for Government Agencies

Although government agencies are treated as other organizations for purposes of Rule 4.2 in most ordinary litigation, the Rule does ***not prevent*** a lawyer from communicating with an agency policymaker about an issue of ***general public policy.*** [Restatement § 101]

(3) Former Employees

Generally, a lawyer ***may*** contact ***former*** employees of an organization, even if they had one of the identified roles at the time they were employed. However, such contact is ***prohibited*** if the employee ***continues*** to regularly communicate with the organization's counsel about the matter. [ABA Opn. 91–359; Restatement § 100, comment g] Furthermore, when talking with either a present or former employee, a lawyer must take care not to violate the organization's legal rights, such as the attorney-client privilege. [Model Rule 4.2, comment 7]

e.g. **Example:** Lawyer represents Plaintiff in a defamation action against the Herald Newspaper Corp. Without getting the permission of the Herald's counsel, Lawyer interviewed the newspaper's former editor-in-chief and convinced him to disclose some privileged communications he had with the newspaper's lawyer about the case. Lawyer acted improperly in prying into the privileged communications. [Model Rule 4.2, comment 7; *and see* Model Rule 4.4, comment 1]

c. Communication Authorized by Law or Court Order

Some communication with a represented person is inevitable (*e.g.,* the law may require service of process on an opposing party, not the person's lawyer). Such contact is authorized by law and is not prohibited by the rule. [Model Rule 4.2; Restatement § 99(l)(c)]

(1) Represented Criminal Defendant

Particular controversy has arisen over whether a prosecutor may talk with a criminal defendant, at the request of that defendant, in the absence of the defendant's counsel. This situation often arises when the defendant wants to enter into a plea agreement but his lawyer refuses to go to the prosecutor. A majority of courts confronted with this situation have held that a prosecutor's duty to refrain from communicating with an indicted defendant known to be represented by counsel cannot be waived by the defendant. [*See* **United States v. Lopez,** 4 F.3d 1455 (9th Cir. 1993)]

(2) Justice Department Efforts

Two U.S. Attorneys General tried to authorize such contacts "by law," but the courts rejected their efforts. Nevertheless, the words "or court order" were added to Model Rule 4.2 to permit lawyers to seek a court ruling interpreting the scope of Rule 4.2 or a court order justifying contact in exceptional circumstances.

2. Person Unrepresented by Counsel

When a person is ***not represented*** by counsel, the lawyer may communicate directly, but:

a. Must Not Imply Disinterest

In the course of communication with the unrepresented person, the lawyer must make clear that she represents someone else and thus is ***not disinterested*** or representing the person being interviewed. If the lawyer knows or reasonably should know that the person misunderstands the lawyer's role in the matter, the lawyer must make reasonable efforts to correct the misunderstanding. [Model Rule 4.3; Restatement § 103]

b. Must Not Give Person Advice

Furthermore, if the person's interests have a reasonable possibility of being ***in conflict*** with those of the lawyer's client, the lawyer ***may not advise*** the person beyond suggesting that he secure counsel to represent his own interests. [Model Rule 4.3]

EXAM TIP GILBERT

If a question involves a lawyer's communication with an ***unrepresented person,*** remember that the lawyer ***may communicate*** directly with the person but that she must be careful in doing so. If the lawyer ***knows, or reasonably should know,*** that the unrepresented person ***misunderstands*** the lawyer's role in the matter, the lawyer must make reasonable efforts to correct the misunderstanding. Likewise, if the lawyer knows or should know that her client's interests are likely to be in conflict with those of the unrepresented person, she must not give legal advice to that person (other than to get a lawyer).

ATTORNEY COMMUNICATIONS WITH THIRD PARTIES

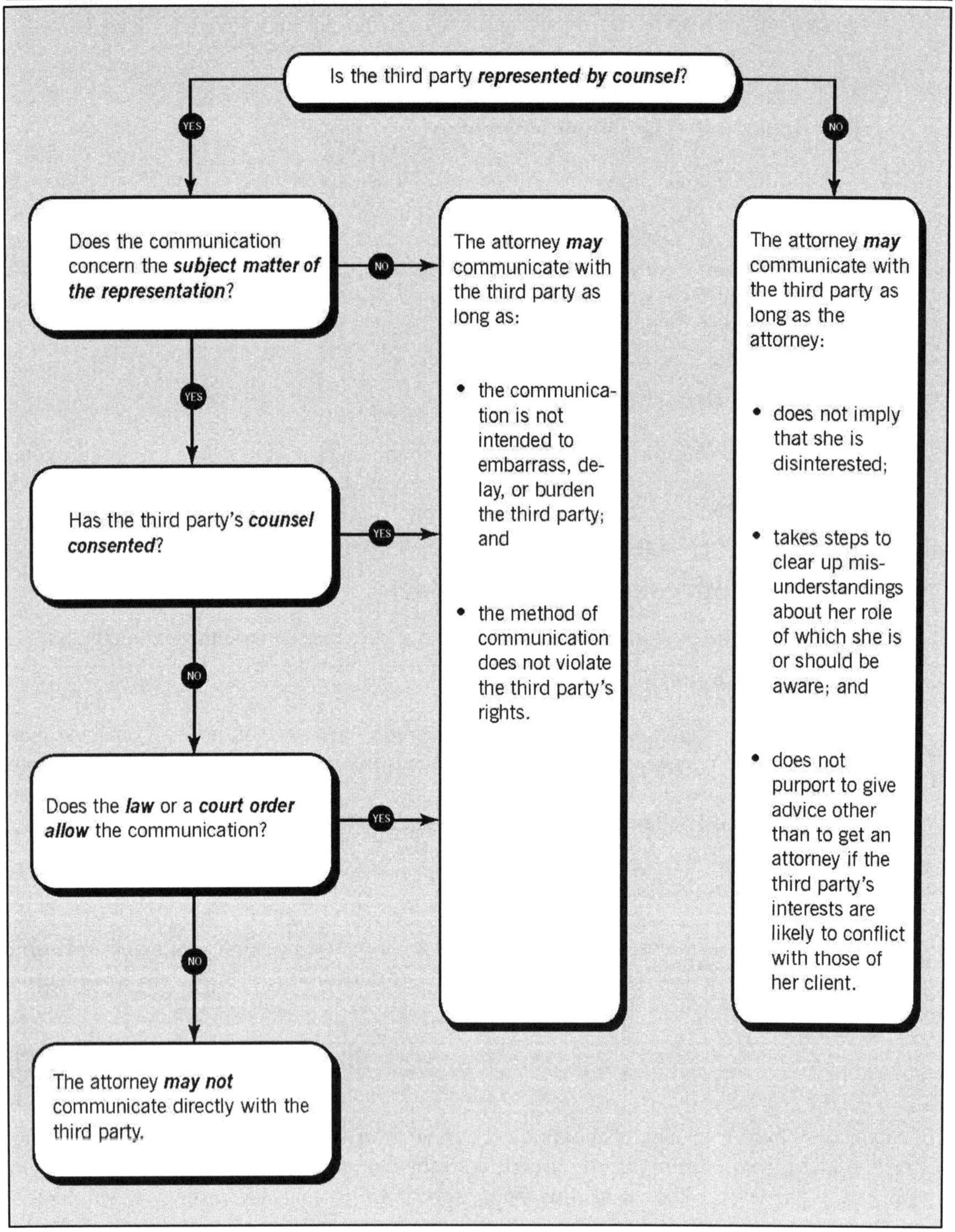

3. Acquisition of Evidence from a Third Party

The Model Rules also say a lawyer may not "embarrass, delay, or burden a third person, or use methods of obtaining evidence that violate the legal rights" of another person. [Model Rule 4.4(a)]

a. Obligation Not to Record Conversations in Violation of Law

A lawyer ***may not record*** any conversation where such recording would ***violate the law.*** This applies to conversations with clients, other lawyers, or any other member of the public (including witnesses and public officials). The ABA has reversed its former position, however, and ***no longer prohibits*** tape recording that is ***not illegal*** (*e.g.,* to document obscene phone calls or threats). [ABA Opn. 01–422]

b. Prosecutorial Duty to Supervise Police

It has also sometimes been held that actions of police officers who violate the rights of suspects will be treated as actions of the prosecutor. Thus, if an officer is considered an agent of the prosecutor, he must not interview a defendant in the absence of the defendant's lawyer.

4. Threats of Criminal Prosecution

A lawyer is prohibited from filing or threatening to file criminal charges solely to obtain an advantage for a client in a civil case. For example, a lawyer for an accident victim may not threaten to go to the police and accuse the driver of drunk driving if he does not agree to a settlement. [*See* **People ex *rel.* Gallagher v. Hertz,** 608 P.2d 335 (Colo. 1979)]

a. Rationale

The ***civil adjudicative process*** is designed to ***settle disputes*** between parties, whereas the ***criminal process*** is designed to ***protect society*** as a whole. Threatening to use the criminal process in order to coerce settlement of private civil matters tends to diminish public confidence in the legal system.

b. Not Limited to Criminal Charges

It is equally improper for a lawyer to file or threaten to file charges that would expose the other party to ***administrative or disciplinary*** sanctions (*e.g.,* threatening to report another lawyer to the disciplinary agency). [Cal. Rule 5–100]

c. Omission of Prohibition in Model Rules

The Model Rules expressly ***omit*** this principle, apparently in the belief that it is primarily a subject of tort and criminal law rather than a matter of legal ethics, but it is unlikely that the law is really different in Model Rules states. [Restatement § 98, comment f]

d. Potential Penalties

Under many penal codes, the threat of criminal proceedings to obtain a settlement constitutes the crime of ***extortion.***

F. Obligation to Avoid Knowing Harassment or Discrimination

1. Lawyers and Law Firms Have Long Been Required to Obey Antidiscrimination Laws

a. Not Exempts as Professionals

In spite of early arguments to the contrary, it has long been clear that nothing about being lawyers or law firms requires different application of the Civil Rights laws to their conduct [*e.g.*, **Hishon v. King & Spalding,** 467 U.S. 69 (1984)]

b. Discrimination as Prejudicial to the Administration of Justice

Until 2016, the Model Rules addressed bias and prejudice as inconsistent with the proper administration of justice and prohibited it in general terms under Model Rule 8.4(d) and comment 3.

2. ABA Model Rule 8.4(g) Adopted in 2016

Model Rule 8.4(g) and new comments 3, 4 & 5 were adopted by the ABA in August, 2016. The provisions reflect an ABA commitment to diversity in the legal profession, as well as a belief that the prohibited "discrimination and harassment by lawyers . . . undermine confidence in the legal profession and the legal system." [Model Rule 8.4, comment 3] The objective is widely shared, but the new provisions leave open questions going forward.

a. The Prohibited Conduct

The rule makes it "professional misconduct" for a lawyer to "engage in conduct that the lawyer knows is harassment or discrimination" as part of "conduct related to the practice of law." [Model Rule 8.4(g)]

(1) Prohibited Bases of Discrimination or Harassment

Eleven bases are proscribed on which lawyers may not harass or discriminate, i.e., (i) race, (ii) sex, (iii) religion, (iv) national origin, (v) ethnicity, (vi) disability, (vii) age, (viii) sexual orientation, (ix) gender identity, (x) marital status and (xi) socioeconomic status. [Model Rule 8.4(g)]

(2) Discrimination Defined

The term "discrimination *includes* harmful verbal or physical conduct that manifests bias or prejudice towards others." [Model Rule 8.4, comment 3 (emphasis added)] What else it includes remains to be determined.

(3) Harassment Defined

The definition of "harassment" is similarly open-ended. It "*includes* sexual harassment and derogatory or demeaning verbal or physical conduct." [Model Rule 8.4, comment 3 (emphasis added)]

(4) Relevance of Antidiscrimination Law Precedents

"The substantive law of antidiscrimination and anti-harassment statutes and case law *may guide* application of paragraph (g)" but those statutes and precedents apparently do not control in disciplinary proceedings. [Model Rule 8.4, comment 3 (emphasis added)]

b. Meaning of "Conduct Related to the Practice of Law"

The phrase that describes conduct subject to the rule is similarly general. It "includes" but is presumably not limited to "[i] representing clients; [ii] interacting with witnesses, coworkers, court personnel, lawyers and others while engaged in the practice of law; [iii] operating or managing a law firm or law practice; and [iv] participating in bar association, business or social activities in connection with the practice of law." [Model Rule 8.4, comment 4]

c. Conduct That Does Not Violate the Rule

The rule and its comments also describe what they continue to permit.

(1) Accepting, Declining or Withdrawing from Representation

Under the rule, a lawyer is permitted to "accept, decline or withdraw from a representation in accordance with Rule 1.16." [Model Rule 8.4(g); *see also* Model Rule 1.16 discussed in Chapter II of this Summary]

(2) Limiting Subjects of a Practice or Limiting Practice to Members of Underserved Populations

The rule also does not prohibit "limiting the scope or subject matter of the lawyer's practice or by limiting the lawyer's practice to members of underserved populations." What is not clear is the meaning of "underserved" and whether a lawyer could open a "men only" or "women only" divorce practice, for example. [Model Rule 8.4, comment 5]

(3) Conduct Undertaken to Promote Diversity

Discrimination undertaken to *promote* "diversity and inclusion" is encouraged, not prohibited. Examples are "initiatives aimed at recruiting, hiring, retaining and advancing diverse employees or sponsoring diverse law student organizations." [Model Rule 8.4, comment 4]

(4) Legitimate Advice or Advocacy

The rule also "does not preclude legitimate advice or advocacy consistent with these Rules." [Model Rule 8.4(g)] But the rule does not explain what "legitimate advice or advocacy" would *not* be "consistent with" the Model Rules.

(5) Use of Peremptory Challenges

Consistent with prior law, the fact that a trial judge finds that a lawyer used peremptory challenges on a discriminatory basis is *not itself* sufficient to prove a violation of Rule 8.4(g), but the exercise of the challenges could separately be charged as such a violation. [Model Rule 8.4, comment 5]

(6) Charging Reasonable Fees

Finally, lest you were worried, nothing in Rule 8.4(g) forbids a lawyer's charging reasonable fees. [Model Rule 8.4, comment 5]

G. Encouragement to Provide Pro Bono Service

1. Duty to Provide Voluntary Pro Bono Service

The Model Rules assert that each lawyer has a personal obligation to serve persons who could not normally afford legal services, but failure to meet the obligation is ***not a disciplinable offense.*** [Model Rule 6.1]

a. Voluntary Contribution of 50 Hours Annually

The Model Rules provide that a lawyer should "aspire to render" at least 50 hours of pro bono service each year, the "substantial majority" of which should be rendered to "persons of limited means" or organizations serving such persons. [Model Rule 6.1(a)]

b. Other Forms of Service

ABA Model Rule 6.1 acknowledges the value of civil rights work and other community service but sees that as coming only after direct service to the poor. [Model Rule 6.1(b)]

2. Accepting Appointment as Counsel

A lawyer's duty to represent a client when the lawyer would not choose to do so is most apparent where the client has a ***constitutional right to counsel*** (*e.g.,* in a criminal trial) but cannot afford to hire a lawyer. Most courts now have paid public defenders or panels of lawyers who volunteer for such cases, but in their absence, it is the ***moral obligation*** of every lawyer to accept court appointment to represent an indigent client. [Model Rule 6.2; **State v. Richardson,** 631 P.2d 221 (Kan. 1981)]

a. Grounds for Rejecting an Appointment

Despite the general obligation to accept court appointment, and lawyers' general reluctance to offend a judge who seeks to appoint them, sometimes it is appropriate for a lawyer to refuse the appointment. ABA Model Rule 6.2 identifies three situations in which an appointment may be refused:

(a) ***The representation would involve violation of a Model Rule***—*e.g.,* where the representation would involve a conflict of interest;

(b) ***The representation would impose an unreasonable financial burden on the lawyer***—*i.e.,* a burden "so great as to be unjust"; or

(c) ***The lawyer's personal feeling of repugnance*** at the client or the client's conduct would affect the lawyer's ability to represent the client adequately.

b. Right of Lawyer to Payment If Appointed to Represent Client

Contrary to prior tradition, some cases have now held that it is unconstitutional to require a lawyer to represent an indigent client without compensation by some public agency. [*See* **Stephan v. Smith,** 747 P.2d 816 (Kan. 1987); **DeLiso v. Alaska Superior Court,** 740 P.2d 437 (Alaska 1987)]

c. Duty in Civil Cases

And while a federal court may "request" a lawyer to represent an indigent client in a civil case, the Supreme Court has held that 42 U.S.C. § 1915 does not permit the court to *order* that the lawyer do so. **[Mallard v. United States District Court,** 490 U.S. 296 (1989)] Some federal courts of appeal, however, have found exceptions to this principle. [*E.g.,* **Tabron v. Grace,** 6 F.3d 147 (3d Cir. 1993)—action against prison officials for failing to protect against assault]

3. Membership in Legal Services or Law Reform Organizations

The broad ABA commitment to make legal services widely available is behind the principle that a lawyer may be a member, officer, or director of an organization that serves the needs even of persons whose interests are often adverse to those of the lawyer's regular clients. [Model Rule 6.3]

a. Requirement to Abstain When Agency Decisions Conflict with Lawyer's Client's Interests

If the lawyer knows that a decision or action of a legal services organization would ***conflict*** with the interest of one or more clients of the lawyer, the lawyer ***must not participate*** in that particular decision or action. [Model Rule 6.3]

b. Law Reform Activities That Benefit Lawyer's Regular Clients

If the lawyer knows that a law reform activity of the organization also would materially ***benefit*** one of the lawyer' regular clients, the lawyer ***may*** participate in the decision, but only after ***disclosing*** the fact of the benefit without identifying the client. [Model Rule 6.4]

4. Short-Term and Limited Services

A lawyer's pro-bono service may involve the lawyer in giving advice for a few hours a month in a nonprofit legal clinic or as part of a call-in help line. Clients may have problems that need immediate attention, and there will be no time to determine whether the lawyer may have a conflict of interest under traditional standards.

a. Model Rules Solution

The Model Rules now provide that a lawyer may give short-term limited legal services of the kind described, *i.e.,* "without expectation . . . that the lawyer will provide continuing representation," unless the lawyer has ***actual knowledge*** of a conflict of interest, *e.g.,* that the lawyer or the lawyer's firm represents someone opposing the pro bono client. [Model Rule 6.5(a)]

b. No Imputation of Conflict

Furthermore, the work done by the lawyer at the legal aid clinic will not disqualify other members of the lawyer's firm from work they might be doing or might be asked to do by someone opposing the legal aid client. [Model Rule 6.5(b)]

H. Other Interactions Between Lawyers and the Legal System

1. Support of Legislation in Public Interest

Lawyers should participate actively in proposing and supporting legislation and programs to improve the legal system, rather than leaving needed reforms only to public-spirited laypersons.

a. Particular Legislation

Because of their unique qualifications, lawyers should, whenever possible, encourage ***simplification of laws*** and ***improvements in legal procedures.***

b. Views of Clients Largely Irrelevant

A lawyer may take personal positions on legislation without regard to the general interests or desires of clients or former clients, ***unless*** to do so will ***materially and adversely*** affect work the lawyer is doing for the client on the issue. Thus, a lawyer may not lobby for legislation for a client in the morning and lobby against the same bill as a citizen in the evening. [Restatement § 125, comment e; *cf.* Model Rule 1.2(b)]

c. Stating or Implying Ability to Improperly Influence Officials

A lawyer must not state or imply that he has the ability to improperly influence a government agency or official or to achieve results by means that violate the law or legal ethics rules. [Model Rule 8.4(e)]

2. Lawyers in Public Service

Service by lawyers in a public capacity is encouraged as a significant method of improving the legal system. However, lawyers who serve as legislators or other public officials must ***not*** engage in activities in which their personal or professional interests are, or foreseeably may be, ***in conflict*** with their official duties. [Restatement § 135]

a. Use of Public Position to Advance Client's Interests Prohibited

Lawyers holding public office owe their primary duty to the public and, therefore, may ***not*** use public office to obtain special advantages for themselves or a client. [Model Rule 8.4, comment 5]

b. Appearances Before Other Public Bodies

The right of a lawyer holding public office to appear as counsel on behalf of clients before a public body is ***narrowly limited.*** For example, it is a crime for a member of Congress to receive compensation for representing a client before a federal agency. [18 U.S.C. § 203(a); **Office of Disciplinary Counsel v. Eilberg,** 441 A.2d 1193 (Pa. 1982)]

3. Involvement in Selection of Judges

Lawyers are uniquely capable of evaluating the qualifications of those seeking or being considered for judgeships and, therefore, owe a special duty to aid in the selection of qualified persons. A lawyer should protest against the appointment or election of those who are not qualified and do everything possible to prevent political considerations from outweighing judicial fitness in the selection process.

a. Defending the Judiciary

Judges are not wholly free to defend themselves against unjust criticism. Thus, it is also the responsibility of the organized bar, and of lawyers individually, to defend judges and the judiciary against ***inaccurate or irresponsible*** charges.

b. Criticizing the Judiciary

The duty to defend the judiciary does not mean that lawyers cannot criticize judges in public statements. However, ***reckless or knowingly false*** accusations are grounds for discipline. [Model Rule 8.2(a); Restatement § 114]

c. Contributions Calculated to Obtain Favoritism Prohibited

A lawyer who makes or solicits a political contribution for a judge for the purpose of later getting legal engagements or appointments from that judge is prohibited from later accepting such engagements or appointments. [Model Rule 7.6]

d. Assisting a Judge in Violation of Judicial Code

A lawyer is subject to discipline for ***knowingly*** assisting a judge or judicial officer in conduct that violates the Code of Judicial Conduct or other law. [Model Rule 8.4(f)]

4. Personally Running for Judicial Office

Where the lawyer is seeking election or appointment to a judgeship (either against another candidate or in a merit system election), the lawyer must comply with the applicable provisions of the ABA Model Code of Judicial Conduct ("CJC") (*see infra*, p. 168 *et seq.*). [Model Rule 8.2(b)]

5. Serving as a Third Party Neutral

One way an increasing number of lawyers participate in administering justice is by serving as mediators, arbitrators, conciliators & evaluators helping parties resolve their disputes. Non-lawyers may serve in these roles as well, and the processes often have their own standards of conduct. Thus, lawyer professional standards speak to the role only briefly.

a. Not Serve as Lawyer in Case Where Served as a Third-Party Neutral

With some exceptions noted earlier in Chapter IV of this Summary, p. 101, a third-party neutral who was personally and substantially involved in a matter may not later act as a lawyer in the matter. [Model Rule 1.12(a)].

b. Inform Unrepresented Parties That the Third-Party Neutral Does Not Represent Them

Unrepresented persons might reasonably believe that a lawyer acting as a third party neutral has usual lawyer duties of confidentiality and loyalty to them. Where the neutral knows or should know a person has that mistaken belief, the lawyer ***must*** explain the neutral's actual role in the proceeding. [Model Rule 2.4]

Chapter Six

Special Obligations of Lawyers in Litigation

CONTENTS	PAGE

Chapter Approach

As seen throughout this Summary, a lawyer often has duties to persons other than the client. The previous chapter discussed duties that apply regardless of whether the subject matter of the representation is in litigation. This chapter presents the special duties of lawyers involved in a litigated matter.

Some things to keep in mind are:

1. A lawyer ***must not assert a frivolous claim or defense*** and ***must not delay proceedings for improper purposes.***
2. A lawyer ***must not knowingly make a false statement of material fact*** to the court, and ***must disclose adverse legal authority.***
3. A lawyer ***may present the client's case in the best possible light,*** but the lawyer ***must not illegally conceal evidence, use false evidence, or ignore professional standards and court rules*** in presenting evidence.
4. A lawyer must not try the case in the media; *i.e.*, the lawyer ***must restrict out-of-court comments*** about a case, especially in criminal proceedings.
5. A lawyer ***must not give or lend money to the client except for litigation expenses.***
6. A lawyer ordinarily ***must not act as both an advocate and a witness.***
7. A lawyer ***must not take actions that could affect the impartiality of the court.***
8. A ***public prosecutor or government attorney*** has a duty, beyond those above, to ***seek justice*** in the proceeding.
9. Many of these rules apply even when an advocate's work is before a legislative committee or otherwise not before a traditional tribunal.

The sources of most of the principles in this chapter are Restatement §§ 105–120 and Model Rules 3.1–3.9.

A. Duty Not to Waste the Court's Time

1. Introduction

Litigation can impose significant financial and other burdens on both litigants and the courts. But a rule that would punish lawyers for filing or defending cases that they wind up losing would deny many clients their day in court and could slow legal changes that benefit the public generally. Progress in civil rights and rights of criminal defendants, for example, came only after litigants lost many early cases. Model Rules 3.1 and 3.2 address this tension between testing the limits of what the law allows and what constitutes wasting a court's time.

2. Lawyer May Only Take Positions That Are "Not Frivolous"

A lawyer may not file, defend or controvert an issue in a case on behalf of a client unless there is a ***"not frivolous"*** basis for doing so, which includes a "***good faith argument*** for an ***extension, modification, or reversal*** of existing law." [Model Rule 3.1; Restatement § 110(a)]

a. Test Gives Lawyers Substantial Latitude to Represent Client Zealously

The "not frivolous" test is objective. It does not inquire into a lawyer's motive for action or whether the lawyer believes her position will prevail. [Model Rule 3.1, comment 2]

b. Expectation of Developing Facts in Discovery

A filing is ***not frivolous, even*** if the lawyer does not have all the facts, if she reasonably expects to be able to determine them in discovery. [Model Rule 3.1, comment 2]

c. Defense of a Criminal Case

There is a strong public interest in seeing that ***all*** persons accused of a crime have the services of counsel, and a criminal defendant has a constitutional right to the effective assistance of counsel, so a lawyer ***may defend*** a criminal client ***whom the lawyer believes to be guilty*** and ***may require the prosecution to prove every necessary element*** of the crime. [Model Rule 3.1 and comment 3; Restatement § 110(2)]

(1) Constitutional Rights Prevail over Limitations the Model Rules Would Otherwise Impose

A lawyer's obligations under Model Rule 3.1 expressly yield to constitutional rights courts hold criminal defendants have. Part of providing the effective assistance of counsel is asserting the defendant's rights. [Model Rule 3.1, comment 3]

(2) Doubts About Client's Innocence

A lawyer who lets personal doubts about the innocence of the client affect defense of the client's case may be unable to provide zealous representation and thus deny his client his constitutional right to effective assistance of counsel. [**Johns v. Smyth,** 176 F. Supp. 949 (E.D. Va. 1959)]

(3) Questionable Grounds for Appeal

Issues may also arise when counsel is appointed for an appeal requested by the defendant. The lawyer must recognize that his duties are those of an ***active advocate supporting the appeal*** to the best of his ability, as opposed to those of an "amicus curiae" advising the court on the merits of the appeal. If a lawyer appointed for a criminal defendant's appeal finds all claims to be frivolous, she must request permission to withdraw and supply a brief covering all grounds that might arguably support an appeal. [**Anders v. California,** 386 U.S. 738 (1967); *but see* **Jones v. Barnes,** 463 U.S. 745 (1983)—lawyer need not press all nonfrivolous issues]

EXAM TIP GILBERT

Note that an exam question raising the issue of frivolous claims or defenses often actually requires you to discuss what is ***not*** frivolous. For example, if the question indicates that the claim or defense cannot be supported by existing law, check the facts to see if the lawyer can make a ***good faith argument that the law should be changed.*** If so, the claim or defense is ***not frivolous.*** And note that the lawyer doesn't have to believe that the argument is necessarily a winning one; it just has to be a sound argument that can be made in good faith. Also watch for facts about a ***criminal lawyer*** who believes her client is guilty of the crime charged. Recall that it is not frivolous for her to conduct the case so that the ***prosecutor must prove every necessary element*** of the crime.

d. Duty to Assert "Technicalities"

In both civil and criminal cases, to the extent that the client's interests are ***advanced*** or protected by reliance on legal "technicalities" the lawyer usually ***owes a duty*** to assert them. However, it is not improper to waive or fail to assert a technicality where, in the lawyer's professional judgment, the issue is weak, distracting, and not in the client's best interests to pursue.

3. Avoiding Unnecessary Litigation Delay

a. The Duty to Expedite Litigation

The Model Rules impose an ***affirmative requirement*** that lawyers make "***reasonable efforts to expedite litigation*** consistent with the interest of the client." [Model Rule 3.2]

(1) Delay for Convenience of the Advocates

Although a lawyer may seek and should grant a delay in the proceedings for personal reasons, e.g., one of the lawyers has to undergo an emergency medical procedure, it is not proper for lawyers "routinely" to fail to expedite a matter for their own convenience. [Model Rule 3.2, comment]

(2) Must Have a "Substantial Purpose Other than Delay"

The test for determining whether a delay that would benefit the lawyer's client is improper is whether, in the eyes of a competent, independent lawyer, the effort a lawyer makes to slow resolution of the matter has "some substantial purpose other than delay." The comment then asserts that financial or other benefits to the client from "otherwise improper delay" is ***not*** a legitimate interest of the client." [Model Rule 3.2, comment]

b. Federal Rule 11

Federal Rule of Civil Procedure 11 requires that a lawyer ***sign every pleading*** and stipulates that the lawyer's signature constitutes a ***certification*** that the pleading "is not being interposed for the purpose of delay." For abuse or violation of this rule, a lawyer or client may be forced to pay attorney's fees and other expenses incurred by the opponent in dealing with the offending pleading.

c. Courts' Inherent Power to Sanction

Courts have been held to have ***inherent power*** to punish lawyers for using delay to get an advantage in the litigation process. [*See* **Chambers v. NASCO, Inc.,** 501 U.S. 32 (1991)]

4. Discovery Abuse

In addition, a lawyer is subject to professional discipline and judicially-imposed payment to his opponent for (i) making a frivolous request in discovery, or (ii) failing to make a diligent effort to comply with a legally proper discovery request by opposing counsel. [Model Rule 3.4(d); Restatement § 110(3)]

B. Duty of Honesty and Candor Before a Tribunal

1. Introduction

Few lawyers are surprised to learn that they may not lie to a judge, but they quickly find it tempting to test the limits of that rule. Advocacy frequently requires framing a factual story, for example, and it is tempting to stress some facts over others, or even leave out facts that tell a different story. Think through the issues of litigation honesty by distinguishing three questions:

(i) What matters require ***"honesty"*** in the sense of representations that are "not knowingly false?"

(ii) What matters require lawyer ***"candor,"*** *i.e.*, volunteering truthful information that might be helpful to the other side?

(iii) When is a lawyer required to correct testimony or other representations that the lawyer thought were truthful when they were made but that turn out to be incorrect?

2. General Rule

The most basic requirement is that, although the lawyer acts as a partisan representative of a client, the lawyer must not "***knowingly*** make a ***false statement*** of ***fact*** or ***law*** to a tribunal." [Model Rule 3.3(a)(1); Restatement § 120(l)(b)]

a. Duty of Honesty, Not Candor

Notice that this is a duty of honesty but not candor. In general, a lawyer is under ***no affirmative duty to volunteer facts*** that would be harmful to the client's case. Such facts are protected by the lawyer's professional duty of confidentiality. Under our adversary system of justice, it is left to opposing counsel to bring such matters to the court's attention. [Model Rule 1.6]

b. Duty Not to Misstate Law

Notice further that a lawyer likewise ***must not knowingly mislead*** the judge ***about the law***. The lawyer must not misquote the language of any statute or decision, nor knowingly cite as authority any decision that has been overruled or any statute that has been repealed. [Model Rule 3.3(a)(1); Cal. Rule 5–200(c); Restatement § 111(1)]

c. Duty to Correct Prior Misstatements of Material Fact or Law

In addition, the law requires a lawyer to "correct" a false statement the lawyer (presumably unintentionally) made to the tribunal earlier in the matter, but only if the statement is ***material*** to the case. Thus, a lawyer may not knowingly make ***any*** false statement of fact or law, but she need only go back and correct ones that are ***material.*** [Model Rule 3.3(a)(1); Restatement § 120(l)(b)]

e.g. **Example:** A lawyer may *never say* the defendant was wearing a red dress when she knows the dress was blue. But the lawyer need not later go back and correct a mistake about the dress color unless the color of the dress has material relevance to the issues in the case.

EXAM TIP GILBERT

Regarding misstatements of fact or law, note that the lawyer's duty differs depending on whether she is first making the statement or attempting to correct a previously made misstatement. The lawyer must not knowingly ***make any*** false statement of fact or law, but her duty to ***correct*** previously made false statements extends ***only to those that are material.***

3. Duty as to Pleadings Generally

Pleadings prepared by a lawyer are, in effect, representations to the court and thus must be truthful and accurate. In federal practice and in many states, a lawyer must sign every pleading, and this signature operates as a certification that there are good grounds to support it, as well as that it is not being interposed for purpose of delay (*see supra*, p. 126). [Fed. R. Civ. P. 11]

4. Special Candor Required in *Ex Parte* Proceedings

When the court is asked to enter a preliminary injunction or considers some other ***ex parte*** motion, it must rely upon the facts as presented by counsel, untested by the usual adversary process. For this reason, counsel for the moving party has a ***duty of candor*** and must "inform the tribunal of ***all material facts*** known to the lawyer" that are likely to be ***relevant*** "whether or not the facts are adverse." [Model Rule 3.3(d); Restatement § 112]

5. Duty to Disclose Adverse Legal Authority

As an officer of the court, a lawyer owes a carefully limited, affirmative ***duty to disclose the law*** relevant to the matter at hand—even if the law is adverse to the client's case.

a. What the Lawyer Must Disclose

The lawyer must disclose:

(i) Legal authority

(ii) In the ***controlling jurisdiction***

(iii) Known by the lawyer

(iv) To be ***directly adverse*** to the position of the client and

(v) Not disclosed by opposing counsel.

[Model Rule 3.3(a)(2); Restatement § 111(2)]

b. Authority Need Not Be on "All Fours"

The adverse decision does not have to be on "all fours" in order that the lawyer is required to disclose it. It is sufficient that it be the kind of precedent that a ***reasonable judge might wish to consider*** in dealing with the case at hand. If it is, the lawyer owes a duty to disclose. [**Katris v. Immigration & Naturalization Service,** 562 F.2d 866 (2d Cir. 1977)]

c. Right to Challenge Soundness of Adverse Authority

The obligation to disclose adverse law does not override the duty of zealous representation. Once the adverse authority is disclosed, the lawyer may attempt to distinguish it or present reasons why it is unsound and should not be followed in the present case.

d. Manner of Presenting Adverse Authority

If the lawyer concludes that adverse authority should be cited, but believes that such decisions are distinguishable from or tangential to her basic position, the lawyer need not distract from the main point of her argument by dealing with the adverse authority exhaustively. The use of footnotes or parenthetical asides may be useful stylistic devices by which a lawyer can fulfill the duty of disclosure while still presenting the client's position in its best light.

EXAM TIP GILBERT

Sometimes an exam question involving the duty to disclose adverse legal authority will mention that a case is directly adverse to the client's position. If so, be sure to check that the case is ***from the controlling jurisdiction***. Thus, if the lawyer's case is in state court, the lawyer needs to disclose only adverse decisions of the higher courts ***of that state***—not decisions from other states or even from the federal courts in that state, as they are not controlling.

DUTY OF HONESTY
AN ATTORNEY MAY BE SUBJECT TO DISCIPLINE FOR: GILBERT

LAW	FACTS	EVIDENCE
Knowingly making a false statement of law to the tribunal	***Knowingly*** making a false statement of fact to the tribunal	***Knowingly*** offering false evidence
Or	***Or***	
Failing to correct a materially false statement of law previously made by the attorney to the tribunal	Failing to correct a false statement of ***material*** fact previously made by the attorney to the tribunal	Failing to disavow material evidence the lawyer learns was false.
Or	***Or***	
Failing to disclose ***directly adverse* law of the *controlling jurisdiction***	Failing to volunteer to the tribunal known harmful facts if the proceeding is ***ex parte***	

6. Duty When a Client or Witness Gives or Intends to Give False Evidence

A lawyer is not only required to be honest in his or her own statements to a court; the lawyer also may not **knowingly "offer"** the false testimony of a witness. [Model Rule 3.3(a)(3); Restatement § 120] This can create a dilemma for the lawyer when it becomes clear that someone has given, or plans to give, false evidence favorable to the lawyer's client. In such a case, the lawyer has a duty to the court not to offer false evidence, but also a corresponding duty—perhaps even a constitutional duty—to minimize injury to the client.

a. False Statement in a *Civil* Case

(1) Intent to Give False Testimony

If a lawyer knows that a client or witness plans to give false testimony in a ***civil*** case, the lawyer's duty is clear; the lawyer may not permit the person to give the false testimony. That may require not calling the witness to testify at all. [Model Rule 3.3(a)(3); Restatement § 120]

(2) When False Testimony Has Already Been Given

Likewise, if the lawyer later learns that a client or witness has given ***materially false evidence*** or has made a ***material mistake*** (*e.g.*, got a date or other important fact wrong in a deposition in a civil case), the lawyer is required to ***"take reasonable remedial measures."*** [Model Rule 3.3(a)(3); Restatement § 120]

(a) Urge Client or Witness to Correct

The lawyer must speak confidentially with her client and urge the client to cooperate in withdrawing or ***correcting the false evidence.*** [Model Rule 3.3, comment 10]

(b) Ask Permission to Withdraw

If the client will not correct the record, the lawyer should consider asking the court's permission to ***withdraw.*** [Model Rule 3.3, comments 10, 15]

(c) Confidential Information May Be Disclosed

If withdrawal is not permitted or will not solve the problem, the lawyer probably must ***disclose*** the situation to the judge, even if that means disclosing client information that would otherwise be protected under the duty of confidentiality. The duty to make disclosures to the tribunal under these provisions—including disclosures about client perjury—expressly overrides the duty of confidentiality under Model Rule 1.6. [Model Rule 3.3(c) and comment 10]

WHAT LAWYER SHOULD DO WHEN CLIENT INTENDS TO COMMIT PERJURY GILBERT

UNDER THE MODEL RULES, IF A CLIENT INTENDS TO COMMIT PERJURY, THE LAWYER SHOULD TAKE THE FOLLOWING STEPS:

- ☑ ***Attempt to dissuade*** client from committing perjury or testifying
- ☑ ***Attempt to withdraw*** from representation, if permitted
- ☑ Let client testify but ***avoid asking about subjects as to which the client intends to lie***
- ☑ ***Disclose*** situation to the judge (unless in a jurisdiction where client may testify in narrative form—*i.e.*, telling story without counsel asking questions)

b. False Testimony in a *Criminal* Case

The issues take on constitutional dimensions when a criminal proceeding is involved and the lawyer has a duty to provide the client effective assistance of counsel.

(1) Attempt to Dissuade

At a minimum, the lawyer must seek to persuade the client or witness not to testify at all, or at least not to commit perjury. [Model Rule 3.3, comment 6; Restatement § 120, comment g]

Example: In the leading Supreme Court case dealing directly with this problem, the lawyer effectively dissuaded his criminal defendant client from lying by threatening to impeach the client's intended lie. Without deciding that this was the best way to handle such a situation, the Court unanimously held that the lawyer's action was not a denial of effective assistance of counsel. [**Nix v. Whiteside,** 475 U.S. 157 (1986)]

Compare: The Supreme Court later held in **Rock v. Arkansas,** 483 U.S. 44 (1987), that a defendant has a constitutional right to testify in his own defense. The *Rock* case did not authorize perjured testimony, but the tension inherent in this area of the law is clear.

(2) Attempt to Withdraw

The lawyer might attempt to withdraw from the representation. This often will not be permitted, especially if the trial is imminent, and it is also likely to make the judge suspicious of the client. However, these problems ordinarily do not make a lawyer's attempt to withdraw improper. [**People v. Schultheis,** 638 P.2d 8 (Colo. 1981)] In fact, the threat itself might persuade the client not to testify.

(3) Avoid Sensitive Subjects

Sometimes, a lawyer can let the defendant testify without asking the witness questions about subjects on which the client intends to lie. The Model Rules ***require*** a lawyer not to offer evidence the lawyer ***knows*** is false, and ***permit*** a lawyer in a civil matter not to offer what she ***reasonably believes*** is false, but the reasonable belief standard does not apply in a criminal matter. [Model Rule 3.3(a)(3); *but see* Restatement § 120(3)—not invoking the exception]

(4) Disclose Situation to Judge

If the lawyer's attempt to withdraw and attempt to dissuade the client from committing perjury have been unsuccessful, the lawyer probably must reveal the situation to the judge, even if that means disclosing the client's confidential information. [Model Rule 3.3(a)(3)]

(a) Exception—Use of Narrative Testimony

Some jurisdictions say that if withdrawal is not permitted, the lawyer should let the client take the stand and tell his story in narrative form. That way, the lawyer is said not to be "offering" the false evidence. Under this approach, the lawyer may not rely on the false testimony in arguing the case. [*See* **Lowery v. Cardwell,** 575 F.2d 727 (9th Cir. 1978); *and see* Model Rule 3.3, comment 7]

(b) Argument for Letting Client Testify

Reasoning that a defendant's constitutional right to testify should be the controlling principle, some argue that a defense lawyer should be allowed to present perjurious testimony and leave its truth or falsity to the jury. [Monroe Freedman, *Understanding Lawyers' Ethics* (1990)] That is an often-admired academic theory, but no jurisdiction has clearly affirmed it as a correct statement of the law.

7. Disclosure of Crime or Fraud upon the Court

If a lawyer learns that her client intends to act, is acting, or has acted to criminally or fraudulently corrupt a proceeding, the lawyer must take ***"reasonable remedial measures,"*** which may include ***disclosure to the tribunal.*** [Model Rule 3.3(b)] Note, however, that this requirement applies to crimes such as jury tampering, rather than the issues of perjured testimony discussed above.

8. Scope and Duration of the Requirements

The Model Rules provide their own statute of limitations for the requirements under Model Rule 3.3(a) and (b), just discussed. The lawyer's duty to correct false testimony or a false statement ends at "the conclusion of the proceeding." For example, the lawyer need not correct a false statement of fact or law after a final judgment has been ***"affirmed on appeal*** or the time for review has passed." [Model Rule 3.3(c) and comment 13]

EXAM TIP GILBERT

Beware of an exam question in which the client prevails in a proceeding, the time has expired for the opposing party to file an appeal, and the client ***then*** tells the lawyer in confidence that he lied. Remember that the lawyer is then under ***no obligation*** to reveal the perjury to anyone because the proceeding is over.

C. Duties of an Advocate Regarding Witnesses and Evidence

1. Suppression of Evidence

A lawyer ***may not unlawfully obstruct*** any party's ***access*** to, nor unlawfully ***alter or destroy,*** relevant evidence. [Model Rule 3.4(a); Cal. Rule 5–220; Restatement § 118]

a. Privilege

Every time a lawyer asserts the attorney-client privilege or work product protection as to items of evidence, she is "obstructing" another party's access to that evidence. That is why the word "unlawfully" is such an important modifier of "obstructing" access. The rule against suppression of evidence reaffirms the right to use "lawful" ways to keep certain information out of the hands of others.

b. Spoliation

Traditionally, people and businesses have not been required to preserve documents indefinitely, absent a good reason they might be relevant in anticipated litigation. But spoliation is the term many jurisdictions give to the unwarranted and injurious destruction of evidence to avoid its litigation availability. A finding that it has occurred can lead to adverse evidentiary presumptions and sanctions for contempt of court. [Restatement § 118, comment c]

c. Electronic Discovery

Large amounts of discovery today consists of data stored in a party's computer network. Courts have been aggressive about imposing obligations not to destroy such data, but they have also been sensitive to practical costs of searching and accessing it. [Fed. R. Civ. P. 26, 34 & 37; **Zubulake v. UBS Warburg,** 229 F.R.D. 422 (S.D.N.Y. 2004)]

d. Asking Potential Witnesses Not to Give Information

A lawyer may not ask a person other than the client not to give relevant information to an opposing party ***unless*** (i) the person is a ***relative, employee, or agent*** of the client, ***and*** (ii) the lawyer reasonably believes that refraining from giving information ***will not affect the person adversely.*** [Model Rule 3.4(f); Restatement § 116(4)]

e. Receipt of an Inadvertently Sent Document

A problem created by broad discovery and new technology is the inadvertent transmission of a privileged or otherwise sensitive document to someone not intended to receive it. For example, a confidential e-mail message might mistakenly be sent to ***all*** counsel instead of just to counsel in a privileged relationship to the client.

(1) Original ABA Advice—Send It Back

The first ABA response to this problem was to say that, as a matter of professional courtesy, the receiving lawyer should refrain from reading it and should destroy the document or send it back. [ABA Opn. 94–382]

(2) Current Requirement—Notify the Sender

Later reflection by the ABA, however, recognized that the former rule put the recipient lawyer in a difficult position through no fault of her own. It required the lawyer to forget what could not be forgotten. Thus, the Model Rules were amended in 2002 to say that the recipient must "promptly notify the sender" of the mistaken transmission, but the burden is then on the sender to get a judicial declaration that the item must be returned, remains privileged, etc. [Model Rule 4.4(b)]

2. Inducing Favorable Testimony

A lawyer should counsel witnesses to testify truthfully and may not seek to influence their testimony by money or any other means. [Model Rule 3.4(b)]

a. Prohibition on Excessive Payments to Witness

Thus, a lawyer may not pay, nor let the client pay, a fact witness more than ***reasonable*** reimbursement for the witness's ***expenses*** and ***loss of time.*** [Model Rule 3.4(b); Restatement § 117(1)]

b. Experts

On the other hand, an expert witness may be paid a reasonable fee for services, both in testifying and pretrial preparation. [Model Rule 3.4(b); Restatement § 117(1)]

c. No Fees Contingent on Outcome of Case

But the lawyer ***may not*** agree to pay a fact or expert witness a fee ***contingent*** upon the content of the witness's testimony and/or the outcome of the proceeding. [Cal. Rule 5–

310(B); Restatement § 117(2); **Person v. Association of the Bar of the City of New York,** 554 F.2d 534 (2d Cir. 1977)—upholding constitutionality of this prohibition]

EXAM TIP GILBERT

If on an exam you see a payment being made to a witness, do not assume it is automatically improper. Remember that a lawyer may: reimburse a witness for ***reasonable expenses*** (*e.g.,* travel, hotel, meals), compensate a witness for ***loss of time***, and pay an ***expert witness a reasonable fee*** for services. However, a lawyer ***must not pay*** a fee even to an expert that is ***contingent*** on the content of the testimony or the outcome of the case.

d. Coaching Witnesses

Discussions with a witness before putting the witness on the stand are normally essential to pretrial preparation and presentation of the evidence. However, such discussions must not turn into "coaching" sessions whereby the witness is improperly influenced to give certain testimony.

(1) Application

It is clearly improper for the lawyer to bend the testimony or put words in the witness's mouth. However, it is ***not improper*** for the lawyer to ***probe the witness's recollection,*** to ***point out fallacies or inconsistencies*** in the witness's version of the facts, and even to ***refresh*** and ***remind*** the witness of key points in the evidence that the witness has trouble recalling. [*See, e.g.,* **People v. McGuirk,** 245 N.E.2d 917 (Ill. 1969)—not improper for prosecutor to help nine-year-old rape victim frame her testimony before trial]

(2) Note

It is often difficult to draw a line between improper coaching and proper preparation of a witness. The important point is that the ***essential nature*** of the witness's testimony ***may not be altered*** or colored by the lawyer's emphasis or suggestions prior to trial.

CONDUCT WITH WITNESSES—EXAMPLES
WHEN PREPARING A WITNESS FOR TRIAL AND WHEN CROSS EXAMINING AN ADVERSE WITNESS, A LAWYER MUST BE CAREFUL NOT TO CROSS THE ETHICAL LINE GILBERT

PROPER CONDUCT	IMPROPER CONDUCT
• Probing a witness's memory	• Coaching a witness
• Refreshing a witness's recollection	• Putting words in a witness's mouth
• Pointing out fallacies or inconsistencies	• Bending the witness's testimony
• Impeaching an adverse witness	• Harassing or degrading an adverse witness
• Undermining an adverse witness's credibility	• Expressing personal opinion as to witness's credibility

3. Strategy and Tactics in Trial

Although the lawyer is expected to be a partisan advocate for the client, there are limits to the tactics the lawyer may employ in the courtroom. Procedural and evidentiary rules are means of insuring that the proceedings are conducted in the interests of justice; professional standards also impose restrictions on the lawyer.

a. Violation of Rules of Evidence or Procedure

A lawyer must not knowingly violate an established rule of procedure or evidence. [Model Rule 3.4(c); Restatement § 105]

(1) Distinguish—May Test Validity of Particular Rule

It is ***not improper*** for a lawyer to ***openly refuse*** to comply with a court order or rule of procedure in order to ***test the validity*** of the order or rule—provided this is done in good faith. [Model Rule 3.4(c)]

(2) Sanctions

The sanctions that may be imposed against lawyers (and/or their clients) for violation of procedural and evidentiary rules depend upon the nature of the violation. Courts may impose ***sanctions against the lawyer personally*** where it appears that the violations are ***deliberate.*** Such intentional conduct may be punished as a ***contempt of court*** (*i.e.*, by fine or imprisonment), and may lead to ***professional discipline*** (*e.g.*, suspension or disbarment).

b. Reference to Matters Unsubstantiated by Evidence

In court appearances, a lawyer must not state or allude to any matter that the lawyer has no reasonable basis to believe will be supported by admissible evidence. [Model Rule 3.4(e); Restatement § 107(2)]

(1) Opening Statement by Counsel

A lawyer should not make references in the opening statement to purported facts in the case without having a ***good faith belief*** that they will be ***supported by admissible evidence.***

(2) Unsubstantiated Testimony from Witness

It is likewise *improper* for the lawyer to imply, in the way the lawyer frames questions to a witness, the existence of ***facts not in the record or incapable of being proved.***

(3) Improper Arguments

It is misconduct for a lawyer to suggest or imply in closing argument to the jury the existence of ***facts not proved.***

c. Personal Knowledge or Opinion of Lawyer

The lawyer is also ***prohibited*** from asserting ***personal knowledge*** of the facts in issue (except when testifying as a witness), or presenting a ***personal opinion*** on the justness of a claim, the credibility of a witness, the culpability of a civil litigant, or the guilt or innocence of an accused. [Model Rule 3.4(e); Cal. Rule 5–200(E); Restatement § 107(1); **Hawk v. Superior Court,** 42 Cal. App. 3d 108 (1974)]

EXAM TIP GILBERT

Don't get confused about this rule. Although a lawyer ***cannot give his personal opinion*** about the credibility of a witness, he can certainly make the point that the witness is not credible by referring to the evidence. Thus, the lawyer ***cannot*** say, "Defendant told you that the light was green, but I don't believe him and you shouldn't either," but he ***can*** say, "Defendant says the light was green, but he stands to lose a lot of money in this case. Two eyewitnesses, who have nothing to gain or lose, testified that it was red. You decide whom to believe."

d. Appeals to Emotion or Prejudice

Some appeal by an advocate to the emotion of jurors is inevitable. However, it is misconduct for a lawyer to arouse the emotions or prejudices of jurors as to matters that are not supported by admissible evidence and thus are legally irrelevant. [Model Rule 3.4(e); Restatement § 107(2)]

(1) References to Defendant's Insurance or Lack Thereof

In most jurisdictions, it is improper for plaintiff's counsel to make any reference to the fact that the defendant is covered by liability insurance to prove negligence or other wrongdoing. Its mention is calculated solely to encourage the jury to award a greater sum. In some jurisdictions, it is equally improper for defense counsel to tell the jury that the defendant is ***not*** insured. [*See* Fed. R. Evid. 41]

(2) "Golden Rule" Argument

Jurors are required to act as objective triers of fact and to exclude personal feelings in arriving at their verdict. Hence, it is ***improper*** for counsel to ask the jury to "bring back a verdict that you would expect if ***you*** were the plaintiff." [**Miku v. Almen,** 193 So. 2d 17 (Fla. 1966)]

e. Cross-Examining an Adverse Witnesses at Trial

The rules of evidence give a lawyer considerable leeway in cross-examining a witness. Indeed, part of the way the adversary system tests the credibility of evidence is by trying to impeach witnesses and undermine their credibility with the jury. Nevertheless, the rules articulate particular certain restraints on the zeal with which such examinations can be conducted.

(1) Examining to Degrade or Harass a Witness

It is misconduct for a lawyer to use cross-examination simply to degrade or harass a witness, or for the purpose of prejudicing the jury. [Model Rule 4.4(a); Restatement § 106, comment c]

(2) Expressing Personal Opinion on Witness's Credibility

It is likewise improper for a lawyer to express a ***personal opinion*** as to the ***credibility*** of the witness's testimony. [Model Rule 3.4(e); Restatement § 107(1)]

4. Requirement of Dignity in Adversary Proceedings

A lawyer's duty to represent the client with zeal must also be balanced against the lawyer's obligation of courtesy and proper behavior toward ***all persons*** involved in the legal process.

a. Advocate Must Not Disrupt Tribunal

In handling a case, the lawyer must not engage in conduct intended to ***disrupt*** the tribunal. [Model Rule 3.5(d); Restatement § 105]

(1) Distinguish—Objections to Questions or Comments by the Judge

It is ***not improper*** for a lawyer to ***object*** to any ***questions*** the trial judge may ask of a witness (whether the witness was called by the court or by another party).

e.g. **Example:** Where the jury had been deliberating in a murder trial for over three weeks, and the judge interrupted their deliberations with a "dynamite" charge and comments regarding credibility of witnesses that was heavily slanted against his client, the defendant's lawyer was entitled to object. [**Cooper v. Superior Court,** 55 Cal. 2d 291 (1961)]

(2) Respect for Court Rulings in Proceedings

Respect for judicial rulings is essential to the administration of justice. Thus, a lawyer may not disregard (nor advise the client to disregard) rulings made by the court in the proceeding. But a lawyer ***may*** properly take steps in ***good faith*** to test the correctness of any ruling or action by the court. [Model Rule 3.4(c); Restatement § 105]

b. Conduct Toward Opposing Counsel

A standard of dignity and courtesy is required in all dealings with opposing counsel. Each lawyer must abstain from offensive conduct toward adversaries. [Restatement § 106, comment d]

(1) Compliance with Local Customs and Practice

A lawyer must comply with local customs of courtesy or practice of the bar or a particular tribunal, unless the lawyer gives opposing counsel timely notice of his intention not to comply.

(2) Compliance with Reasonable Requests

Likewise, a lawyer should accede to reasonable requests from opposing counsel regarding court proceedings, settings, continuances, waiver of procedural formalities, or similar matters that do not prejudice the client's rights or interests. [Model Rule 3.2, comment 1]

5. Settlement Restricting Lawyer's Right to Practice

The law expressly prohibits an offer or agreement made as part of settling a client's claim that restricts the lawyer's future rights to practice. [Model Rule 5.6(b); Restatement § 13(2)]

e.g. **Example:** Lawyer has done a particularly good job investigating a product for her client's product liability claim. Defendant wants to settle the matter and include a provision that the lawyer will not file any future cases based on this defect on behalf of future plaintiffs. The defense lawyer may not offer and the plaintiff's lawyer may not enter into such an agreement.

D. Improper Contacts with Court Officials and Jurors

1. Introduction

Proper functioning of the adversary system depends on the ***impartiality*** of judges, court officials, and jurors and on the litigants' ***equal access*** to the tribunal. Most of the following provisions should be obvious.

2. No Gifts or Loans to Court Personnel

A lawyer may not make a gift or loan to a judge, hearing officer, or other employee of a tribunal unless permitted by law (*e.g.*, a gift to a friend or relative that is appropriate for the occasion and the relationship). [Model Rule 3.5(a); Restatement § 113(2); Cal. Rule 5–300]

a. Exception—Political Contributions

A lawyer may contribute to the ***campaign fund*** of a candidate for judicial office, provided the contributions comply with all requirements of the ABA Code of Judicial Conduct. [Model Rule 8.4(f)]

3. Communication with Judge or Hearing Officer

In an adversary proceeding, the lawyer may only communicate with a judge or hearing officer regarding the ***merits of the case*** in the course of the proceedings, except as other communications are authorized by law or court order. The most frequent instance in which such communications are authorized is in connection with seeking a temporary restraining order or making another *ex parte* application to the court. [Model Rule 3.5(b); ABA Code of Judicial Conduct, Rule 2.9]

4. Contacts with Jurors

To safeguard the impartiality of the judicial process, jurors and prospective jurors must be protected against extraneous influence. Therefore, a lawyer owes a duty to the legal system to avoid improper communications or contacts with jurors, and a duty to disclose to the appropriate court any such conduct by others. [Model Rule 3.5(a); Cal. Rule 5–320; Restatement § 115]

a. Communications Before Trial

Before the trial of a case, lawyers connected with the matter ***must not communicate*** (or cause anyone else to communicate) with any person known to be a member of the jury panel from which a jury for the case will be selected. Any investigation of members of the jury panel to determine their backgrounds and the existence of any factors that would be grounds for a challenge (*e.g.*, bias, relationship to party, etc.) must be conducted with "circumspection and restraint" so as not to discourage jury service.

b. Contacts During Trial

Other than addressing the jurors as part of the official proceedings (*e.g.*, in opening and closing argument), a lawyer who is connected with the case ***may not communicate*** (or cause another to communicate) with a member of the jury during the course of a trial.

EXAM TIP GILBERT

Note that this no contact with jurors rule is strict: There should be ***no communications*** with jurors or prospective jurors except as part of official proceedings ***during and before trial.*** Thus, for example, if the lawyer sees a juror in the elevator, she should not talk to the juror even about unrelated topics and regardless of who initiates the conversation.

c. Communications After Trial

(1) To Determine Basis for Challenging Jury Verdict

A jury verdict may be subject to challenge for certain kinds of irregularities in the jury deliberations, *e.g.*, improper influence from outsiders or a verdict arrived at by flipping a coin. (*See* Civil Procedure Summary.) To discover such irregularities, the lawyer may interview the jurors after the trial if not prohibited by law or court order. [Model Rule 3.5(c)(1); Restatement § 115(3)(b)]

(2) To Improve Advocacy Skill

Another reason for permitting contact with jurors after trial is to inform lawyers of the factors that led to the jury verdict and thus enable the lawyers to improve their skill and efficiency for other clients. [ABA Opn. 319]

(3) Limitations

However, a lawyer may not interrogate any juror who does not wish to be interviewed. Moreover, in questioning those jurors willing to talk, the lawyer must take great care to avoid questions or comments that are calculated to ***harass or embarrass*** the jurors or to influence their conduct in future jury service. [Model Rule 3.5(c); Restatement § 115(3)(a)]

d. Communications with Members of Juror's Family

The same restraints on communications with jurors and prospective jurors apply as well to contacts with members of their families.

E. Limitations on Advancing Money to Client

1. Introduction

A controversial but longstanding limitation on a trial lawyer's conduct forbids the lawyer from giving financial support to a client during litigation. Such support was traditionally prohibited out of concern for "stirring up litigation." Today, the concern is that the more financially involved the lawyer becomes, the more difficult it is to exercise independent judgment in handling the case.

2. Advancing Litigation Expenses

The Model Rules ***permit*** a lawyer to advance court costs and other litigation expenses, repayment of which ***may be contingent*** on the outcome of the case. Furthermore, if the client is indigent, the lawyer need make ***no provision for repayment*** of the expenses. [Model Rule 1.8(e); Restatement § 36(2)]

3. No Other Financial Support

However, the law has consistently forbidden paying living expenses or meeting other financial needs of the client, even when the payments are based on genuine compassion. [*See* **State of Oklahoma v. Smolen,** 17 P.3d 456 (Okla. 2000)—lawyer loaned client $1,200 after client's house burned down]

a. Criticism of Traditional Rule

Prohibiting a lawyer who is handling a case from lending money to cover the client's living expenses may leave the client without means of support. As a result, the client may be forced to accept an inadequate settlement. This would defeat both the client's interest and that of the lawyer who is handling the matter on a contingent fee basis.

b. Some Evidence the Law Is Changing

In at least a few cases, courts have suggested that there is little justification for this prohibition. [*Cf.*, **Osprey v. Cabana Limited Partnership,** 532 S.E.2d 269 (S.C. 2000)—allowing third-party lender to advance living expenses in exchange for an interest in judgment]

F. Lawyer as Witness and Advocate

1. Nature of the Problem

When a lawyer representing a client in litigation also witnessed key events in a case, the lawyer may have to assume inconsistent roles. The function of the lawyer as ***advocate*** is to advance and ***argue*** the client's case, while the function of a ***witness*** is to state facts ***objectively.*** The advocate-witness may be forced to argue his own credibility, may be more easily impeached, and therefore may be less effective both as counsel and as witness.

2. Prohibition on Appearance in Both Capacities

The general rule is that a lawyer may ***neither accept nor continue employment*** in litigation if the lawyer ***is likely to be a necessary witness*** in the case. [Model Rule 3.7; Restatement § 108; *but see* Cal. Rule 5–210(c)—permitting client consent to dual role]

a. Doubts Resolved in Favor of Lawyer Withdrawing from Case

The lawyer does not have a choice of which role to assume. The lawyer ***must act as a witness*** in the matter if that testimony would be material to resolving the matter. [Model Rule 3.7(a); Restatement § 108(1)(b)]

b. Representation by Another Lawyer in Witness-Lawyer's Firm

The force of this rule is significantly moderated by the fact that the disqualification is ***not imputed;*** *i.e.*, another lawyer in the witness's firm ***may*** act as advocate in the trial unless to do so would involve a conflict of interest with a current or former client of the firm. [Model Rule 3.7(b); Restatement § 108(3)]

3. Exceptions to General Rule

In some situations, the lawyer may appear as a witness on behalf of the client while continuing to serve as advocate.

a. Testimony on Uncontested Matter

A lawyer who intends to testify solely on ***an uncontested matter*** (*i.e.*, one as to which there is no reason to expect evidence in opposition, *e.g.*, as witness to execution of an instrument or to establish receipt of correspondence) may properly act as both witness and counsel. [Model Rule 3.7(a)(1); Restatement § 108(2)(a)]

e.g. **Example—will execution:** It is permissible for a lawyer to testify as a witness to the ***execution of a decedents will*** and to express an opinion as to the decedent's testamentary capacity where such testimony is necessary for the record and those issues are not in dispute.

cf. **Compare—will contest:** In the event of a ***will contest*** in which testamentary intent or capacity is at issue, the lawyer who drafted the will ***cannot*** appear as an attorney for any party to the will contest. The lawyer is a crucial witness on the controverted issue of testamentary intent or capacity, and therefore, appearing as an advocate would be improper.

b. Testimony on Nature and Value of Legal Services

The lawyer is ***not barred*** from representing a client as both counsel and witness when testimony is required about the nature and value of legal services rendered by the lawyer or his law firm (*e.g.*, where the client sues a third party to recover legal expenses as a result of third party's breach of contract). [Model Rule 3.7(a)(2); Restatement § 108(2)(a)]

c. Preventing Substantial Hardship to Client

The law also permits the lawyer to testify with respect to even a contested matter if failure to do so, or the need to withdraw as counsel, would "work as a substantial hardship on his client because of the distinctive value of the lawyer or his firm as counsel in the particular case." In practice, this is a high standard, not often met. [Model Rule 3.7(a)(3) and comment 4; Restatement § 108(2)(b) and comment h]

WHEN LAWYER MAY APPEAR AS WITNESS FOR CLIENT — GILBERT
GENERAL RULE: A LAWYER MAY NOT ACCEPT OR CONTINUE EMPLOYMENT WHEN HE KNOWS OR IT IS LIKELY THAT HE MAY BE CALLED AS A WITNESS EXCEPTIONS:
☑ When testimony relates only to an ***uncontested matter;***
☑ When testimony pertains to the ***nature and value of legal services;***
☑ To prevent a ***substantial hardship to client.***

4. Lawyer Called as Witness by Opposing Party

A separate problem is presented when the lawyer is called as a witness ***other than*** on behalf of the lawyer's client (*e.g.*, the adverse party calls the lawyer as a hostile witness to prove the content of the meeting between the client and the opposing party).

a. Possibility That Testimony Will Create Conflict of Interest

If the lawyer's testimony would conflict with that of the client, the lawyer may act as counsel only with the informed consent of the client. [Model Rule 3.7, comment 6; Restatement § 108(3) & (4)]

b. Lawyer's Firm Sometimes Also May Not Act as Counsel

In such situations, the usual rule permitting another lawyer in the witness-lawyer's firm to act as counsel may not apply. Cross-examining and testing the credibility of one's own law partner would present a conflict requiring the client's informed consent, and in some cases may be too great a conflict to be waived at all. [Model Rule 3.6, comment 7; Restatement § 108(3); *see* pp. 79–80, *supra*]

G. Limitations on Trial Publicity

1. Introduction

Impartial adjudication of disputes can be adversely affected when advocates make public comments about their cases, unrestrained by the rules of evidence. Thus, a series of restrictions are imposed on out-of-court statements in connection with pending criminal and civil proceedings. [Model Rule 3.6; Restatement § 109]

2. General Rule

A lawyer may not make an out-of-court statement likely to be reported by the news media if the lawyer knows or reasonably should know that the statement would have a ***"substantial likelihood of materially prejudicing an adjudicative proceeding."*** [Model Rule 3.6(a); *see also* Restatement § 109(1)]

a. Tension with the First Amendment

The public's important right to know about government acts such as criminal trials makes it important that restrictions on comments be no greater than necessary. In extreme cases, however, the Court has held that prejudicial publicity denied the defendant due process of law. [*See, e.g.*, **Sheppard v. Maxwell,** 384 U.S. 333 (1966)]

b. Constitutionality of Model Rule Standard Upheld

The Supreme Court has upheld the constitutionality of the "substantial likelihood of material prejudice" standard as applied to pretrial statements by lawyers. However, the Court held that a state standard permitting lawyers to describe only the "general nature" of a defense "without elaboration" was void for vagueness. [**Gentile v. Nevada State Bar,** 501 U.S. 1030 (1991)]

3. Criminal Proceedings

a. Information That May Be Disclosed

A lawyer associated with the investigation of a criminal matter (*e.g.*, a district attorney) is forbidden to make any out-of-court statement capable of public dissemination that does more than state ***without elaboration:***

(i) The matter being investigated;

(ii) Information in a ***public record***;

(iii) The fact that an ***investigation is in progress***;

(iv) The scheduling or result of any step in the litigation;

(v) A request for ***assistance*** in apprehending a suspect or other assistance;

(vi) A ***warning*** of any substantial danger to an individual or the public;

(vii) The ***identity*** of the accused; and

(viii) ***Arrest information,*** if any.

[Model Rule 3.6(b); *compare* Restatement § 109, comment c—urging caution about lists such as these]

b. Matters That May Not Be Disclosed

Particularly sensitive matters identified by the Model Rules include: (i) the ***prior arrest record*** of the accused, (ii) the existence of a ***confession*** or the ***possibility of a guilty plea,*** (iii) ***results of tests*** performed or the ***refusal to submit to such tests,*** (iv) any ***opinion as to the guilt*** of the accused, and (v) other information that would be *inadmissible at trial.* [Model Rule 3.6, comment 5]

c. Lawyers Affected

These restrictions apply to any lawyer—whether part of the prosecution or defense—and any lawyer associated with the office or agency prosecuting the case. [Model Rule 3.6(a), (d)]

d. Special Duty of Prosecutors

In addition, the Model Rules now say that prosecutors, "except for statements that are necessary to inform the public of the nature and extent of the prosecutor's action and that serve a legitimate law enforcement purpose," must "refrain from making extrajudicial comments that have a ***substantial likelihood of heightening public condemnation*** of the accused." [Model Rule 3.8(f)]

e. Latitude Given Defense Lawyers

Under what is informally called the "anti-police-leak rule," defense lawyers now may "make a statement that a reasonable lawyer would believe is required to protect a client from the substantial undue prejudicial effect of recent publicity not initiated by the lawyer or the lawyer's client." However, such a statement must "be limited to such information as is necessary to mitigate the recent adverse publicity." [Model Rule 3.6(c)]

4. Civil and Administrative Proceedings

By their terms, most of the above limitations on pretrial publicity apply equally to civil litigation. However, it is likely that the number of civil cases in which publicity will be found to violate the "substantial likelihood of material prejudice" standard will be far fewer than the number of criminal cases. [*See, e.g.,* **Hirschkop v. Snead,** 594 F.2d 356 (4th Cir. 1979)—rule of Virginia Code of Professional Responsibility held unconstitutional as applied to other than criminal cases]

H. Special Duties of Prosecutors and Other Government Lawyers

1. Special Limitations on Prosecutorial Function

The constitutional protections afforded criminal defendants, as well as traditional concerns that public officials act with fairness and a concern for justice help set prosecutors apart from lawyers representing private clients.

a. Restraint in Exercise of Governmental Power

As a representative of the sovereign, the prosecutor is obliged to use ***restraint*** in the discretionary exercise of governmental powers, and particularly in the ***selection of cases to prosecute.***

(1) Probable Cause Required

A public prosecutor may not institute criminal charges when she knows (or it is obvious) that such charges are ***not supported by probable cause.*** [Model Rule 3.8(a); Restatement § 97(3)]

(2) Must Not Require Waiver of Rights

Similarly, a prosecutor may not seek to get an unrepresented accused to ***waive important pretrial rights***, such as the right to a preliminary hearing. [Model Rule 3.8(c)]

b. Must Help Accused Obtain Counsel

The prosecutor must reasonably assure that the accused knows how to obtain counsel and has had a chance to do so. [Model Rule 3.8(b)]

c. Dual Role During Trial

At trial, the prosecutor is both an advocate and a representative of the broad public interest. Thus, tradition says the prosecutor's actions must be ***fair***, rather than calculated merely to prevail in the pending action.

2. Duties Respecting Witnesses and Evidence

In light of the special responsibility to see that justice is done, the prosecutor also has special duties with respect to witnesses and evidence in criminal proceedings.

a. Obligation to Disclose Evidence Beneficial to Defense

The prosecutor has a constitutional as well as a professional obligation to make timely disclosure to the defense of any available evidence known to the prosecutor that may negate guilt, mitigate the degree of the offense, or reduce the appropriate punishment. [Model Rule 3.8(d); Restatement § 97(4); **Brady v. Maryland,** 373 U.S. 83 (1963)]

b. Obligation to Pursue "Harmful" Evidence

Similarly, a prosecutor may not intentionally fail to pursue evidence merely because such evidence may damage the prosecution's case or aid the accused.

c. Access to Government Witnesses

The prosecutor ordinarily must also permit defense counsel to ***interview*** government witnesses and may not properly counsel such witnesses to refuse to talk to the defense. [**Gregory v. United States,** 369 F.2d 185 (D.C. Cir. 1966)]

d. Limit on Use of Subpoena to Get Defense Records

One common practice of United States Attorneys was to subpoena defense lawyers' files or call the lawyers before a grand jury to testify about fee arrangements and other information about their clients. Model Rule 3.8(e) now ***prohibits*** such conduct unless the prosecutor reasonably believes:

(1) The information is ***not privileged;***

(2) The evidence is ***essential*** to an ongoing investigation or prosecution; and

(3) There is ***no other feasible way*** to get the information.

3. Duty to Correct Prior Injustice

Recent advances in DNA science and evidence testing have contributed to finding many cases where the fact a defendant was wrongfully convicted can be proved to a high degree of certainty. Prosecutors are now required to help correct such past injustices.

a. "New, Credible and Material Evidence"

A prosecutor who learns of "new, credible and material evidence creating a reasonable likelihood that a convicted defendant did not commit" the offense for which he was convicted must: (i) promptly disclose the evidence to an appropriate court or prosecutor, and (ii) if the case was in the prosecutor's jurisdiction, promptly notify the defendant and investigate whether the defendant was convicted of an offense he did not commit. [Model Rule 3.8(g); Restatement § 97(4)]

b. "Clear and Convincing Evidence"

If clear and convincing evidence establishes that a person was wrongly convicted in the prosecutor's jurisdiction, the prosecutor has an affirmative duty to "seek to remedy the conviction." [Model Rule 3.8(h)]

EXAMPLES OF SPECIAL RESPONSIBILITIES OF PROSECUTORS GILBERT
TO ASSURE THAT A DEFENDANT IS TRIED BY FAIR PROCEDURES AND THAT GUILT IS DECIDED ON PROPER AND SUFFICIENT EVIDENCE, A PROSECUTOR:
☑ ***Must make reasonable efforts*** to assure that an accused is advised of the ***right to counsel*** and is given an opportunity to obtain counsel; ☑ ***Must timely disclose*** to the defense all evidence and information known to the prosecutor that tends to ***negate guilt, mitigate the degree of an offense, or reduce the appropriate punishment;*** ☑ ***Must not*** institute a criminal charge that is ***not supported by probable cause;*** ☑ ***Must not seek a waiver of important pretrial rights*** from an unrepresented accused; ☑ ***Must not subpoena a lawyer*** to give evidence about a client ***unless*** the information ***is not privileged, is essential,*** and ***cannot be obtained*** in any other way; ☑ ***Must seek to reverse a conviction of a person wrongfully convicted.***

I. Advocate in a Non-Adjudicative Proceeding

1. Introduction

Most people are used to thinking of advocates as representing clients before courts or other tribunals, but many advocates also work behind the scenes at state legislatures, before administrative agencies considering policy changes, or before officials in executive agencies. The Model Rules impose requirements on lawyers' conduct in such settings that echo some of those applicable before tribunals. [Model Rule 3.9 and comment 1]

2. Duty to Disclose Representative Capacity

In any such appearance or communication with a public body, the lawyer ***must disclose*** that the lawyer is representing interests that may be affected by the action or legislation under consideration. [Model Rule 3.9; Restatement § 104]

3. Same Requirements of Honesty as in Model Rule 3.3(a) Through (c)

As discussed earlier in this chapter, a lawyer may not make a false statement of law or fact to a tribunal, must reveal directly adverse controlling legal authority, may not offer false testimony, and must use "reasonable remedial measures" to correct any material misstatements. Those same rules apply in a non-adjudicative setting. [Model Rule 3.9]

4. Same Requirements of Fairness as in Model Rule 3.4(a) Through (c)

A lawyer in a non-adjudicative proceeding is likewise held to the same standards of not falsifying evidence, not obstructing access to evidence and obeying the rules of a tribunal as seen earlier. [Model Rule 3.9]

5. Same Requirement of Impartiality and Decorum as Required by Model Rule 3.5

A lawyer in a non-adjudicative proceeding is also held to legal prohibitions on improper influence of the relevant decision makers. [Model Rule 3.9]

Chapter Seven

The Business of Practicing Law

Chapter Seven

CONTENTS	PAGE

Chapter Approach

This chapter covers the basic rules of running a modern law office. It is hard to think of some of the issues in this chapter as dealing with "ethics" at all, but they are the subject of professional rules that you will need to know and follow. One of the most important aspects of the "business" of practicing law—the charging of legal fees—was addressed earlier in Chapter II of this Summary (*see supra*, p. 48 *et seq.)*. The five key issues in this Chapter relate to:

1. The ***ways that lawyers associate themselves*** to practice law and the obligations of ***supervisors*** in those practice organizations;
2. The ***marketing of a law practice*** and limits on that marketing;
3. Lawyer ***specialization;***
4. ***Fee sharing outside a law firm;*** and
5. ***Departing from*** a law firm.

The sources of most of the principles in this chapter are Restatement §§ 9–13 and Model Rules 5.1–5.4 and 7.1–7.5.

A. Associations of Lawyers for the Practice of Law

1. Introduction

Much of the ABA Code of Professional Responsibility (1969) was written as though law were practiced primarily by sole practitioners in a general practice. That, of course, is no longer true. The Model Rules recognize that law firms, legal services agencies, legal clinics, and other groups, corporations, and government agencies are all settings for the practice of law. The form these organizations take—and want to take—promises to require future rule changes. The current form of some associations, and the rules of ethics that apply to them, are discussed below.

2. Law Firms and Professional Law Corporations

a. Roles in a Traditional Law Firm

Partly as a result of the benefits to be derived from specialization and partly for reasons of efficiency (*e.g.*, sharing overhead), partnerships and other associations of lawyers are common.

(1) Partners

(a) Normally Share Fees

Partners are the principals in a traditional firm. Partners normally share the fees generated by the firm. This financial interest in each other's work is one of the justifications for imputation of conflicts of interest (*see supra*, p. 96).

(b) Normally Share Liability for Malpractice

1) General Partnership Law

Partnership law holds all members of a general partnership liable for the torts (*e.g.,* malpractice) of any one of them. In part, that's why law firms tend to carry high levels of malpractice insurance coverage.

2) Practice Through Professional Law Corporations

In most states today, lawyers may form a corporation or limited liability company ("LLC") to carry on the practice of law. "Shareholders" in such entities typically are insulated from liability for malpractice in which they were not personally involved.

(c) Holding out as Partners

Lawyers may not hold themselves out as partners unless they in fact are partners. If non-partners violate this rule, they will be treated as partners liable for each other's malpractice. [Model Rule 7.5(d); **Gosselin v. Webb,** 242 F.3d 412 (1st Cir. 2001)]

EXAM TIP GILBERT

You may see a question that involves lawyers who are not associated with each other in a law practice but who share office space, secretarial help, a photocopier, etc. Remember that, although this is permitted, they ***must not imply that they are associated*** in a law firm (*e.g.,* by sharing a firm name) or they risk being treated as partners when one of them gets sued for malpractice (*i.e.,* they will all be liable for the damages).

---

(2) Associates

Reference to a lawyer as an "associate" is proper only where the lawyer has an ongoing relationship with a law firm (or another lawyer) other than as a partner. Normally, an associate performs legal services for the firm's clients as a salaried employee of the firm.

(a) Rights of Associates

In the past, little was said about the rights or status of associates. However, associates have been held entitled to: (i) ***form a union*** to bargain with their law firm under federal labor laws [**Foley, Hoag & Eliot,** 229 N.L.R.B. 456 (1977)]; and (ii) sue their law firms for ***discrimination*** under Title VII of the Civil Rights Act of 1964 [*see, e.g.,* **Lucido v. Cravath, Swaine & Moore,** 425 F. Supp. 123 (E.D. Va. 1977).

(b) Protection Under Model Rule 8.4(g)

As discussed in Chapter V of this Summary, pp. 116–118, *supra*, Model Rule 8.4(g) establishes extensive regulation of harassment and discrimination in the practice of law. Law firm associates are likely to be some of the principal beneficiaries of this protection.

(3) Lawyers Who Are "Of Counsel" to a Law Firm

The term "of counsel" signifies a lawyer's continuing relationship with a law firm ***other than as a partner or associate.*** The term describes many kinds of relationships, but often the title is taken by a lawyer who formerly was a partner in the law firm and now has only occasional client responsibility. The lawyer may or may not maintain an office with the firm, but he or she will be subject to the rules of imputed conflicts of interest.

b. Association with Nonlawyers in Practice

The restrictions on unauthorized practice of law by nonlawyers were discussed in Chapter I of this Summary. [*See supra*, p. 2 *et seq*]. Similar concerns about nonlawyer practice ***restrict*** the extent to which a lawyer ***may associate*** in practice with nonlawyers.

(1) Partnerships with Nonlawyers Prohibited

The Model Rules authorize use of nonlawyer legal assistants (often called "paralegals"). This benefits the client through more efficient service at reduced cost, and the lawyer through increased income. [Model Rule 5.3; ABA Opn. 320] But the Model Rules flatly prohibit ***partnerships*** between lawyers and nonlawyers ***if any*** of the partnership ***activities include the practice of law.*** [Model Rule 5.4(b); Restatement § 10(2)]

(a) Distinguish—Partnerships Not Involving Practice of Law

A lawyer is free to enter into a partnership with a nonlawyer if the partnership confines itself ***solely to nonlegal activities*** (*e.g.*, investments, operation of a restaurant, etc.).

EXAM TIP GILBERT

Whenever you see an exam question involving a lawyer and a nonlawyer forming a partnership, you should suspect trouble. Be sure to check the facts carefully to see if ***any legal service*** is provided by the partnership—even one that is only incidental to the main partnership activities. If so, the lawyer is subject to discipline, even if she alone provides the service and even if she does it only occasionally. Thus, if Lawyer and Nonlawyer form a partnership to sell life insurance policies, that is fine, but if every now and then Lawyer sets up a trust for a client purchasing life insurance, Lawyer is subject to discipline for associating with Nonlawyer for the practice of law.

---

(2) Law Corporations

A corporation that allows professional practice is similarly ***prohibited*** from allowing a nonlawyer to (i) own an interest in the corporation, (ii) act as a director or officer, or (iii) direct or control the practice of a lawyer. [Model Rule 5.4(d)]

c. Sharing Fees with Nonlawyer Prohibited

Both the ABA Code and Model Rules also prohibit the division of legal fees with a nonlawyer, Thus, a lawyer may not pay a non-lawyer investigator a special bonus for finding the evidence that allowed the lawyer to win an important case. [Model Rule 5.4(a)] This prohibition is subject to the following ***exceptions***:

(1) **Employment on Flat Salary Basis Permitted**

A lawyer is ***permitted to employ*** nonlawyers whose salaries will come from fees earned by the lawyer as long as their compensation is ***not tied to fees collected*** for particular legal services. For example, a paralegal can be paid by the hour but cannot be given 10% of the fee collected in a case. [Model Rule 5.4(a)]

(2) **Profit Sharing Permissible in Firm Plans**

A broad exception to this rule against "fee splitting" permits salaried employees of a lawyer or law firm to participate in a retirement or profit-sharing plan, even though the plan will inevitably be based upon sharing income with the lawyer-employer. [Model Rule 5.4(a)(3)]

(3) **Payments to Estate of Deceased Lawyer Permissible**

Another exception permits the surviving members of a law firm to pay the estate of a deceased lawyer a sum of money for a reasonable period of time after his death. [Model Rule 5.4(a)(1)] And a lawyer who buys the practice of a dead, disabled, or missing lawyer may pay the purchase price to the lawyer's estate or representative, even though the estate and representative are technically nonlawyers. [Model Rule 5.4(a)(2)]

(4) **Sharing Court-Awarded Fee with Nonprofit Organization Permitted**

When a court awards attorney's fees to a lawyer, the lawyer may also share the fees with a nonprofit organization that hired him or recommended him as counsel in the matter. [Model Rule 5.4(a)(4)]

3. Supervisory Relationships in a Practice Organization

The Model Rules contain important provisions on supervisory responsibilities in a law firm, law office, or professional corporation. For purposes of imposing professional discipline, ***unlike*** the shared ***malpractice liability*** of partners, a lawyer is ***not vicariously liable*** for the conduct of others in the firm. Instead:

a. Partner's Responsibility to Ensure Conformity with Professional Standards

A law firm partner or lawyer with managerial authority has a duty to make reasonable efforts to assure that the firm has measures in place to ensure that all lawyers in the firm will conform to professional standards. [Model Rule 5.1(a); Restatement § 11(1)]

(1) **Direct Supervisor of Another Lawyer**

A lawyer, whether or not a partner or manager, who directly supervises another lawyer must make reasonable efforts to see that the other lawyer conforms to professional standards. [Model Rule 5.1(b); Restatement § 11(2)]

EXAM TIP GILBERT

Note that a supervisory lawyer who has ***no knowledge*** of a subordinate lawyer's misconduct may still be ***subject to discipline*** if he has not made ***reasonable efforts*** to ensure the subordinate lawyer's conformity to professional standards.

(2) Responsibility for Another Lawyer's Ethical Violation

A lawyer is ***responsible for another lawyer's violation*** of the Model Rules if the lawyer:

(i) ***Ordered,*** or with knowledge ***ratified,*** the other's conduct; or

(ii) Is a ***partner*** in the firm, or a ***direct supervisor*** of the other lawyer, and ***fails to take reasonably available remedial action*** to avoid or mitigate consequences of the action.

[Model Rule 5.1(c); Restatement § 11(3)]

(3) Responsibility Concerning Nonlawyer Assistants

The duties of partners and supervising lawyers are the ***same*** with respect to nonlawyers under their supervision as with respect to lawyers. [Model Rule 5.3; Restatement § 11(4)]

b. Responsibility of a Subordinate Lawyer

Every lawyer is ***bound by the Model Rules*** even if directed to act contrary to them by another person, including a direct supervisor. [Model Rule 5.2(a); Restatement § 12(1)]

(1) Where the Ethical Duty Is Clear

If the relevant rule clearly points only one way, e.g. don't make a false statement of law or fact to a tribunal, a subordinate lawyer must comply with that rule no matter who directs the lawyer to lie. And a majority of discipline cases seem to find, looking back, that a subordinate lawyer should have known the direction received should have been disobeyed.

(2) Where the Duty Is "Arguable"

If the question of the subordinate lawyer's professional duty is ***arguable,*** the lawyer may rely on the ***reasonable*** interpretation of that duty by a supervising lawyer, even if it is later found to have been incorrect. Questions whether a situation poses a conflict of interest, for example, are sometimes close and the law firm has to either take the case or not. [Model Rule 5.2(b) and comment 2; Restatement § 12(2)]

EXAM TIP GILBERT

Although a subordinate lawyer will not be subject to discipline for following a supervisory lawyer's reasonable resolution of a ***debatable ethics question,*** keep in mind that this is ***no excuse for clearly unethical conduct.*** If a supervisory lawyer orders a subordinate lawyer to commit a clear ethics violation, the subordinate lawyer will be subject to discipline if he carries out the order.

4. Firm Name

Traditionally, a firm name could not contain names other than those of persons who were, in fact, lawyers in the firm. Thus, neither a lawyer nor a law firm engaged in private practice could do business under a trade name (*e.g.,* "The Winners") or a misleading name (*e.g.,* "Associates of Perry Mason"). The Model Rules now ***permit*** use of a trade name as long as it is ***not misleading*** and does ***not imply connection with a government agency or a legal services organization*** (*e.g.,* "City Legal Clinic"). [Model Rule 7.5(a)]

a. Names of Deceased or Retired Members

A firm name ***may include*** the names of ***deceased or retired members*** whose names are part of the firm's continuing identity. [Model Rule 7.5, comment 1]

b. Lawyers Holding Public Office

But the name of a lawyer who enters public service for a substantial period, and thus is not engaged in firm business, ***must be removed*** from the firm name. [Model Rule 7.5(c)]

c. Multi-State Firms

A firm comprised of lawyers licensed in different jurisdictions may use the same firm name in each jurisdiction. However, "identification of the ***lawyers in an office*** of the firm" on the firm's letterhead ***must make clear any jurisdictional limitations*** of the members and associates serving in that office. [Model Rule 7.5(b)]

d. Law Corporations

A professional corporation or association may (and in some states must) include the abbreviation "P.C." or "P.A." in its name.

5. Offering Law-Related Services

For many years, law firms have engaged in activities beyond the traditional practice of law. The Model Rules call these ancillary business activities "law-related services" and define them as services that "in substance are related to the provision of legal services, and that are not prohibited as unauthorized practice of law when provided by a nonlawyer." Services might include providing title insurance, financial planning, lobbying, accounting, trust services, real estate counseling, economic analysis, social work, tax return preparation, and patent, medical, or environmental consulting. [Model Rule 5.7(b) and comment 9]

a. Model Rules Presumed Applicable

A lawyer is "subject to the Rules of Professional Conduct with respect to the provision of" law-related services if the services are rendered as part of the delivery of legal services to clients. [Model Rule 5.7(a)(1) and comment 3]

b. Services Provided Separately from the Provision of Legal Services

The Rules are even applicable if the law-related services are provided to clients separately from the provision of legal services, unless the lawyer takes reasonable measures to make clear that the services are not legal services and that protections such as the attorney-client privilege do not apply. [Model Rule 5.7(a)(2) and comments 4–8]

EXAM TIP GILBERT

When answering a question involving ***law-related services,*** remember that a lawyer is ***subject to the Rules of Professional Conduct*** when providing law-related services to her clients in circumstances that are not distinct from her provision of legal services. The Rules also apply even when the law-related services ***are distinct*** from her provision of legal services, ***unless the lawyer takes reasonable steps*** to assure that people who receive the law-related services understand that those services are not covered by the Rules of Professional Conduct.

6. Group and Prepaid Legal Services Plans

Group and prepaid legal services plans are designed to make legal services easily available to middle-income citizens who are union members or members of other voluntary associations.

a. Past Opposition to Group Legal Services Plans

For many years, the bar argued that group legal services plans would interfere with a client's free choice of counsel and would divide the lawyer's loyalty between the individual client and the group from which future referrals might come. Thus, lawyers were largely prohibited from participating in group plans.

b. Constitutional Right to Provide Group Services

On four separate occasions, the United States Supreme Court held that, under certain circumstances, the right to furnish group legal services is protected under the "freedom of expression and association" guaranteed by the First and Fourteenth Amendments to the United States Constitution. [**NAACP v. Button,** 371 U.S. 415 (1963); **Brotherhood of Railroad Trainmen v. Virginia,** 377 U.S. 1 (1964); **United Mine Workers v. Illinois State Bar Association,** 389 U.S. 217 (1967); **United Transportation Union v. State Bar of Michigan,** 401 U.S. 576 (1971)]

c. Present Status

These Supreme Court decisions clearly required the organized bar and state courts to expand the opportunities for group plans to meet the increased need for legal services while still preserving professional standards. There are now two main types of group and prepaid legal services plans:

(1) Closed Panel Plans

Under a closed panel plan, an organizing group (*e.g.*, a trade union) hires a lawyer or group of lawyers to handle the members' legal work on an annual flat fee basis or according to an agreed schedule of fees for various types of work. The clients ordinarily may not choose which lawyer will represent them.

(2) Open Panel Plans

In an open panel plan, a number of lawyers practicing in a geographic area agree to do legal work for clients that is ordinarily wholly or partly paid for by legal insurance (*i.e.*, the client pays a periodic premium and thereby becomes entitled to a set amount of legal services during the policy period). This type of plan allows the client to select a lawyer from the panel of lawyers who have agreed to take work on this basis.

d. Model Rules Treatment of Group Plans

The Model Rules place ***no specific limits*** on lawyer participation in such plans, other than the generally applicable rule that a lawyer may not let a group that recommends employment direct or regulate the manner in which the lawyer represents her clients. [Model Rules 5.4(c)] The Model Rules do, however, expressly permit a lawyer to participate in a group plan that (i) is not owned or directed by any of the participating lawyers, and (ii) does not market itself by in-person or telephone contact to persons who are "known to need legal services in a particular matter covered by the plan." [Model Rule 7.3(d)]

B. Regulation of Lawyers Seeking Employment—Solicitation and Advertising

1. Traditional Position of Organized Bar—Only Allow Passive Acceptance of Employment

The organized bar ***traditionally*** took the position that a lawyer was ***not permitted to actively publicize his or her services.*** In effect, it was presumed that every lawyer had an established clientele, or that a lawyer's reputation for good work would inevitably lead others to seek out the lawyer. ***Direct publicity*** by lawyers was ***strictly controlled.***

a. Criticisms of Traditional Approach

The traditional "passive" standard was criticized as:

(1) Unfair to lawyers without ***established practices;***

(2) Inappropriate for lower- and middle-income clients who might be ***unaware of their need for legal services*** or who might have ***no idea how to locate a competent lawyer;***

(3) In conflict with ***consumers' need to receive information*** about lawyers, their fees, and their services; and

(4) ***Anticompetitive.***

b. Beginnings of Change

The above criticisms developed strength in the mid-1970s as consumer groups and some lawyers combined to oppose the restrictions on lawyer advertising.

(1) Consumers' First Amendment "Right to Know"

The critics' position was further strengthened by two subsequent Supreme Court decisions that, although not specifically concerned with advertising by lawyers, held that commercial advertising was entitled to First Amendment protection. [**Bigelow v. Virginia,** 421 U.S. 809 (1975); **Virginia State Board of Pharmacy v. Virginia Citizens Consumer Council,** 425 U.S. 748 (1976)]

(2) Relaxation of Traditional Restraints—*Bates*

In 1977, the Supreme Court at last squarely confronted the issue of lawyer advertising. In **Bates v. State Bar of Arizona,** 433 U.S. 350 (1977), disciplinary action had been brought against lawyers for placing a newspaper ad that listed fees for routine, standardized legal services. In finding the lawyers ***not*** subject to discipline, the Supreme Court held that:

(1) Advertising by licensed lawyers may ***not be "subjected to blanket suppression"***;

(2) *Truthful* advertising conveying the *availability and terms* (fees) for routine legal services is *protected* by the First Amendment; but

(3) *Reasonable restrictions may be imposed* on the time, place, and manner of legal advertising; and

(4) Advertising that is ***"false, deceptive, or misleading"*** is subject to *restraint.*

2. Lawyer Advertising and Publicity—Current Status of the Law

a. Only False and Misleading Advertising Prohibited

(1) False Advertising

The Model Rules permit all advertising except that which is "false and misleading," defined as containing a "material misrepresentation of fact or law." [Model Rule 7.1]

(a) Misleading Advertising

Even technically truthful statements can be misleading and thus prohibited if they "omit a fact necessary to make the statement considered as a whole not materially misleading." [Model Rule 7.1]

(b) Use of Examples That Create False Expectations

A lawyer may not report past verdicts or make comparisons with other lawyers that (i) Are ***likely to create an unjustified expectation*** about the results the lawyer can achieve, or (ii) ***Compare the lawyer's services*** with those of other lawyers in ways that imply the comparison can be factually substantiated. In some cases, disclaimers or qualifiers may avoid or minimize the problem [Model Rule 7.1, comments 2, 3]

EXAM TIP GILBERT

An important point to remember is that even truthful advertisements can be ***misleading.*** For example, if the lawyer states in her ad that in her last personal injury case the jury awarded a $200,000 verdict, even if true, this might create an ***unjustified expectation*** that the lawyer can obtain the same result for other clients. Qualifying language would be needed.

b. Manner of Dissemination

Under the Model Rules, advertising may be done through any public media, including websites or the Internet generally, and in any written communication not involving "solicitation" (*see infra*, p. 160). [Model Rule 7.2(a)]

The Supreme Court has appeared to confirm the Model Rules approach to lawyer advertising when it held both that illustrations in lawyer advertising are entitled to the same constitutional protections as text, and that an appeal may be made in an advertisement encouraging persons with a particular kind of injury to consult the lawyer.

c. Lawyer's Name Required

Lawyer advertising must include the name of at least one lawyer responsible for its content. [Model Rule 7.2(c)] Other permissible information is listed in the chart, *infra.*

EXAMPLES OF ACCEPTABLE ADVERTISING INFORMATION
THE MODEL RULES PERMIT THE FOLLOWING INFORMATION IN ADVERTISEMENTS:
☑ The lawyer's ***name***, address, and telephone number; ☑ The lawyer's area of ***practice***; ☑ How the lawyer's ***fees are determined***; ☑ The ***cost of specific services*** and ***payment arrangements***; ☑ Names of ***references***; ☑ Names of regular ***clients*** (***with their consent***). [Model Rule 7.2, comment 2]

d. Additional Limits on State Regulation

A state ***may not*** (i) ***Require*** that lawyer advertising ***be "dignified";*** or (ii) limit lawyer advertising ***except*** "in the service of a ***substantial government interest,***" and even then, "only through means that ***directly affect that interest.***" [**Zauderer v. Office of Disciplinary Counsel,** 471 U.S. 626 (1985)].

e. But a State Limit Has Been Upheld—The *Went For It* Case

In 1995, for the first time since *Bates*, the Supreme Court ***upheld state limits*** on lawyer advertising. The Court said that it applied the substantial government interest standard and concluded that the state's limitation on direct mail advertising within 30 days of an accident or disaster was valid. [**Florida Bar v. Went For It, Inc.,** 515 U.S. 618 (1995)]

3. Directly Paying for Recommendations Prohibited

In contrast to the questions of relatively impersonal advertising just discussed, Model Rule 7.2 regulates a lawyer's paying others to recommend the lawyer's services to their friends and acquaintances. A lawyer ***may not*** give others "anything of value" to recommend him.

a. But a Lawyer May:

(1) Pay the reasonable costs of advertising permitted by Model Rule 7.2;

(2) Pay the usual charges of a legal services plan or not-for-profit or qualified lawyer referral service;

(3) Buy a law practice pursuant to Model Rule 1.17, discussed later in this Chapter, p. 166; and

(4) Refer clients to another lawyer or nonlawyer professional under a nonexclusive reciprocal arrangement about whose existence and nature the client is informed. [Model Rule 7.2(b)]

b. In Addition, a Lawyer May:

(1) Pay public-relations and other marketing personnel;

(2) Pay lead generators, including for Internet-based client leads, so long as the lead generator does not also recommend the lawyer. [Model Rule 7.2, comment 5]

4. Direct Contact Solicitation

The term "solicitation" was once used to refer to any conduct on behalf of a lawyer designed to help obtain new clients. It thus traditionally included all advertising. However, after *Bates*, "solicitation" has come to mean ***in-person or other direct real-time contact with a potential client,*** whether by the lawyer or the lawyer's agent, that is not protected as advertising. [Model Rule 7.3]

a. Constitutionality of Regulation

In the case that established the principle, the United States Supreme Court considered a lawyer who harassed a young woman in her hospital room until she signed his engagement agreement. The Court confirmed the validity of prohibiting in-person solicitation of clients for cases in which a fee will be charged and the solicitation "in fact is misleading, overbearing, or involves other features of deception or improper influence." [**Ohralik v. Ohio State Bar Association,** 436 U.S. 447 (1978)]

b. Model Rules

Thus, the Model Rules prohibit "in-person, live telephone or real-time electronic contact" with potential clients where a ***"significant motive"*** for the contact is the ***"lawyer's personal gain."*** [Model Rule 7.3(a)]

(1) Permitted Exceptions

A lawyer may have such otherwise-prohibited contact with (i) another lawyer, or (ii) a person with whom the lawyer has a "family, close personal or other prior professional relationship." [Model Rule 7.3(a)]

e.g. **Example:** A lawyer may make unsolicited telephone calls to persons for whom she has previously drafted wills, advising them of changes in tax laws affecting the tax treatment of the will provisions, and may accept employment to revise the wills accordingly. [***In re* Madsen,** 370 N.E.2d 199 (Ill. 1977)]

(2) Duress Prohibited

The Model Rules prohibit contact with any prospective client if (i) the person has made known to the lawyer a ***desire not to be solicited***; or (ii) the solicitation involves ***coercion, duress, or harassment.*** [Model Rule 7.3(b)]

(3) Warning to Be Affixed

All written or recorded communications with a prospective client ***known to be in need of legal services in a particular matter*** must also say ***"Advertising Material"*** on the envelope or the recording. [Model Rule 7.3(c)]

MODEL RULES APPROACH TO DIRECT CONTACT SOLICITATION

GILBERT

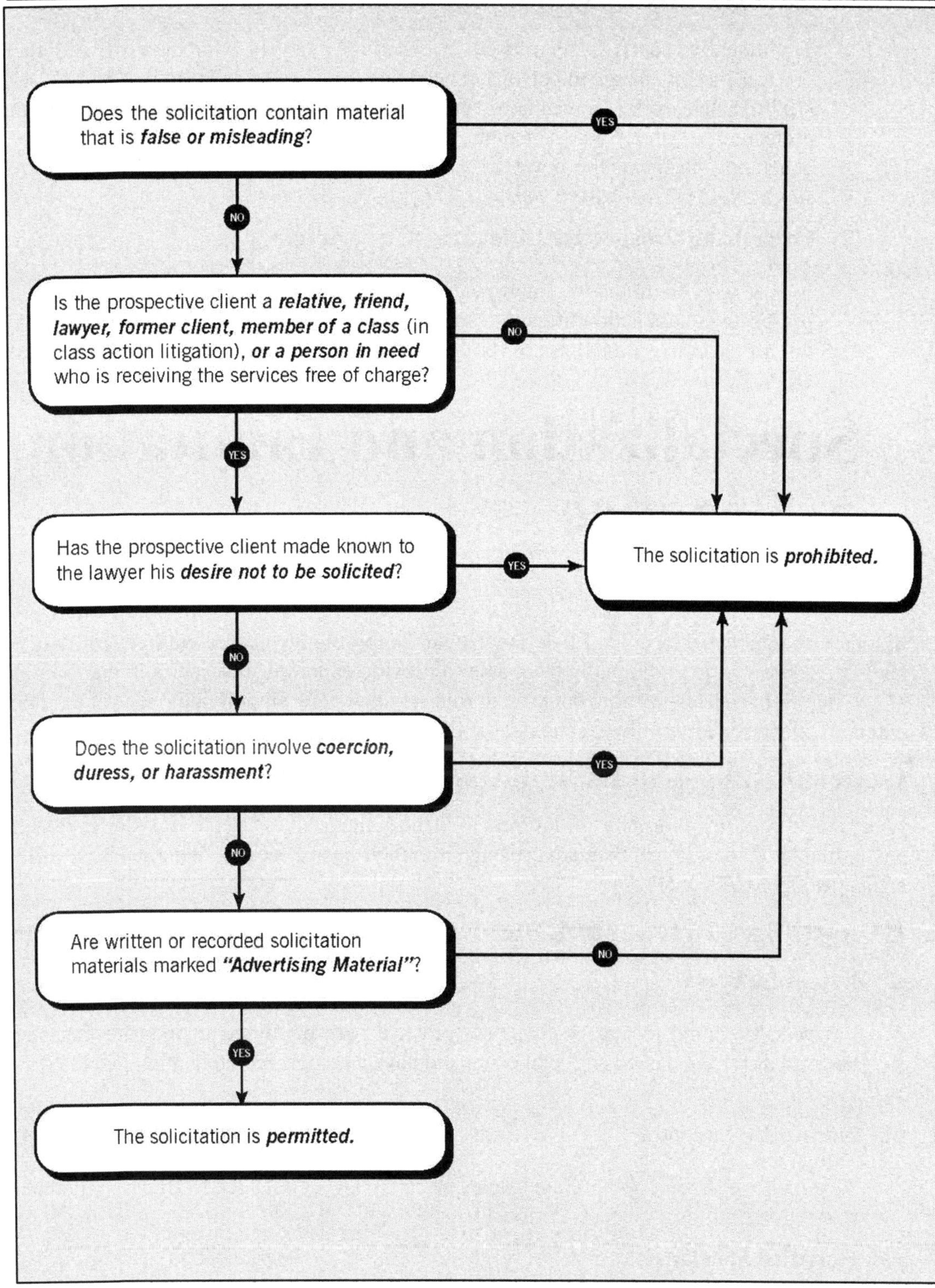

c. **Other Exceptions to General Prohibition on Solicitation**

(1) **Services Offered to Persons in Need**

Traditionally, courts have refused to discipline lawyers who have offered their services ***free of charge*** to persons in need thereof. [*See* ***In re*** **Primus,** 436 U.S. 412 (1978)] Such work is a means of "political expression and association" within the protection of the First Amendment. Furthermore, unlike solicitation of fee-generating business, the potential for overreaching is too slight. [***In re*** **Primus,** *supra*; **NAACP v. Button,** *supra*, p. 156]

(2) **Organizing Prospective Litigants—Class Action**

It was also traditionally improper for lawyers to ***initiate*** the organization of prospective class action litigants, but the Supreme Court has held that a court may not set excessive limits on lawyer contact with prospective class members. [**Gulf Oil v. Bernard,** 450 U.S. 907 (1981)]

C. Specialization and Limitation of Practice

1. Introduction

In today's complicated legal world, no lawyer can be thoroughly competent in every field of law. Large firms have traditionally been able to provide expert legal services in many fields of law by de facto specialization, but present rules regulate how an individual lawyer may tell potential clients the kinds of work she is qualified and willing to do.

2. General Rule—No Designation of Specialty

As a general rule, it is ***improper*** for lawyers to identify themselves as specialists or experts in any particular field of law in their advertising or on their business cards, letterheads, or office signs. [Model Rule 7.4(d)]

3. Exceptions to General Rule

a. **Patent Lawyers**

Lawyers "admitted to engage in patent practice" are permitted to indicate this fact, because they have passed a special exam and have a recognized credential. [Model Rule 7.4(b)]

b. **Admiralty Lawyers**

As a matter of tradition, the Model Rules permit a lawyer engaged in admiralty practice to designate this as a specialty. [Model Rule 7.4(c)]

c. **Certified Specialists**

Lawyers may hold themselves out as specialists if they have been certified by an appropriate authority.

(1) State Certification Programs

A number of states have programs to certify lawyers as specialists; *e.g.,* California certifies specialists in taxation, criminal law, family law, and workers' compensation. Such programs typically require proof of qualifying experience in the specialty field (such as five years of practice, more than 50% of which is devoted to the specialty) and/or the passing of a written examination.

(2) Certification by Private Organizations

Although the law once required certification by an authority ***sanctioned by the state,*** the Supreme Court has held that a state may not limit specialty certification to state agencies, and a lawyer may not be disciplined for noting on a letterhead that the lawyer has been "certified" as a specialist by an independent private organization if the claim is both ***verifiable*** and ***true.*** [**Peel v. Attorney Registration & Disciplinary Commission of Illinois,** 496 U.S. 91 (1990)]

(3) Model Rules Requirements

The ABA has amended the Model Rules to recognize private certification as well as state-sanctioned certification. However, a lawyer may not hold himself out as a specialist unless the certifying organization is identified and has been accredited by a state authority or the ABA. [Model Rule 7.4(d)]

EXCEPTIONS TO NO DESIGNATION OF SPECIALTY RULE (GILBERT)
THE GENERAL RULE IS THAT LAWYERS MAY *NOT* IDENTIFY THEMSELVES AS SPECIALISTS OR EXPERTS IN A FIELD *EXCEPT FOR:*
☑ ***Patent*** lawyers ☑ ***Admiralty*** lawyers ☑ Lawyers ***certified as specialists*** by a certifying body ***approved by a state authority or the ABA.***

4. Limitation of Practice

In contrast to specialization, both the ABA Code and Model Rules recognize the concept of "***limited practice***" that describes what the lawyer is and is not prepared to undertake and carries with it ***no implication of special skill.*** The Model Rules ***do not limit*** or prescribe the fields of law by which a lawyer may describe her practice except that the description may not be false or misleading. [Model Rule 7.4(a)]

EXAM TIP GILBERT

Keep in mind the different rules for ***designating a specialty*** and ***limiting a practice*** to certain areas of law: A lawyer ***cannot call herself a specialist or an expert*** except in the very limited areas of patent and admiralty law or when she has been certified by an appropriate state or ABA authority, but she may ***freely limit her practice*** as long as her statements are truthful and not misleading. The reason for the difference is that calling oneself a specialist is thought to mislead clients by indicating that the lawyer has special knowledge or skill, which she may or may not have. On the other hand, merely stating that one limits practice to certain areas, or does not handle certain types of cases, does not in and of itself imply special knowledge or skill.

D. Division of Fees with Lawyers Outside One's Firm

1. Introduction

"Fee splitting" has long been attractive to many lawyers for reasons closely related to specialization. If a lawyer's client needs help in an area of law where the lawyer is not up-to-date, the lawyer would like to send the client to someone who is skilled in the area and who would share what the client pays with the referring lawyer.

a. Concern About Referral Fees

The traditional concern about referral fees has been that a lawyer who receives compensation in return for referring a case or client may refer potential clients to the lawyer who pays the most, rather than to the lawyer who is most competent.

b. Sharing Work on the Case

For many years before the Model Rules, the referring lawyer could do some work on the case and the receiving lawyer would do the rest. Each lawyer would be paid in proportion to the work each did. [See Model Rule 1.5(d)(1)—division "in proportion to the services performed"]

2. Model Rules Requirements for Fee Splitting

Under the Model Rules, lawyers who assume ***joint responsibility*** for a matter may share the fee in ***whatever proportions they agree***, regardless of how much work each does. [Model Rule 1.5(e)(1)]

a. Joint Responsibility as Sharing Malpractice Liability

The meaning of joint responsibility is simple—the referring lawyer agrees to be jointly liable for any malpractice committed by the lawyer to whom the matter is referred. [**Elane v. St. Bernard Hospital,** 672 N.E.2d 820 (Ill. 1996)]

b. Analogy to Practice in a Law Firm

The rationale for this standard is that it encourages the referring lawyer to send the matter to someone who will handle it competently. Furthermore, it is what a lawyer expects of partners in a law firm where it is common to refer work on a case to a lawyer other than the one to whom the client first came.

c. Client Must Consent in Writing to Terms of the Referral

Unlike the practice in most law firms, however, the Model Rules require that the client be told the ***share of the fee that each lawyer will receive***, and the client's agreement to the arrangement must be **"*confirmed in writing*."** [Model Rule 1.5(e)(2) and comment 7]

d. Total Fee Must Be Reasonable

Finally, the total fee received by the referring and receiving lawyers must be reasonable. That is unremarkable, because it is true of any legal fee, but notice that it is not an absolute requirement that the fee need be no higher than it would have been if only a single lawyer were involved.

E. Departing from a Law Firm

Far more than in earlier years, lawyers today join and leave law practice organizations. That reality has implications for conflicts of interest and screening, considered in Chapter IV of this Summary, but it also affects the relationships among lawyers while at a particular firm.

1. Noncompetition Agreements

Many non-law business organizations protect their customer relationships by having each employee sign a covenant not to complete if they leave the organization. Law firms ***can't do*** that. To ensure that lawyers are not bound to their firms forever, the ABA Model Rules *forbid* agreements that *restrict* the right of a lawyer to practice after termination of the relationship, except as a condition for continued payment of retirement benefits. [Model Rule 5.6(a)]

2. How to Leave a Law Firm

Law firms and other practice organizations typically have detailed partnership agreements whose terms control most aspects of their work. Partnerships are also governed by principles of agency law, however, that impose fiduciary obligations on the partners and may limit the otherwise plenary right to leave the law firm. [Restatement § 9(1) & (2)]

a. Not Take Property of the Partnership

Ordinarily, as part of leaving a law partnership, a lawyer may not take partnership assets such as office supplies, books or client files.

b. Contacts with Clients Prior to Leaving the Firm

Among the most important assets a law partnership has are its relationship with clients. The same fiduciary duty that prohibits stealing pencils is sometimes cited as prohibiting contact with firm clients in an effort to get them to follow the departing lawyer to her new firm.

(1) Clients Are Not Merchandise

The problem with that logic, however, is that clients are not property; clients are entitled to choose whom they want to be their lawyers. Thus, the ethical question becomes how to give clients freedom to make that choice, and how to give both the old firm and the departing lawyer a fair chance to attract them.

(2) Contact with Clients Only After Giving Notice to Firm

The basic rule has become that a lawyer or group of lawyers who is leaving a firm may contact only clients on whose matters the lawyer is "actively and substantially" working, and only after giving "adequate and timely" notice to the firm of the lawyer's intent to depart and to contact firm clients. [Restatement § 9(3)]

c. Contacts After the Lawyer Has Left the Firm

After a lawyer has left the firm, a lawyer may contact firm clients just as any other lawyer could, i.e., subject to the limitations on lawyer advertising and solicitation. [Restatement § 9(4)]

3. Sale of a Lawyer's Practice

a. How the Issue Arises

A lawyer who retires or otherwise leaves practice may wish to sell that practice to a *nonpartner* for a price that reflects "*goodwill*," *i.e.,* future fees the new lawyer will earn because of the firm's reputation. Sale of goodwill was once prohibited, based on the principle we have just seen, *i.e.*, that "clients are not merchandise" who are subject to valuation and sale.

b. How Model Rule 1.17 Deals with the Issues Presented

Model Rule 1.17 allows a lawyer (typically in a solo-practice) who wants to leave law altogether, retire, or move to a new area, to get the kind of financial benefit available to a partner in a private law firm. That partner may be paid the current value of the capital she contributed to the firm, so Model Rule 1.17 now says that a solo or small firm lawyer may sell her practice at a price that includes goodwill *if:*

i. ***The selling lawyer entirely ceases practice,*** or ceases practicing in the ***area of practice being sold,*** and in the jurisdiction where the practice has been conducted;

ii. ***The practice or area of practice is sold in its entirety*** to one or more lawyers or law firms;

iii. ***Written notice is given to each client*** that the client may retain other counsel and need not continue with the lawyer buying the practice (but the client's silence may be taken as consent to the sale); and

iv. ***Clients' fees are not increased*** because of the sale. [Model Rule 1.17]

c. Practical Importance of This Rule

This rule has not been widely adopted by states around the country, but it is one of those items in the Model Rules that bar examiners like to test to determine whether you really have studied as thoroughly as they hope you have.

Chapter Eight

The Special Responsibilities of Judges

CONTENTS	PAGE

Chapter Approach

Judges are lawyers first and thus subject to the rules of ethical conduct for lawyers. On assuming the bench, they become subject to additional ethical norms. This chapter discusses those additional obligations of judges and limitations on their activities both on and off the bench.

The obligations fall generally into the following groups:

1. The judge's actions ***acting officially***;
2. Bases for judicial ***disqualification***;
3. The judge's ***unofficial*** and ***money-making*** activities; and
4. ***Political activities*** of the judge.

The source of the material in this Chapter is the ABA Model Code of Judicial Conduct (2007). Federal judges are subject to rules that are similar, but not identical to the ABA Model Code.

A. Introduction

1. State Judges

The ***ABA Model Code of Judicial Conduct*** (***"CJC"***) provides detailed rules to regulate the conduct of judges in order to preserve the ***independence*** and ***integrity*** of the judiciary. As is true with the Model Rules relating to the conduct of lawyers, the CJC becomes legally binding on judges only as it is adopted by individual states.

a. Format of Code of Judicial Conduct

The CJC, as amended in 2007, is made up of four Canons. Like the Model Rules, it follows a Restatement-type format, with black-letter rules and accompanying comments.

b. Application to Part-Time Judges

Some lawyers serve as a judge only part of the time, *e.g.*, retired judges who are subject to recall as needed. Those lawyers are subject to the CJC when they serve as a judge, but are excused from some CJC provisions when they do not, *e.g.*, prohibitions regulating the practice of law, involvement in political campaigns or serving as a mediator.

c. Relevance of Code of Judicial Conduct to the MPRE

Like the Model Rules, the content of the CJC is regularly tested on the Multistate Professional Responsibility Examination ("MPRE").

2. Federal Judges

The standards governing federal judges are prescribed by federal statute and by a Code of Conduct for Federal Judges adopted by the U.S. Judicial Conference. They are discussed at pp. 186–187, *infra*.

3. Arbitrators and Other "Private" Judges

The conduct of lawyers who serve as arbitrators, mediators, or other third-party neutrals is regulated by ABA Model Rule 2.4. The conduct of third-party neutrals is *not regulated by the CJC*.

B. General Norms

1. Promote Public Confidence in Judiciary

A judge must ***obey the law,*** including the CJC, and must behave in a manner that promotes public confidence in the ***independence, integrity, and impartiality*** of the judiciary. [CJC Rules 1.1, 1.2]

2. Avoid Appearance of Impropriety

A judge must avoid impropriety and even the "appearance of impropriety." The "appearance of impropriety" standard has been criticized as vague, but the CJC makes it an objective test and defines it as conduct that "would create in reasonable minds a perception that the judge violated this Code or engaged in other conduct that reflects adversely on the judge's honesty, impartiality, temperament, or fitness to serve as a judge." [CJC Rule 1.2 and comment 5]

3. May Not Abuse the Prestige of Judicial Office

A judge may not use the prestige of the office to advance the personal interests of the judge or others, whether, *e.g.,* in business affairs or in seeking to avoid traffic tickets. [CJC Rule 1.3 and comment 1]

a. References and Recommendations

A judge may provide a recommendation or reference based on personal knowledge and may use official letterhead if that would not reasonably be seen as an attempt to exert pressure. [CJC Rule 1.3, comment 2]

b. For-Profit Books

A judge who writes or contributes to a for-profit book should not allow the publisher to exploit the judge's office in advertising; indeed, the judge's contract with the publisher should give the judge sufficient control over advertising to prevent such exploitation. [CJC Rule 1.3, comment 4]

4. Avoid External Influence

A judge may not permit "family, social, political, financial, or other interests or relationships" to influence affect the judge's decisions, or "convey or permit others to convey the impression that any person or organization is in a special position to influence the judge." [CJC Rule 2.4]

5. May Not Testify as a Character Witness

A judge may not testify as a character witness ***unless subpoenaed*** to do so, and the judge should "discourage" parties from requiring the judge to so testify. [CJC Rule 3.3 and comment 1]

EXAM TIP GILBERT

Whenever an exam question involves a judge's conduct ***off the bench*** that is completely separate from her judicial duties, be sure to remember that a judge is the subject of constant public scrutiny and should manifest integrity and impartiality in ***all of her activities,*** whether official or personal, to preserve public confidence in the judiciary.

C. Judge's Official Actions

1. Priority of Judicial Duties

A judge must put her judicial duties ahead of all other personal or extrajudicial activities. [CJC Rule 2.1]

2. Behavior on the Bench

A judge must be faithful to the law and perform all judicial duties ***fairly, impartially, competently, and diligently***. [CJC Rules 2.2, 2.5(A)]

a. Hear All Cases

A judge must hear and decide all assigned cases ***unless disqualified*** from a case. [CJC Rule 2.7]

b. Order and Decorum in Court

A judge must maintain order and decorum in the courtroom. [CJC Rule 2.8(A)]

c. Right to Be Heard

A judge must assure every person with a legal interest in a proceeding "the right to be heard according to law." [CJC Rule 2.6(A)]

d. Encouraging Settlement

A judge may encourage parties and counsel to settle a matter but may not act in a manner that coerces any party to settle. If the judge's involvement during settlement influences the judge's decisionmaking ability, disqualification may be appropriate. [CJC Rule 2.6(B) and comment 3]

e. Relations with Others

A judge must be ***patient, dignified, and courteous*** to litigants, lawyers, jurors, witnesses, and others with whom the judge deals in an official capacity. He also must require the same conduct of lawyers appearing in the court, court staff, and any other persons subject to the judge's direction and control. [CJC Rule 2.8(B)]

f. Performance of Duties Without Bias or Prejudice

A judge must not, by words or conduct, ***manifest bias or prejudice or engage in harassment*** based on race, sex, gender, religion, national origin, ethnicity, disability, age, sexual orientation, marital status, socioeconomic status, political affiliation, or any other factor not relevant to an issue in the proceeding. The judge must be careful to avoid suggesting bias through, *e.g.,* attempts at humor and body language. [CJC Rule 2.3 and comment 2]

g. Prohibiting Lawyers and Court Personnel from Manifesting Bias

A judge must prohibit court personnel and lawyers appearing before the judge from manifesting bias or prejudice. Note that lawyers may engage in legitimate advocacy when the above factors are at issue in a proceeding. [CJC Rule 2.3; Model Rule 8.4(g)]

h. Commending or Criticizing Jurors

A judge ***may not commend or criticize jurors*** for their verdict unless he does so in a court order or opinion. [CJC Rule 2.8(C)]

3. Ex Parte Communications

The judge ***may not initiate, permit, or consider*** ex parte communications with parties or their lawyers, ***except*** as otherwise authorized by law, and in the following specific situations [CJC Rule 2.9(A)]:

a. Scheduling Matters and Emergency Situations

The judge may speak with parties ex parte when necessary for administrative purposes, to schedule matters, or to deal with emergency situations that ***do not address substantive matters***, provided that (i) the judge reasonably believes that ***no party will be advantaged*** thereby, and (ii) the judge ***arranges to notify the other parties*** promptly of the substance of the communication and ***gives them a chance to respond***. [CJC Rule 2.9(A)(1)]

b. Discussions in the Context of Settling Cases

With the ***consent of the parties***, the judge ***may meet individually*** with the parties and their lawyers in an effort to ***settle a matter.*** [CJC Rule 2.9(A)(4)]

c. Inadvertent Receipt of Information

A judge who inadvertently receives ex parte information bearing on the substance of a matter must ***promptly notify the parties*** of the substance of the communication and allow them an opportunity to respond. [CJC Rule 2.9(B)]

4. Communications Outside Presence of Parties and Their Lawyers

a. Consultation with Disinterested Expert on the Law

The judge may obtain the written advice of a disinterested expert on the law applicable to a case before the court if the judge ***gives the parties advance notice of the person to be consulted and the subject matter of the advice solicited,*** and gives the parties an opportunity to respond to the notice and the advice received. [CJC Rule 2.9(A)(2)]

b. Consultation with Clerks or Other Judges

The judge may discuss a case with fellow judges and with court personnel who assist the judge with her responsibilities (*e.g.*, the judge's law clerk), provided the judge makes reasonable efforts not to receive factual information that is not part of the record. [CJC Rule 2.9(A)(3)]

5. No Independent Investigation of Facts

A judge must not independently investigate the facts in a case and must consider only the evidence presented. [CJC Rule 2.9(C)]

e.g. **Example:** While reading the transcript of a case, Judge X is confused about the testimony of a witness and telephones the witness for clarification of the issue. Judge X's conduct is improper.

e.g. **Example:** Judge B is presiding over a breach of contract action. To learn more about the character of the parties and the facts of the case, he conducted Internet research and gathers information beyond that which is likely to be disclosed during the trial. Judge B's conduct is improper.

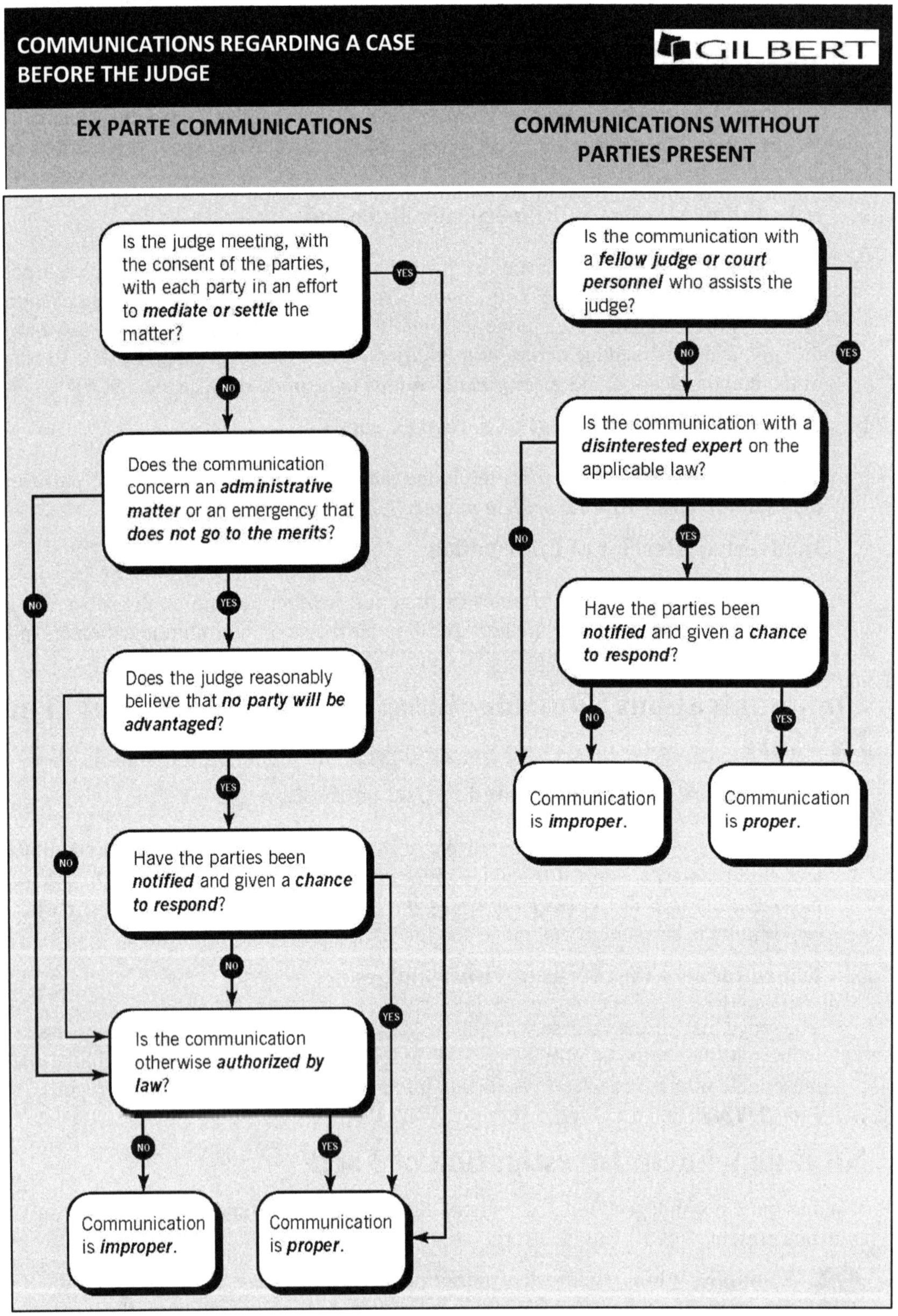

6. Relations with News Media

A judge must not make a public statement, and must require that court personnel refrain from making comments, about a pending or impending matter that might reasonably be expected to

affect the matter's outcome or impair its fairness. Also, a judge must not make a nonpublic statement that might substantially ***interfere with a fair trial.*** [CJC Rule 2.10(A), (C)]

a. No Pledges or Promises About Cases or Issues

A judge must not make public pledges, promises, or commitments about cases or issues "likely to come before the court" that are ***inconsistent with impartial performance*** of the judge's duties. [CJC Rule 2.10(B)]

b. Distinguish—Permitted Public Statements

A judge may make other public statements, such as ***explanations of the status of proceedings or court procedures.*** The judge may also comment on a case in which the judge is a party and may respond to criticism of the judge's conduct in a matter. [CJC Rule 2.10(D), (E)]

7. Supervisory and Administrative Duties of the Judge

The judge must require that court personnel and other judges subject to the judge's supervision act in a manner consistent with the CJC. [CJC Rule 2.12]

a. No Unnecessary Appointments

A judge appointing receivers, trustees, and the like may not do so unnecessarily, must ***base appointments on merit,*** and must ***avoid nepotism and favoritism.*** [CJC Rule 2.13(A)]

b. No Reward for Campaign Contributions

A judge ***may not appoint a lawyer*** to such a paid position if the judge knows or learns that the lawyer or his spouse or domestic partner ***contributed more than a sum prescribed by state law*** to the judge's campaign, unless the lawyer has been selected in rotation from a list compiled without regard to political contributions, or unless no other lawyer can be found who is willing, competent, and able to accept the position. [CJC Rule 2.13(B)]

c. No Excessive Compensation

A judge must not approve compensation for appointees ***beyond the fair value of services rendered.*** [CJC Rule 2.13(C)]

8. Responding to Judicial or Lawyer Misconduct

A judge must inform the appropriate disciplinary authority when the judge ***knows*** that a lawyer or another judge has committed a violation of the Rules of Professional Conduct or CJC that raises a ***substantial question*** regarding the lawyer's or judge's ***honesty, trustworthiness, or fitness*** as a lawyer or judge in other respects. [CJC Rule 2.15(A), (B)]

a. Substantial Likelihood of Violation

A judge must take "appropriate action" when the judge learns information indicating a ***substantial likelihood*** that a lawyer or judge has violated the Rules of Professional Conduct or CJC. [CJC Rule 2.15(C), (D)]

b. Disability and Impairment

A judge with ***reasonable belief*** that the performance of a lawyer or another judge is impaired by substance abuse or by a mental, emotional, or physical condition must take action to help the judge or lawyer. Appropriate action may include a confidential referral to an assistance program or notifying a person with supervisory duties over the judge or lawyer. [CJC Rule 2.14 and comment]

9. Cooperation with Disciplinary Authorities

A judge must cooperate with judicial and lawyer disciplinary agencies and may not retaliate against any person who assists in such an investigation. [CJC Rule 2.16]

D. Judicial Disqualification

1. Bases for Disqualification

A judge is disqualified to act in any proceeding in which the judge's ***"impartiality might reasonably be questioned."*** The CJC lists several such situations, but states that there may be others. [CJC Rule.2.11(A)]

a. Personal Bias Concerning a Party

The judge is disqualified if she "has a personal bias or prejudice concerning a party or a party's lawyer." [CJC Rule 2.11(A)(1)]

(1) Distinguish—Policy Issue

A judge is ***not necessarily disqualified*** where the bias is with respect to a ***policy issue***. Thus, an African-American judge is not ordinarily disqualified to sit in a civil rights case, and either a male or female judge may hear a sex discrimination case.

(2) Extrajudicial Source Factor and Pervasive Bias Exception

Normally, to be disqualified for bias, the judge's alleged bias also must come from an ***"extrajudicial source"***; what the judge learns in a courtroom inevitably is a part of the judge's decision and is ordinarily not "bias or prejudice." However, a ***"pervasive bias" exception*** applies even to the extrajudicial source doctrine. Whenever the judge has a ***"clear inability to render fair judgment,"*** the judge's disqualification is required. [**Liteky v. United States,** 510 U.S. 540 (1994); **United States v. Microsoft Corp.,** 253 F.3d 34 (D.C. Cir. 2001)]

EXAM TIP GILBERT

Although a judge may be disqualified because of a bias acquired from an ***extrajudicial*** source, remember these caveats:

(i) ***Not every*** opinion derived from a source outside of judicial proceedings is cause for disqualification (*e.g.*, bias concerning a policy issue).

(ii) A judge's opinions based on facts introduced during the proceedings may be ***so extreme*** and undeserved that disqualification is necessary because a ***fair judgment is impossible*** (pervasive bias exception).

b. Knowledge of Disputed Evidentiary Facts

A judge is also disqualified if the judge has ***knowledge about disputed facts*** in the case. [CJC Rule 2.11(A)(1)]

c. Prior Involvement in the Matter

A judge may not hear a case in which the judge ***served as a lawyer*** before coming on the bench or in which she ***previously presided*** in another court. Also, a judge may not hear a case if she was ***associated*** in law practice with a lawyer who handled the case at the time they practiced together or if the judge served as a ***material witness*** in the case. [CJC Rule 2.11(A)(6)]

d. Cases Involving Judge's Relatives

The judge is disqualified if the judge's spouse, domestic partner, or someone within the third degree of relationship to either of them, or the spouse or domestic partner of such a relative is:

(i) A party to the proceeding, or the officer, director, general partner, managing member, or trustee of a party;

(ii) Acting as a lawyer in the proceeding;

(iii) Known by the judge to have a more than de minimis interest that could be substantially affected by the proceeding; or

(iv) Likely to be a material witness in the case.

[CJC Rule 2.11(A)(2)]

(1) "Third Degree of Relationship"

The "third degree of relationship" is calculated according to the civil law system and includes parents, grandparents, great-grandparents, siblings, aunts and uncles, nieces and nephews, children, grandchildren, and great-grandchildren. [CJC Terminology]

(2) Scope of Obligation to Inquire

The judge must make *reasonable efforts* to be informed about the financial interests of her spouse, domestic partner, and minor children residing in the judge's household. [CJC Rule 2.11(B)]

(3) "De Minimis" Interest

A de minimis interest is an insignificant interest that ***does not raise a reasonable question regarding the judge's impartiality.*** [CJC Terminology]

e. Financial Interest in Party or Subject Matter of Litigation

A judge is disqualified if she knows that she or a family member has an ***economic interest*** in a party or in the subject matter of the proceeding. [CJC Rule 2.11(A)(3)]

(1) Whose Interest Can Be Disqualifying

The disqualifying interest may be that of the judge's ***spouse, domestic partner, parent, child, or any other family member residing in the judge's household***. An interest that the judge has acting as a ***fiduciary*** (*i.e.*, an executor, administrator, trustee, or guardian) is also disqualifying.

(2) Economic Interest Defined

A judge has an economic interest if she has more than a *de minimis* legal or equitable interest. Ordinarily, the following are ***not disqualifying*** interests [CJC Terminology]:

(a) Mutual Fund

Ownership of a mutual fund does not constitute a financial interest in the firms whose securities are held by the fund, unless the judge is a manager of the fund or the case could substantially affect the value of the fund.

(b) Nonprofit Organization

An office in an educational, charitable, fraternal, or civic organization does not constitute an interest in the securities held by the organization.

(c) Policyholder or Depositor

The judge's interest as a policyholder in a mutual insurance company or depositor in a mutual savings association is not disqualifying unless the interest could be substantially affected by the result of the case.

(d) Government Securities

A judge who holds government securities is not disqualified from hearing cases involving the government unless the value of the securities could be substantially affected by the judgment in the case.

f. Persons Making Contributions to Judge's Election Campaign

A judge who is subject to public election must disqualify herself if she knows, or learns through a timely motion, that a party, a party's lawyer, or the firm of the party's lawyer has, within a designated number of prior years, made contributions to the judge's election campaign that ***exceeds*** the jurisdiction's specified amount. [CJC Rule 2.11(A)(4)]

g. Statement Committing Judge to Reach Particular Result

A judge must withdraw from hearing a case if the judge has made a public statement, other than in open court or a judicial decision or opinion, that commits or appears to commit the judge to rule in a particular way in the case. [CJC Rule 2.11(A)(5)]

CHECKLIST OF BASES FOR DISQUALIFICATION OF A JUDGE GILBERT

A JUDGE MAY BE DISQUALIFIED FOR:

- ☑ Having a ***personal bias or prejudice*** against a party or his lawyer
- ☑ Having ***knowledge of facts in dispute***
- ☑ Having a ***prior involvement*** in the matter
- ☑ Having a ***relative involved in the case*** (as a likely witness, a party, or an officer, managing member, general partner, director, or trustee of a party; as a lawyer in the case; or having an interest that could be substantially affected)
- ☑ Having an ***economic interest in a party or the subject matter*** of the proceeding or having a family member with such an interest
- ☑ Receiving ***excessive campaign contributions*** from a party or its lawyer
- ☑ Making a ***public statement indicating that the judge will rule in a particular way*** in a case

2. Remittal of Disqualification

If the judge is disqualified for any reason ***"other than personal bias or prejudice"*** concerning a party, the parties may consider whether to *waive* the judge's disqualification. [CJC Rule 2.11(C)]

a. Procedure

The judge, instead of immediately withdrawing, may disclose on the record the basis of the disqualification and ask the parties and their lawyers to consider, outside the presence of the judge and court personnel, whether to waive the disqualification. [CJC Rule 2.11(C)]

b. Agreement of the Parties and Counsel

If, outside the presence of the judge, all parties and lawyers agree that the judge should not be disqualified, the agreement is included in the record of the case, and the judge may hear the matter. [CJC Rule 2.11(C)]

3. Rule of Necessity

Case law has created a ***rule of necessity*** that ***overrides the rules of disqualification.*** Under this rule, a judge who would otherwise be disqualified because of a conflict of interest may hear a case if there is no other way for the case to be heard (*i.e.*, no other judge is able to hear the case or every judge who might be assigned would also be disqualified). The judge must make reasonable efforts to transfer the matter to a judge who is not disqualified as soon as possible. [CJC Rule 2.11, comment 3]

e.g. **Example:** A state trial judge is assigned to hear a case concerning the constitutionality of a statute that will raise the salary of all trial judges in the state. The judge may hear the case because the reason for disqualification applies equally to all other judges to whom the case might be assigned.

E. Extrajudicial Activities of the Judge

1. In General

A judge may engage in nonjudicial activities, whether or not associated with law, provided that such activities do not:

(i) ***Violate the law***;

(ii) ***Interfere with proper performance*** of the judge's duties;

(iii) ***Lead to frequent disqualification*** of the judge;

(iv) Appear to ***undermine the judge's independence, integrity, or impartiality***;

(v) Appear to ***be coercive***; or

(vi) Make ***unauthorized use of court premises, staff, or other resources,*** unless such use is legal or incidental to activities that concern the law, the legal system, or the administration of justice.

[CJC Rule 3.1]

2. May Speak, Write, Lecture, and Teach

The judge may speak, write, lecture, and teach on ***both legal and nonlegal subjects***, as long as the activities do not violate any other judicial standards. [CJC Rule 3.1, comments] The judge may accept reasonable compensation for these activities provided acceptance of the compensation does not appear to undermine the judge's independence, integrity, or impartiality. [CJC Rule 3.12]

3. May Not Consult with Legislators or Executive Officials

The judge may ***not appear*** in a public hearing or otherwise consult with legislators and executive officials, *except* (i) on matters concerning the law, the legal system, or the administration of justice; (ii) in connection with matters about which the judge acquired knowledge in the course of judicial duties; or (iii) when appearing pro se on the judge's own behalf or in a fiduciary capacity. [CJC Rule 3.2]

4. May Not Serve on Government Commissions

A judge may ***not serve*** on a government commission, board, committee, or other governmental position unless it involves the law, the legal system, or the administration of justice, but a judge ***may serve*** as an official ***representative*** at ceremonies or in connection with ***historical, educational, or cultural activities.*** [CJC Rule 3.4]

5. May Not Use or Disclose Nonpublic Information

A judge must not intentionally disclose or use nonpublic information acquired in the course of performing judicial duties for personal gain or for any other purpose unrelated to judicial duties unless necessary to protect the health and safety of the judge, his family, or staff. [CJC Rule 3.5 and comments]

6. May Not Be a Member of a Discriminatory Organization

A judge may ***not be a member*** of any organization that "practices ***invidious discrimination*** on the basis of race, sex, gender, religion, national origin, ethnicity, or sexual orientation." When a judge learns that an organization so discriminates, the judge must immediately resign from the organization. [CJC Rule 3.6(A) and comment 3]

a. When Discrimination Is "Invidious"

Discrimination is "invidious" if it arbitrarily excludes persons from membership in an organization on any of the prohibited grounds. Judges must be attentive to whether an organization is so acting. The organization's membership rolls do not alone determine the issue; rather, the judge should verify reality, *e.g.*, the manner in which the organization selects it members. [CJC Rule 3.6, comment 2]

b. Distinguish—Permissible Organizations

A judge may be a member of a ***completely private*** organization whose membership limitations could not be constitutionally prohibited ***or*** an organization that is "***dedicated to the preservation of religious, ethnic, or cultural values*** of legitimate common interest to its members." [CJC Rule 3.6, comment 2]

e.g. **Example:** Judge Alvarez belongs to the Lansing Library Reading Group, open only to Lansing citizens, who meet each month to talk about a specific work. Judge Brant belongs to the American Indian Society, whose members promote cross-cultural awareness and are descendants of Native Americans. Judge Connors is a member of the alumni association of Heathmoor Women's College). None of these organizations practices invidious discrimination, and the judges' memberships are permissible.

c. May Not Use Facilities of a Prohibited Organization

A judge may not use the facilities of an organization that the judge would not be permitted to join, except that the judge may attend isolated events at such facilities, *e.g.*, a wedding reception, if attendance does not reasonably suggest an endorsement of the organization's practices. [CJC Rule 3.6(B)]

JUDGE'S MEMBERSHIP IN DISCRIMINATORY ORGANIZATIONS—EXAMPLES GILBERT

PERMISSIBLE	IMPERMISSIBLE
Monday night men-only poker club consisting of judge and his college chums	Men-only social club with 6,000 members and dining and health club facilities
Women's support group for breastfeeding mothers	Women's bar association that refuses to admit male members
Talmudic study group that limits membership to members of the judge's temple	Country club that excludes members on the basis of race or religion

7. May Participate in Educational, Religious, Charitable, Fraternal, and Civic Organizations

Subject to the general limitations regarding extrajudicial activities (*see supra*, p. 177), a judge ***may be a member of***, and ***serve*** as an officer, director, trustee, or nonlegal advisor of nonprofit educational, religious, charitable, fraternal, and civic organizations. [CJC Rule 3.7(A)]

a. Distinguish—Organization That Often Litigates

A judge may ***not serve*** as an officer, director, trustee, or advisor of an organization: (i) engaged in litigation that would ordinarily come before the judge, or (ii) engaged frequently in litigation in the court on which the judge serves or a court subject to the judge's appellate jurisdiction. [CJC Rule 3.7(A)(6)]

b. May Participate in Planning Organization's Fundraising and Investment Decisions

The judge may assist the organization in planning fundraising and making investment decisions. [CJC Rule 3.7(A)(1)]

c. May Appear at Events of Organization

The judge may ***attend or speak at events*** of the organization and may ***receive an award*** or other recognition from the organization. The judge also may ***permit his title to be used in connection with the event*** unless the purpose of the event is fundraising, in which case the judge's title may be used only if the event concerns the law, legal system, or administration of justice. [CJC Rule 3.7(A)(4)]

d. Limits on Raising Money for Organization

The judge may ***solicit contributions*** for the organization but only from members of his family and from other judges over whom he does not have supervisory authority. The judge also may ***solicit memberships*** for the organization, or ***make recommendations to a fund-granting organization***, but only if the organization concerns the law, legal system, or administration of justice. [CJC Rule 3.7(A)(2), (3), (5)]

EXTRAJUDICIAL ACTIVITIES OF JUDGE GILBERT
SPEAKING, WRITING, LECTURING, AND TEACHING:
• Must ***not violate any other judicial standards***; and • Acceptance of ***compensation must not undermine judge's independence, integrity, or impartiality***
APPEARING AT HEARING BEFORE OR CONSULTATION WITH EXECUTIVE OR LEGISLATIVE OFFICIALS:
• Must concern the ***law, legal system, or administration of justice***; or • Must be in connection with matters ***about which the judge acquired knowledge in the course of judicial duties***; or • Pro se to ***protect judge's own interest*** or in a fiduciary capacity
SERVING ON GOVERNMENTAL COMMISSION:
• Must relate to the ***law, legal system, or administration of justice***; or • Represents governmental unit on ***purely ceremonial grounds*** or for a historical, educational, or cultural activity
USING OR DISCLOSING NONPUBLIC INFORMATION:
• Only if ***necessary to protect health and safety*** of the judge, his family, and staff
MEMBERSHIP IN ORGANIZATIONS:
• Organization ***must not practice invidious discrimination*** on the basis of race, sex, gender, religion, national origin, ethnicity, or sexual orientation • May be a member or serve as director, officer, trustee or advisor of ***nonprofit*** educational, religious, charitable, fraternal, and civic organizations

F. Money-Making Activities of the Judge

1. In General

As with other "outside" activities of a judge, all financial activities are subject to the requirements that they do not: (i) ***interfere with judicial duties,*** (ii) ***lead to frequent disqualification***, or (iii) ***involve the judge in dealings with persons likely to come before the court.*** [CJC Rule 3.11(C)]

2. Investments

With the above qualifications, a judge ***may*** hold and manage financial investments, including those of the judge's family. However, the judge must manage investments so as to minimize circumstances in which she would be disqualified and divest herself of investments that might require frequent disqualification. [CJC Rule 3.11(A) and comment 2]

3. Participation in a Business

A judge ***may not*** serve as officer, director, manager, advisor, or employee of any business ***except a closely-held family business or investment trust.*** Even in such cases, the judge must divest herself of investments that might require frequent disqualification. [CJC Rule 3.11(B) and comment 2]

4. Acting as Arbitrator or Mediator

A judge ***may not*** act as an ***arbitrator or mediator*** unless expressly authorized by law. [CJC Rule 3.9]

5. Practice of Law

A judge ***may not practice law***, but may act pro se and may give legal advice to family members without compensation. [CJC Rule 3.10]

6. Fiduciary Activities

A judge ***may not*** act as executor, administrator, trustee, guardian, or other fiduciary ***except for a member of the judge's family***, and even then only if the work ***will not interfere*** with the judge's official duties and not come before a court on which the judge serves or one under the judge's appellate jurisdiction. [CJC Rule 3.8(A), (B)]

a. Limitation on Financial Activities

A judge acting as a fiduciary is subject to the same restrictions on financial holdings and transactions as when acting for herself. [CJC Rule 3.8(C)]

b. Duty upon Becoming a Judge

A judge must comply with the rules on fiduciary service "as soon as reasonably practicable, but in no event later than one year after becoming a judge." [CJC Rule 3.8(D)]

7. Other Extrajudicial Activities

In addition to being paid reasonable compensation to speak, write, and teach *(see supra*, p. 178), a judge may engage in other extrajudicial activities provided the compensation is reasonable for the work performed and the activities do not undermine the judge's independence, integrity, or impartiality. [CJC Rule 3.12]

8. Gifts, Bequests, Favors, or Loans

A judge ordinarily may accept gifts, loans, bequests, benefits, or other things of value unless acceptance is prohibited by law or would ***appear*** to a reasonable person ***to undermine the judge's independence, integrity, or impartiality.*** [CJC Rule 3.13(A)]. The following gifts, etc., may be accepted:

(1) ***Items with little intrinsic value***, *e.g.,* a plaque or certificate [CJC Rule 3.13(B)(1)];

(2) ***Gifts from someone whose relationship with the judge would already require disqualification*** [CJC Rule 3.13(B)(2)];

(3) ***Ordinary social hospitality*** [CJC Rule 3.13(B)(3)];

(4) ***Commercial or financial opportunities,*** including loans from financial institutions that are available on the same terms to people who are not judges [CJC Rule 3.13(B)(4)];

(5) ***Complimentary books and materials supplied by publishers for official use*** [CJC Rule 3.13(B)(7)];

(6) ***Gifts, awards, or benefits associated with the separate activity of the judge's spouse, domestic partner, or other family member*** residing in the judge's household that only incidentally benefits the judge [CJC Rule 3.11(B)(8)];

(7) ***Rewards and prizes from random drawings*** [CJC Rule 3.13(B)(5)];

(8) ***Scholarships and similar benefits*** awarded on the same terms as for others [CJC Rule 3.13(B)(6)];

(9) ***A gift incident to a public testimonial*** [CJC Rule 3.13 (C) (1)];

(10) ***A free invitation*** to the judge and a guest ***to attend a bar-related function*** or ***event associated with any other educational, religious, charitable, fraternal, or civic activity of the judge*** [CJC Rule 3.13(C)(2)]; and

(11) ***A gift or other benefit from a lawyer or party whose interests, if they have or are likely to come before the judge, would require the judge's disqualification.*** [CJC Rule 3.13(C)(3)].

9. Reimbursement of Expenses and Waivers of Fees

A judge may accept reimbursement of ***necessary and reasonable expenses for participation in extrajudicial activities*** such as educational seminars**.** Reimbursed expenses are limited to actual expenses of the judge and, where appropriate, the judge's spouse, domestic partner, or guest. [CJC Rule 3.14(A), (B)]

a. Factors for Judge to Consider When Accepting Reimbursement or Fee Waiver

In determining whether to accept reimbursement or a fee waiver, the judge should consider whether or not, *e.g.,* the entity is an accredited school rather than a trade association, the organization is funded by multiple groups rather than a few, the program is primarily educational rather than recreational, differing viewpoints are presented, and the subject matter involves contested matters likely to come before the judge. [CJC Rule 3.14, comment 3]

10. Reporting Compensation, Gifts, and Reimbursements

A judge ***must publicly report*** the amount or value of: (i) ***compensation*** received for extrajudicial activities; (ii) the receipt of *certain gifts*; and (iii) ***reimbursement of expenses and waiver of fees or charges*** for her extrajudicial activities to the extent required by. [CJC Rule 3.15(A)]

a. Time for Making Report

The CJC requires public reporting at least ***annually.*** However, reports of reimbursement of expenses and waiver of fees or charges must be made within 30 days after the conclusion of the event or program. [CJC Rule 3.15(C)]

b. Gifts that Must Be Reported

The amount or value of the following gifts must be publicly reported: (i) gifts incident to a public testimonial; (ii) free invitations to attend bar-related functions or other educational, religious, charitable, fraternal, or civic events; and (iii) gifts or other benefits from a lawyer or party whose interests are likely to come before the judge. [CJC Rule 3.15(A)(2)]

c. Reporting Expense Reimbursements and Waiver of Fees or Charges

A judge must also publicly report the amount of expenses reimbursed and fees waived for the judge and the judge's spouse, domestic partner or guest, as permitted by Rule 3.14. [CJC Rule 3.15(A)(3)]

d. Exception to Reporting Requirements

Gifts and reimbursements of expenses and waiver of fees may be ***accepted without publicly reporting*** them if their value, either alone or in aggregation with other items from the same source, does not exceed a dollar amount determined by other state law. [CJC Rule 3.15(A)]

G. Involvement of Judges and Judicial Candidates in Political Activities

1. In General

The rules on political activity of judges apply as well to ***lawyers running for judicial office.*** [CJC Rule 4.1(A); Model Rule 8.2(b)] Except as permitted by law or by the CJC with respect to a judge's or judicial candidate's own candidacy for election, the following rules apply:

a. No Office in Political Organization

A judge or judicial candidate may not act as a leader in, hold office in, seek endorsement from, or publicly identify herself as a member of a political organization. [CJC Rule 4.1(A)(1), (6), (7)]

b. No Endorsements of Political Candidates or Speeches for Political Organizations

A judge or judicial candidate may not speak on behalf of a political organization or publicly endorse or oppose a candidate for public office (*but see infra*, p. 184). [CJC Rule 4.1(A)(2), (3)]

c. No Political Fundraising

A judge or judicial candidate ***may not raise money*** for, ***pay an assessment*** to, ***make a contribution*** to, or ***attend or purchase tickets*** for events for a political organization or for another candidate for public office (*but see infra*, p. 184). [CJC Rule 4.1(A)(4), (5)]

d. Limits on Use of Campaign Resources

A judge or judicial candidate may not use campaign contributions for her ***private benefit*** and may not use court staff, facilities, or resources in a campaign. [CJC Rule 4.1(A)(9), (10)]

e. Limits on Statements

A judge or judicial candidate may not make any statement that is: (i) knowingly ***false or misleading***; (ii) in ***reckless disregard for its truth***; or (iii) reasonably ***expected to affect the outcome or impair the fairness of a matter*** before a court. [CJC Rule 4.1(A)(11), (12)]

f. Limits on Pledges, Promises, or Commitments

A judge or judicial candidate may not make a pledge, promise, or commitment about matters likely to come before the court that is ***inconsistent with the impartial performance of her judicial duties.*** [CJC Rule 4.1(A)(13)]

g. Ensure No Violation of These Rules by Others

A judge or judicial candidate must take reasonable measures to ensure that other persons do not act on behalf of the judge in ways that would violate the above rules. [CJC Rule 4.1(B)]

2. Election Campaign for Judicial Office

a. In General

A candidate for election or reelection ***must***: (i) act consistently with the ***independence, integrity, and impartiality*** of the judiciary; (ii) comply with all ***election laws***; (iii) review the ***content of campaign statements and materials***; and (iv) take reasonable measures to ensure that ***others do not act on behalf of the candidate*** in ways the candidate could not act. [CJC Rule 4.2(A)]

b. Permitted Activities

A candidate for judicial office ***may***, unless prohibited by law:

(1) ***Form a campaign committee*** to raise money and manage the campaign [CJC Rules 4.2(B)(1), 4.4(A)];

(2) ***Speak and appear in media advertising, websites, and promotional literature*** supporting his candidacy [CJC Rule 4.2(B)(2)];

(3) ***Publicly endorse or oppose other candidates*** for the same judicial office and organize with them to form slates to campaign more effectively [CJC Rule 4.2(B)(3) and comment 7];

(4) ***Attend or buy tickets*** for political events; ***contribute*** to a political organization or candidate; and ***seek, accept, or use endorsements*** of anyone other than a partisan political organization [CJC Rule 4.2(B)(4)–(6)]; and

(5) ***If the election is held on a partisan basis, identify*** himself as a candidate of a political organization and ***accept the endorsement*** of that organization [CJC Rule 4.2(C)].

3. Solicitation of Campaign Contributions

It is ***improper*** for a candidate for judicial office ***personally*** to solicit campaign contributions or endorsements. [CJC Rule 4.1(A)(8)]

a. Distinguish—Committees to Raise Campaign Money

A judicial candidate's campaign committee ***may solicit and accept*** reasonable financial contributions that do not exceed limits established by the CJC or other law. [CJC Rule 4.4(B)(1)]

b. Time Periods for Raising Money

Committee fundraising is limited by the CJC to a period established by state law, but includes a period ***after*** the election in which the judge is running. Thus, this creates a questionable situation of lawyers sending contributions after they know who will be their judge for the next multi-year term. [CJC Rule 4.4(B)(2)]

c. Compliance with Reporting Requirements

A judicial candidate must direct his campaign committee to comply with all laws for disclosure of campaign contributions. [CJC Rule 4.4(B)(3)]

4. Candidates Seeking Appointment to Judicial Office

A person seeking appointment to judicial office ***may***:

a. ***Communicate with the appointing or confirming authority***, including any committee designated to screen candidates [CJC Rule 4.3(A)]; and

b. ***Seek endorsement from any person or organization*** other than a partisan political organization [CJC Rule 4.3(B)].

5. Judge Seeking Nonjudicial Office

a. No Running for Nonjudicial Office

A judge must ***resign*** as judge when seeking election to any nonjudicial office. [CJC Rule 4.5(A)]

b. Judge Seeking Other Government Office

A judge who becomes a candidate for a nonjudicial ***appointive*** office (*e.g.*, an ambassador) is ***not required to resign*** as judge until he actually gets the appointment, if she complies with all other requirements of the CJC. [CJC Rule 4.5(B)]

EXAM TIP GILBERT

When answering a question dealing with the political involvement of a judicial candidate, remember the reasons for the ***limitations*** imposed and the ***exceptions*** to the limitations:

(i) All judicial candidates ***must avoid*** political activity that may create the appearance of ***political bias*** or ***impropriety,*** and because the impartiality of judges is essential to the preservation of public confidence in the judiciary, incumbent judges are subject to additional restrictions;

(ii) Judicial candidates must be careful to avoid making statements that are ***false, misleading, in reckless disregard for truthfulness, or that are expected to affect the fairness of a matter,*** and may not make ***pledges or promises*** about matters likely to come before them;

(iii) Judicial candidates subject to ***public election*** need support for their candidacies, and, therefore, there are ***exceptions*** allowing both judge and nonjudge candidates to ***speak on their own behalf, establish campaign committees*** to solicit public support and financial contributions, publicly ***endorse or oppose*** other candidates, attend ***political events***, and accept the ***endorsement*** of an organization;

(iv) Judicial candidates ***seeking appointment*** or reappointment need to apprise the appointing authority of their qualifications, and ***exceptions*** permit these candidates to communicate with and ***provide information to the appointing authority*** and ***seek endorsement from organizations*** that regularly make recommendations for appointments.

(v) A judge seeking ***election*** to a nonjudicial office must first ***resign as judge***.

H. Standards Applicable to Federal Judges

1. No Practice of Law

A federal judge or justice may not practice law; one who engages in the practice of law is guilty of a "high misdemeanor." [28 U.S.C. § 454]

2. Circumstances in Which Disqualification Is Required

Most of the standards for disqualification of a federal judge—*e.g.,* personal bias toward a party, having served as a lawyer in the matter, and financial interest in the outcome—are *substantially the same* as the standards under the CJC and will not be repeated here. A few disqualification standards, however, are ***different*** or are stated differently:

a. Litigant's Right to File an Affidavit of Bias or Prejudice

A federal district judge must recuse himself upon a litigant's filing of a "timely and sufficient affidavit" asserting that the judge "has a personal bias or prejudice either against him or in favor of any adverse party." The affidavit must be accompanied by a certificate of counsel that the affidavit is made in good faith. [28 U.S.C. § 144]

b. Impartiality Subject to Question

A federal judge, including a Supreme Court Justice, must recuse herself whenever her "impartiality might reasonably be questioned." [28 U.S.C. § 455(a)]

c. Views Expressed While in Government Service

Disqualification is also required whenever the judge or justice, while in other government service, "participated as counsel, adviser, or material witness" concerning the case or "expressed an opinion concerning the merits of the particular case in controversy." [28 U.S.C. § 455(b)(3)]

d. Divesting a Disqualifying Financial Interest

If a disqualifying financial interest is discovered only after substantial time has been devoted to a case, the judge may avoid disqualification by disposing of the interest. [28 U.S.C. § 455(f)]

3. Discipline of Federal Judges

Federal judges are appointed by the President and hold office for life, during good behavior. A federal judge may be removed from office only by impeachment. However, each federal circuit now has a disciplinary process that can impose sanctions such as the inability to hear cases where the judge's conduct warrants. [28 U.S.C. § 372]

a. The Code of Conduct for Federal Judges

To help standardize disciplinary standards among the federal circuits, the Judicial Conference of the United States has adopted a Code of Conduct for Federal Judges that is similar to the CJC but less detailed. The federal Code of Conduct is not itself tested on the MPRE.

Review Questions and Answers

Review Questions

FILL IN ANSWER

1. Indicate whether the following statements are true or false:
   a. While the courts generally administer regulations governing the legal profession, the inherent power of regulation lies with the legislative branch. ________
   b. Under an "integrated" bar system, membership in the state bar association is voluntary, but all local bar groups are members of the state association. ________
   c. The ABA Model Rules of Professional Conduct directly regulate the conduct of all practicing lawyers. ________
2. State X requires that applicants for admission to practice law be residents of the state in which they are applying at least six months prior to admission. Is the requirement constitutional? ________
3. May State X insist upon graduation from an accredited law school as a condition for practicing law? ________
4. If a question is raised regarding an applicant's moral character, the burden of establishing good character rests with the applicant. True or false? ________
5. An adverse determination on moral character by the state bar is final and may not be reviewed by the courts. True or false? ________
6. Wylie applies for admission to practice in State Y. On his application, Wylie notes that he was once arrested for shoplifting but was subsequently acquitted. May the State Y Bar Association consider these charges in assessing Wylie's moral fitness? ________
7. Zelda likewise applies for admission in State Y and notes that she was convicted of petty theft at age 14. Could this be enough to bar Zelda's admission to practice? ________
8. Stanley, an applicant for admission in State Y, was once arrested for indecent exposure, but the charges were immediately dropped when the complaining party was adjudged mentally disturbed. Stanley's record is otherwise impeccable, and he is embarrassed to raise the exposure incident on his application. May he properly omit it? ________
9. Carol seeks admission in State A. She is a member of the Communist Party and acknowledges this fact. Is this enough to bar her admission? ________
10. State X admits lawyers from State W without a bar examination, but requires an examination for State Y lawyers seeking to practice within State X. Does the State X policy have constitutional defects? ________
11. State A requires that any out-of-state lawyer seeking admission pro hac vice associate local counsel and have at least two years of trial experience in her home state. Are these requirements enforceable? ________
12. Admission to the bar of a state entitles a lawyer to practice in the federal courts of that state. True or false? ________

13. Smith, a lawyer licensed to practice in State X, opens an office in State Y for the purpose of advising clients solely on matters of patent law. Can State Y prevent Smith from practicing in the state? ________

14. Professor Canon tells his students that "the ABA places great reliance on history and custom in determining what constitutes the practice of law." Is he correct? ________

15. Harry, a local grocer, is sued personally by a patron allegedly injured by a protruding nail on a display shelf. Can Harry appear personally to defend himself in court? ________

16. Would the result be different if Harry were appearing as president of his grocery corporation? ________

17. Scam-O Title Company, without assistance from a lawyer, completes a standardized mortgage form for the sale of a house to Arthur (who is also unrepresented by counsel). Is this permissible? ________

18. Samantha, a nonlawyer, enterprising local businesswoman and recent divorcee, opens a "divorce clinic" in which she advises spouses considering divorce on their property rights and obligations. Is Samantha guilty of the unauthorized practice of law? ________

19. Might the result be different if Samantha instead had written a book on the subject and advertised it for sale? ________

20. Lawyer Jones is appointed to the federal district court bench. Thereafter, Jones continues to appear in state court from time to time on behalf of clients. Is Jones's conduct proper? ________

21. Might the result be different if Jones were a law student rather than a federal judge? ________

22. Lawyer Ling is asked to represent Zeke, an itinerant worker charged with the rape-slayings of six women in the local community. If Ling has strong feelings on the subject of rape, can she properly refuse to represent Zeke? ________

23. Orville files a lawsuit for his client, Wilbur. Shortly thereafter, defense counsel asks that the case be dismissed. May Orville proceed to execute the necessary documents without Wilbur's authorization? ________

24. In discussing a pending lawsuit with opposing counsel, Lawyer admits that her client was "partially at fault" in the matter at issue. Can opposing counsel introduce this admission at trial? ________

25. Would the result be different if the response were made by Lawyer in written answers to interrogatories propounded by opposing counsel? ________

26. Client asks Lawyer to represent her in a tax dispute with the I.R.S. Lawyer has never handled tax matters but is presently enrolled in a continuing education course on the subject. May he properly take the case? ________

27. Lawyer Winston is assigned to represent Zach, an indigent accused of manslaughter. At trial, the prosecution seeks to introduce evidence obtained in a search of Zach's hotel room. Winston objects but fails to cite a recent case which would have supported exclusion. If the evidence is admitted and a conviction results, should it be set aside? ________

28. Lawyer's failure to answer a civil complaint results in a default judgment against her client. If the failure was due to Lawyer's inexcusable negligence, should the default be set aside? ________

29. To insure zealous representation, must a lawyer personally share the viewpoints of her client? ________

30. Lawyer Anita represents her client Boris in negotiating the purchase of an apartment complex. Boris gives Anita $50,000 to be applied toward purchase of the property. Can Anita deposit the funds in her personal bank account? ________

31. David hires Ted to represent him as a plaintiff in a products liability case at the rate of $100 per hour. After a brief review of the facts and one phone call to the defendant, Ted realizes he can settle the case immediately for a substantial sum. May Ted properly change his arrangement with David to a contingent fee? ________

32. Assume instead that the original agreement called for a flat fee of $10,000. Ted settles the case with 10 hours of work, and David refuses to pay the full fee. Can Ted successfully sue for the $10,000? ________

33. If the court finds the $10,000 fee to be unreasonable and clearly excessive, is Ted subject to disciplinary action? ________

34. Amore, a leading divorce lawyer, is asked by Stella to represent her in an action for increased alimony from her husband. Amore agrees to do so for 20% of the increase obtained for the following two years. Is this a proper fee arrangement? ________

35. Elwood agrees to handle the probate of an estate in State X which imposes a maximum statutory attorney's fee of 3% of the estate assets. During the probate, Elwood handles a number of tax problems for the estate and arranges the sale of certain assets therein. May he properly bill the estate for a fee in excess of the statutory maximum? ________

36. Bob represents Ted in a State Y breach of contract suit, obtaining a judgment in Ted's favor. Ted subsequently refuses to pay the agreed fee for Bob's services. State Y recognizes charging liens but not retaining liens. May Bob enforce a lien on the judgment to satisfy his fees in the matter? ________

37. Can Bob foreclose on the judgment for unpaid fees on a business reorganization he previously performed for Ted? ________

38. Client asks Lawyer to file suit against Client's neighbor, Gladys, for breach of contract. After reviewing the facts, Lawyer decides that the case has no merit and is being brought solely to pressure Gladys regarding a boundary dispute. Despite Lawyer's advice, Client refuses to drop the matter. May Lawyer continue to represent Client in the lawsuit? ________

39. If a lawyer wants to withdraw from a case, must she obtain court permission to do so? ________

40. If a client consents to his lawyer's withdrawal, must the lawyer return any unearned portion of the client's original retainer fee? ________

41. Lawyer Jones is retained by Smith to represent him in a contract dispute with Williams. The retainer agreement specifies that Jones will be paid $2,000 for her work and will have Smith's authority to conduct the matter as Jones sees fit. Shortly thereafter, Smith decides that he wants another lawyer.

    a. May Smith discharge Jones if there is no cause shown for the discharge? ________

b. If Jones is discharged without cause, can she represent Williams in the dispute? ________

42. Suppose that Jones and Smith had agreed to a 30% contingency fee on Smith's recovery, whereupon Jones is discharged without cause. Smith retains Lawyer Brown, who ultimately obtains $30,000 for Smith. Is Jones entitled to $9,000 from Smith? ________

43. Colleen consults Lawyer Able regarding a potential lawsuit against Baker. In the initial interview, Colleen gives Able sensitive information regarding her business strategies and sales. Colleen then decides to employ David as her lawyer in the matter.

    a. The Better Business Bureau subsequently contacts Able regarding Colleen's business operations. May Able disclose the information presented in the prior interview? ________

    b. Abie's administrative assistant, Rosemary, types up notes on the Able-Colleen discussion. Thereafter, she tells her boyfriend Tom about Colleen's operations. If Tom is one of Baker's employees, is Able subject to discipline? ________

    c. If there are friends of Colleen present when her business operations are discussed, may Able disclose such discussions at a later time? ________

44. Max is the lawyer for Blimpo Corporation. Blimpo's president asks Max to prepare a memorandum discussing the business and legal ramifications of a proposed merger. Can Max be compelled to disclose the memorandum in a subsequent lawsuit against Blimpo? ________

45. Lawyer Jafar is retained by Stanley to defend him on an indictment for income tax evasion. While reviewing the facts, Stanley admits to Jafar that he previously lied under oath in a civil case regarding his income and disbursements. Is this information privileged? ________

46. At Stanley's trial, the court asks Jafar whether he has any information regarding prior crimes committed by the client. Jafar asserts the attorney-client privilege, whereupon the court orders him to respond. May Jafar reveal his previous discussions with Stanley? ________

47. Wallace contacts his lawyer, Xavier, by telephone and tells him that he is fleeing to another state to avoid prosecution for embezzlement. Xavier cannot persuade Wallace to change his mind. Is Xavier under a duty to disclose this information if sought by the proper authorities? ________

48. Arthur asks his lawyer, Roger, to represent him in negotiating for the lease of an office complex. After contacting the present owners of the building, but without telling Arthur, Roger decides to purchase a 10% ownership interest in the property as a personal investment. Thereafter, Roger consummates a lease on office space for Arthur. Has Roger engaged in improper conduct? ________

49. Suppose instead that Arthur owns the office building and asks Roger to represent him in litigation with certain of his tenants. While the matter is in progress, Roger offers to purchase a 10% interest in the building. Arthur agrees and signs the contract drawn up by Roger. Has Roger breached his professional duties? ________

50. Yolanda asks her lawyer, Yasmin, to draft a will leaving one-half of her total estate to Yasmin. May Yasmin proceed to prepare the document? ________

51. Might the result be different if Yasmin were Yolanda's granddaughter and sole heir? ________

52. Professor Canon tells his class that "a lawyer may properly represent clients with potentially different interests in a nonlitigation matter as long as the lawyer is satisfied that no actual conflict exists." Is the professor correct? ________

53. Frank and Jesse are indicted for armed robbery, and Lawyer Earp is appointed to defend them at trial. Although Frank is a convicted felon and Jesse is not, Earp believes she can properly represent both, and the two defendants acquiesce. Should the court nevertheless consider appointing separate counsel for each? ________

54. Would the result be different if Frank and Jesse jointly retained Earp to represent them? ________

55. Sergio represents Acme Finance, a secured creditor of Fido Corporation. Fido institutes bankruptcy proceedings, and one of its other creditors asks Sergio to handle its claim against Fido. Should he do so? ________

56. Edgar represents Charlie in a breach of contract suit against Candice. While the matter is pending, Candice asks Edgar to handle her alimony claim against David. If the two matters are unrelated, may Edgar take the alimony case? ________

57. Jorge is asked to negotiate a lease for client Lessee. May he also represent Landlord in the matter if both Lessee and Landlord consent to dual representation? ________

58. Would the result be different if the matter involved a litigated dispute between Lessee and Landlord over the terms of an existing lease? ________

59. X is general counsel for Flim-Flam Brokerage Co., which is under investigation for securities fraud. The president of Flim-Flam is subpoenaed to testify before a grand jury about his knowledge of the matter and asks X to advise him. Should X do so? ________

60. Lawyer Willis is retained by Tightwad Insurance to represent its insured, Baker, in a personal injury suit brought by Able. Prior to trial, Able offers to settle the case for $10,000. Realizing that Baker's policy limit is $12,000, Willis adamantly refuses to discuss any settlement. At trial, Able receives a judgment of $75,000. Is Willis subject to discipline? ________

61. When a lawyer is retained by parents to represent their minor child in juvenile court proceedings, the lawyer has a client responsibility to both the minor and the parents and so should honor the parents' decisions about the case. True or false? ________

62. Lawyer Ellen formerly served as general counsel for Widget Corp. As a member of a new law firm, she is now asked to represent the plaintiff in an antitrust case against Widget. May she do so? ________

63. Would the result be different if another lawyer in the firm was then asked to represent the plaintiff and Ellen took no part whatever in the case? ________

64. Mary and Ted are married lawyers who work at different firms. Mary is lead counsel for a client in a case against a client represented by Ted's firm, but Ted is doing no work on the case. Does this situation present a conflict of interest? ________

65. Lawyer Bigwig has joined Law Firm after serving as general counsel of the U.S. Department of Energy. Law Firm has been representing several clients in cases against the Department of Energy. May Bigwig work on those cases at Law Firm? ________

66. In a negotiation with opposing counsel, Lawyer says that his client's property lies in the path of "absolutely certain development" that will make it worth millions in a few years. Lawyer has no reason to believe that it is nearly that valuable. Is Lawyer subject to discipline for his excessive claim? ________

67. Lawyer Tom files a lawsuit for client P against D, who is represented by lawyer Ralph. Shortly thereafter, Tom calls D to discuss D's willingness to settle the case at the onset. Is Tom subject to discipline? ________

68. Lawyer calls her opposing counsel in a case and tells him that she will institute disbarment proceedings for misappropriation of funds unless he agrees to a settlement with Lawyer's client. If the settlement terms are fair to both parties, is Lawyer subject to discipline? ________

69. Blimpo Corporation retains Lawyer Helen to appear before a Food and Drug Administration hearing in support of new drugs that Blimpo wants to place on the market. As a public relations matter, Blimpo asks Helen not to reveal that she is representing the corporation. Must Helen nevertheless disclose her capacity at the hearing? ________

70. Lawyer is elected to the state senate but continues to maintain a private, part-time law practice. May Lawyer properly represent a client before a state administrative board? ________

71. Following a trial in which a judgment was entered against his client, Lawyer Mason is asked to analyze the case for news reporters. Mason replies that "the case was clear to most people—but apparently it was a little too complicated for the court." Is Mason subject to discipline for his remarks? ________

72. Attorney files a lawsuit for her client, Mei. The opposing party fails to respond to the complaint or request additional time to answer. Is Attorney obligated to seek a default judgment in favor of her client? ________

73. Assume instead that the defendant answers and the case proceeds. The court orders both parties to appear for a pretrial conference at a specific time and date. Attorney fails to appear. Is she subject to sanctions? ________

74. Lawyer Clark knows that if she can prolong a case for six more months, her opponent will be so damaged economically that he will settle for much less. She files a motion in the appellate court for mandamus to have the trial judge recuse himself in the case. She knows there is no basis for the motion, but she also knows it will take six months for the court to act. Has she done anything that would subject her to discipline? ________

75. Able is appointed to represent an indigent defendant, Baker, on an appeal requested by Baker. Able examines the record and all the facts, and concludes that the appeal is frivolous. May Able withdraw by advising the client that he finds no merit in the appeal? ________

76. Attorney Alma files an antitrust case for her client, Sam, against Z Corp., alleging damages due to Z's market restraints. In his deposition, Sam testified that the damages were very high, but Sam later told Alma that his injuries resulted from ineffective sales personnel during the period in question. Should Alma disclose this information to anyone? ________

77. Attorney Alma files an antitrust suit for her client, Sam, against Z Corp. Z Corp. files a motion for summary judgment. In preparing an opposing brief, Alma discovers that there are several cases adverse to Sam's position. By construing the facts favorably to Sam, Alma believes the cases are distinguishable from the present action. Should Alma disclose the cases in her brief? ________

78. Lawyer is appointed to defend D on a charge of selling narcotics. On the stand at trial, D testifies that he has never used narcotics in his life. During a recess, D admits to Lawyer that he has used cocaine for several years. Should Lawyer disclose this to the court? ________

79. Albert, the lawyer for a plaintiff in a products liability case, hires Bert as an expert witness on the defects in a defendant's product. Albert tells Bert that his client is presently short of funds but will pay Bert 5% of any recovery he obtains in the case. Is this arrangement improper? ________

80. Roscoe, a flamboyant trial lawyer, comments in his closing statement to the jury that "the defendant's chief witness, Smith, is just as crooked as the defendant himself, and his perjury on the stand proves it. I think his testimony is preposterous." Is this proper? ________

81. In her closing statement, Lawyer Jones tells the jury that "my client is poor and an innocent victim in this case—treat him as you would want to be treated if you were in his shoes." Is this improper? ________

82. Lawyer Dan is contacted by opposing counsel, who requests an extension of time to answer the complaint filed by Dan's client. Dan orally agrees to the extension, but no written stipulation is entered. Thereafter, Dan notices the defendant's default for failure to answer within the statutory period. Is Dan subject to discipline? ________

83. During the trial of his client's personal injury claim, Attorney Smith attempts to introduce certain evidence helpful to the claim. Defense counsel objects, and the court refuses to admit the evidence. Smith asks the court to reconsider its ruling "because Your Honor is totally wrong." Is Smith subject to discipline? ________

84. During a trial, the local newspaper publishes an editorial attacking the defendant's lawyer, Quickly, as "a known opportunist who would say anything to gain publicity for himself and his client." Quickly appears on a television show and refers to the editorial as "totally false and an obvious attempt to injure my reputation." Is Quickly subject to discipline for his statement? ________

85. Perry Prosecutor has filed multiple murder charges against Barry Bumm. Perry calls a press conference and announces the facts of the charges and the name and address of the accused. Has the prosecutor acted properly? ________

86. Lawyer Irving is asked by Clyde to handle his securities fraud claim on a contingency arrangement. May Irving properly advance the costs of litigation to Clyde while the case is in progress? ________

87. Helen is a lawyer for Baker Corporation, which is sued in a products liability case. By chance, Helen was present when the accident in question occurred. Can she properly represent Baker in the litigation? ________

88. Lawyer anticipates that she may be called as a witness concerning a minor dispute involving service of process in a lawsuit she has filed. This fact becomes known after Lawyer has already done substantial work on the case (for which she has been paid). May she continue to represent the client in the litigation? ________

89. During a trial, Judge Hangem calls opposing counsel A and B into chambers for a conference. As they are leaving, B decides to ask the judge about expediting discovery in another case B has before the court. Is this proper? ________

90. Lawyer Marvin represents the defendant in a personal injury lawsuit. Prior to the trial in his case, Marvin encounters a member of the jury panel outside the courthouse and asks him if he has ever been a plaintiff in a personal injury case. If Marvin does not otherwise discuss the case, is his communication proper? ________

91. Shortly after a verdict for plaintiff is returned, Marvin decides to call several of the jurors and discuss the factors they found significant in the case. May he properly do so? ________

92. Prosecutor Allen is preparing to try an accused for first degree murder. While interviewing a prospective witness, Allen learns that the accused may not have been present at the scene of the crime. Is he obligated to disclose this information to defense counsel? ________

93. Allen decides that Charlie will be his chief witness. Can Allen properly instruct Charlie not to discuss the case with defense counsel unless Allen is present? ________

94. Felix and Oscar are lawyers sharing offices and secretarial help. Occasionally, Oscar refers tax matters to Felix. May the two use a letterhead reading "Law Offices of Felix and Oscar"? ________

95. Civil rights legislation and the federal labor laws do not apply to the relationship between an associate and her law firm. True or false? ________

96. Indicate whether the following statements are true or false:

    a. The original opposition to group services plans was based on the fact that the intermediary obtained a profit from the provision of legal services. ________

    b. "Open panel" group plans are now permissible, but "closed panel" plans are still prohibited. ________

    c. The ABA Code and Model Rules permit partnerships between lawyers and nonlawyers as long as the practice of law is merely incidental to the primary partnership activities. ________

    d. In certain situations, it may be permissible for a lawyer to share legal fees with a nonlawyer. ________

97. Attorney Melina wants to list certain biographical information, including her educational background and publications, in a local directory. Does it matter whether she chooses the city directory or a bar directory of lawyers for this purpose? ________

98. Lawyer Eager files an antitrust class action with two named plaintiffs. Thereafter, Eager sends a letter to a trade association of similar business entities, informing them of the lawsuit and his willingness to "discuss the case" with any interested party. Is Eager guilty of solicitation? ________

99. Block is a lawyer who is state-certified as a tax specialist. May she properly list this tax specialty on her business cards? ________

100. May a lawyer leaving one law firm to join a new one inform the clients for whom he has done work that the clients may follow the lawyer to the new firm? ________

101. Nancy, a tax lawyer in River City, systematically refers all personal injury matters involving her clients to Alice, a trial lawyer. Alice then pays Nancy 30% of whatever fee she collects in each such case. Is this arrangement proper? ________

102. Lawyer Jones suspects her partner, Smith, of misappropriating certain funds of his clients. Does Jones have an obligation to report Smith's misconduct to disciplinary authorities? ________

103. At the disciplinary hearing, Smith pleads that he was faced with enormous medical expenses incurred by his sick child and would not otherwise have borrowed the money. Should the state bar consider this plea in assessing sanctions against Smith? ________

104. During the hearing, the examining lawyer seeks to introduce a taped telephone conversation between Smith and a friend, made via a wiretap set by Jones. Should this evidence be admitted? ________

105. Assuming the state supreme court imposes a one-year suspension on Smith, can the local federal court disbar Smith? ________

106. Paolo asks his lawyer, Luther, for an opinion on the tax effects of a complicated leasing transaction. Paolo follows Luther's opinion and is later held to have violated certain regulations applicable to the transaction. Can Paolo hold Luther liable for malpractice? ________

107. Lawyer Smith agrees to represent Jones, the defendant in a personal injury lawsuit. In responding to plaintiff's motion for summary judgment, Smith fails to note a recent case favorable to Jones. If summary judgment is entered against Jones, is Smith liable for the amount of the damages? ________

108. Arthur asks Lawyer Leonard to defend him in a large lawsuit. Leonard explains that the legal issues are extremely complicated, and that he must have Arthur's agreement not to sue for malpractice before he will take the case. In return, Leonard agrees to charge only 80% of his normal hourly fee. Provided Arthur consents after full disclosure, is the agreement enforceable? ________

109. Judge Smith gives a speech at a dinner for a local labor union whose members frequently appear before her. She also has her picture taken with the union president, knowing that it will be posted in the union hall with a "we have a friend at court" caption. Are Judge Smith's actions proper? ________

110. Judge Quashem, a candidate for reelection to the bench, appears at a fund-raising dinner to exchange endorsements with the party's candidates for nonjudicial offices. Is the judge's conduct proper? ________

Answers to Review Questions

1.a. **FALSE** — Ultimate regulatory power lies with the ***judicial branch***, since the practice of law is intimately connected with the administration of justice. [p. 14]

b. **FALSE** — An integrated bar system involves ***compulsory*** membership by all lawyers in the state bar association. [p. 15]

c. **FALSE** — The Model Rules are not directly binding on lawyers. However, over 30 states have adopted the Rules, so they form an ***indirect*** basis for regulation of much of the legal profession. [p. 18]

2. **NO** — The Supreme Court has held that residency requirements for admission to the bar violate the Privileges and Immunities Clause. [p. 10]

3. **YES** — Such a requirement has been deemed to meet the test of a "rational relationship" to fitness to practice law. [p. 10]

4. **TRUE** — The reasoning is that the applicant is in the best position to supply the facts about himself. [p. 11]

5. **FALSE** — An applicant is entitled to judicial review, usually by the highest state court. [p. 12]

6. **YES** — ***Any*** past conduct—including charges on which there is a subsequent acquittal or dismissal—may be deemed relevant to a character investigation. [p. 12]

7. **YES** — Theft is often considered conduct that reflects upon the ability to practice law. However, it could be argued that (due to Zelda's age at the time) this was mere "adolescent misbehavior," and hence not sufficient per se to block her admission. [p. 12]

8. **DEPENDS** — Stanley was not convicted of a crime, and the conduct did not involve dishonesty, but if he is asked about arrests, this must be disclosed—and failure to do so ***would*** be sufficient to bar Stanley's admission. [p. 12]

9. **NO** — Membership in the Communist Party is not sufficient per se to exclude an applicant from practicing law. [p. 13]

10. **NOT NECESSARILY** — If the State X policy is based on ***reciprocity*** (*i.e.*, State W automatically admits State X lawyers, but State Y does not), the policy does not violate equal protection. [p. 6]

11. **YES** — Limitations on admission pro hac vice are generally valid, unless applied to block adequate representation in civil rights cases. [p. 7]

12. **FALSE** — While no separate examination is required, admission to practice in the federal courts is ***distinct***, and a separate application must be

made. (A few federal courts also require completion of certain courses prior to admission.) [p. 8]

13. **NO** A state ordinarily may prevent an out-of-state lawyer from maintaining a continuous practice of law in the state, but here, ***federal regulations*** govern Smith's practice, and State Y cannot prevent her from maintaining an office for that purpose. [p. 9]

14. **SOMEWHAT** Some courts still follow the "history and custom" test, but the ABA also emphasizes the ***need for professional judgment*** as the relevant criterion. [pp. 2–3]

15. **YES** Representation "in propria persona'' is always available to an individual in court proceedings. [p. 2]

16. **YES** A corporation ***cannot*** appear for itself in court through its ***nonlawyer*** officers or directors. [p. 4]

17. **SPLIT OF AUTHORITY** Most courts permit title companies to complete standardized mortgage or deed forms according to information furnished by the parties. Others, however, find this impermissible, on the ground that this is "drafting"—requiring a lawyer's expertise on choice of forms—rather than "scrivening." [p. 4]

18. **YES** Giving individualized advice about legal rights and obligations is usually regarded as the practice of law. [p. 3]

19. **YES** Courts have held that publication of such a book by a layperson is not the practice of law because it necessarily gives general advice rather than advise about specific cases. [p. 3]

20. **NO** Full-time judges may not practice law even though they are also licensed attorneys. [p. 8]

21. **YES** Ordinarily, law students are also prohibited from appearing in court for clients. However, an exception is made where the student does so in connection with an ***authorized law school training program.*** [p. 4]

22. **YES** Although she might have an obligation to accept the case unless there is a valid ***professional reason*** not to do so, a lawyer normally is ***not obliged*** to take any case. [pp. 37, 118]

23. **NO** If the dismissal is with prejudice, it must be authorized by Wilbur. On the other hand, Orville probably has implied authority to execute a dismissal ***without prejudice*** if he considers it to be ***in Wilbur's interests.*** [p. 40]

24. **DEPENDS** If Lawyer was ***authorized*** to make the statement, it would be admissible; otherwise, it is not admissible. In either event, it is probably not conclusive on the issue. [p. 42]

25. **YES** This is a ***judicial admission***, which is binding upon the client unless the court permits an amendment or withdrawal. [p. 42]

26.	**PROBABLY NOT**	A lawyer may accept employment where he expects in good faith to become qualified to perform the necessary services. However, taking a single CLE course is unlikely to be sufficient to become competent to handle this matter.
27.	**PROBABLY NOT**	Unless the evidence was critical to the conviction, failure to cite the case would be unlikely to be a sufficient basis for setting aside the conviction. A mere mistake is not ineffective assistance of counsel. [p. 33]
28.	**SPLIT OF AUTHORITY**	Many courts require a reasonable excuse for the failure to answer in order to set aside a default. Others, however, will not charge a client with his lawyer's gross negligence if doing so denies justice in the particular case. [p. 33]
29.	**NO**	A lawyer has no obligation to approve or adopt a client's moral viewpoints.
30.	**NO**	The funds must be deposited in a ***separately identified*** trust (or other bank) account. [p. 46]
31.	**PROBABLY NOT**	Certainly the change would be improper if Ted did not inform David of the prospects for a quick settlement. And even with disclosure, Ted would have the burden of proving that the new agreement was a reasonable one. [p. 49]
32.	**PROBABLY**	Courts will review a fee agreement to determine its reasonableness. Whether Ted can collect the full $10,000 depends on all the circumstances, but the fact the case settled quickly does not render the fee unreasonable.
33.	**YES**	The charging of unreasonable and clearly excessive fees may subject a lawyer to discipline. [p. 49]
34.	**POSSIBLY**	Courts increasingly permit contingent fees in domestic relations matters ***after*** a divorce has been granted, *i.e.*, for collecting or renegotiating alimony. However, the law changes slowly in this area and the propriety of a contingent fee is thus not completely clear. [p. 52]
35.	**PROBABLY**	Elwood has apparently performed extraordinary services for the estate and is therefore entitled to an additional reasonable fee for that work if the engagement letter so provides. [p. 53]
36.	**YES**	A charging lien can be affirmatively enforced against a judgment awarded to the client for fees in that matter. [p. 55]
37.	**NO**	Charging liens are ***limited*** to fees and costs incurred in the particular matter in which recovery is obtained. Note that if State Y recognized retaining liens, Bob could withhold documents or other items he received as lawyer for the reorganization—and use this as "leverage" in obtaining any fees unpaid by Ted. [pp. 54–55]

38. **NO** — Lawyer has an obligation to withdraw under these circumstances, and she is subject to disciplinary action if she continues with the frivolous lawsuit. [p. 56]

39. **YES** — If the matter is ***pending*** before the court (*i.e.,* a complaint on file), permission of the court must be obtained for withdrawal. [p. 59]

40. **YES** — Whatever the basis for withdrawal, the lawyer is not entitled to retain any unearned portion of fees paid in advance—unless paid solely to insure the laywer's availability for the case. [p. 60]

41.a. **YES** — A client has the unilateral right to discharge his lawyer at any time, without cause, and despite any agreement for an "irrevocable" retainer. [p. 59]

b. **NO** — Despite the discharge without cause, Jones's fiduciary duties to Smith continue—including the duty not to represent conflicting interests. [p. 59]

42. **SPLIT OF AUTHORITY** — Some courts would allow Jones the full 30% contingency (*i.e.,* $9,000), while others would limit recovery to the reasonable value of her services (quantum meruit). [p. 60]

43.a. **NO** — The attorney-client privilege and the professional duty of confidentiality apply to information obtained from a ***prospective*** client, even though the lawyer is not subsequently employed. [pp. 38, 73]

b. **PERHAPS** — Able may disclose such information to his office staff, but he has a duty to prevent such employees from disseminating it to others. If Able has not exercised reasonable care in this regard (*e.g.,* by careful hiring and proper warnings), he is subject to sanctions. [pp. 74, 154]

c. **NO** — The presence of others may waive the "confidentiality" requirement so that the attorney-client privilege would not apply. However, Abie's professional duty of nondisclosure is broader, and is ***not*** affected by the fact that others were present at the interview. [pp. 14, 64, 72]

44. **NO** — ***Mixed communications*** between a corporation and its counsel are within the attorney-client privilege, although discussion of business issues alone are not. [p. 65]

45. **YES** — A client's confidential admission to counsel that he perjured himself in a prior proceeding is privileged information. [p. 66]

46. **SPLIT OF AUTHORITY** — Some courts hold that a lawyer must refuse to disclose privileged information, whatever the personal consequences to him may be (*e.g.,* citation for contempt). However, the Model Rules allow disclosure of such information in response to a ***court order***, and the Comments to the Model Rules state that a lawyer may comply with a final order of a court requiring such information. [p. 67]

47. **DEPENDS** As a general matter, the whereabouts of a client is privileged information. Note, however, that if the violation of a court order is involved (*e.g.,* Wallace was previously released on bail upon Xavier's motion), Xavier ***must*** advise the court of his client's whereabouts. [p. 72]

48. **YES** It is improper for a lawyer to use his client's confidential information to acquire an adverse interest in the subject matter of his employment, since there is at least the potential for a conflict of interest (*e.g.,* Roger's interest as part owner may conflict with his negotiating the most favorable lease terms for Arthur). [p. 74]

49. **DEPENDS** Because of the opportunities for overreaching by counsel, such transactions with a client are subject to a ***presumption of undue influence*** by the lawyer and are examined very closely by the court. Hence, under the Model Rules, the terms of the purchase must be objectively fair to Arthur, he must have had a chance to consult with outside counsel in the matter, and he must have consented in writing. [p. 86]

50. **NO** Yasmin must insist that Yolanda obtain the assistance of another lawyer in drafting the will, since Yasmin is named as a beneficiary.

51. **YES** Most courts permit a lawyer to prepare wills for relatives, provided that any bequest therein to the lawyer is ***reasonable under the circumstances*** and that there is no hint of overreaching. Here, Yolanda's bequest appears to be less than Yasmin's intestate share and hence a reasonable gift. [p. 87]

52. **NO** Under the Model Rules, the test is whether there is a "significant risk" that the client's interests may conflict. A lawyer may undertake such representation only after he has the ***informed consent*** of all the clients concerned, confirmed in writing.

53. **YES** The court has a duty to see whether differing interests appear and to appoint separate counsel if they do.

54. **YES** In this situation, the duty is on Earp (as retained counsel) to consider and disclose any conflicts. However, the court also should remain sensitive to conflicts to avoid a later claim of ineffective assistance of counsel.

55. **DEPENDS** The propriety of representing both creditors depends on whether there are conflicts of interest involved. If the second client is not a secured creditor, and/or if Fido's assets cannot satisfy the claims of both, dual representation would be improper. [p. 83]

56. **PROBABLY NOT** Even though Candice's success on her alimony claim might benefit Charlie, it is a conflict of interest to represent opposing clients in unrelated matters. The conflict may be waived, however, with the informed consent of each client, confirmed in writing. [pp. 81, 84]

57. **PROBABLY NOT** Jorge must ***fully disclose*** to Lessee and Landlord the possible conflicts in representing both parties to the lease negotiations. But if this done, and ***informed*** consent is given by the parties and confirmed in writing, dual representation is probably permissible. [p. 84]

58. **YES** Once the matter goes to court, the conflict between adversaries is not subject to waiver, even with the informed consent of each client. [p. 79]

59. **NO** As general counsel, X owes his loyalty to Flim-Flam. Since the company may have its own defenses and a potential action against the president in this matter, he should retain independent counsel for the grand jury appearance. [p. 85]

60. **YES** A lawyer who rejects a settlement proposal without letting the client make the final decision may be guilty of both unethical conduct and civil malpractice. The lawyer must inform the insurer of its duty to the insured regarding settlement, and must use her best efforts to see that the interests of the insured are protected. Willis's adamant refusal to discuss any settlement was improper. [pp. 91–92]

61. **FALSE** The client responsibility is owed solely to the ***child,*** regardless of who pays the lawyer's fees. The lawyer should consult with the child and let the child make most of the decisions. [pp. 92–93]

62. **PROBABLY NOT** A lawyer is prohibited from representing someone where the lawyer would be taking a position materially adverse to a former client in a matter closely related factually or legally to the prior one, or where there is some other substantial risk that the lawyer will use confidential information obtained in the prior representation against the former client. Unless it can be shown that this antitrust case is unrelated to any matter handled by Ellen at Widget and that the case does not involve confidential information she received while employed by the company, Ellen may not take the case. [p. 94]

63. **NO** The prohibitions applicable to Ellen apply as well to any lawyer affiliated with her—*i.e.,* if there is a conflict as to her representation, it applies to the firm as well. [p. 96]

64. **NO** While the relationship between husband and wife is obviously close, it does not present a disqualifying conflict unless Mary and Ted are personally representing the opposing clients. [p. 96]

65. **POSSIBLY** Bigwig may not work on any matter in which she was ***personally and substantially*** involved while in the government. However, even an agency counsel is not involved in every matter in the office, so Bigwig's involvement would have to be determined case by case. Furthermore, even if Bigwig would be personally disqualified from working on some matters at Law Firm, the firm itself would not be disqualified by imputation if Bigwig is screened against involvement in those matters. As a practical matter, federal statutes, not legal ethics rules, will dictate the answer to this question.

66. **PROBABLY** A lawyer may not knowingly make a false statement of material fact even in the course of a negotiation. Some statements are obviously puffing and would be taken as such by the other side, but this is a very concrete claim, not a general prediction that the property value will rise.

67. **YES** If a lawyer knows the opposing party is represented by counsel, the lawyer ***must not*** communicate directly with that party on any matter in controversy without the consent of opposing counsel. [p. 111]

68. **PROBABLY NOT** Zealous representation does not permit the threat of criminal or other charges (including disbarment) to gain advantages for a lawyer's client. This is an improper use of the legal process and is punished as extortion, regardless of whether the final results are reasonable. But explicit prohibition of it was left out of the Model Rules. [p. 115]

69. **YES** Unless the identity of the client is privileged information (which is not the case here), Helen has a duty to reveal her representative capacity at administrative proceedings. [p. 146]

70. **DEPENDS** Lawyer must avoid any foreseeable conflict between his private interests and his public duties as legislator. In practice, the issue will probably be decided as a matter of state legislation, not legal ethics rules. [p. 120]

71. **POSSIBLY** While snide or petty comments might be considered simply bad manners, intemperate criticism of a court can be disciplined as a threat to public confidence in the judicial system. [p. 121]

72. **NO** Attorney may feel it is in Mei's best interest ***not*** to seek a default, and Attorney will not be disciplined or held liable for civil malpractice if she does not seek a default judgment. But ultimately, the decision whether to pursue the default judgment should be left up to thc client.

73. **YES** Failure to appear at a court-ordered hearing, particularly without advance notice to the court, is punishable as contempt of court and possibly as neglect of the client's case. [p. 32]

74. **YES** The Model Rules impose a requirement to expedite litigation. Benefits to the client from ***improper delay*** may not be taken into account by a lawyer. [p. 126]

75. **NO** The lawyer must seek permission to withdraw, accompanied by a written brief to the court citing any grounds that might arguably support an appeal. [p. 125]

76. **YES** In a matter pending before a tribunal, a lawyer must, under the Model Rules, take ***reasonable remedial measures*** when the lawyer becomes aware that a witness has made a false statement of material fact to the tribunal, including a statement made in a deposition. This duty continues up to the conclusion of the proceedings, and it applies even to otherwise protected confidential information.

Unless the client agrees to rectify the situation himself, the lawyer must reveal the deceit to the court or the other party. [p. 130]

77.	**PROBABLY**	A lawyer must disclose ***directly adverse*** legal authority in the ***controlling jurisdiction.*** Exactly how relevant the cases are is unclear in this question, but doubts involving the applicability of adverse decisions usually should be resolved in favor of disclosure. The lawyer may then go on to distinguish the cases or otherwise attempt to avoid the result suggested by the cases. [pp. 128–129]
78.	**PROBABLY**	Assuming this is a material fact, Lawyer must, under the Model Rules, attempt to persuade D to correct his testimony. If D refuses, Lawyer should seek to withdraw. If the court will not permit withdrawal, there is a strong argument that Lawyer must disclose the perjury to the court.
79.	**YES**	Fees for any witness contingent on the outcome of the case or the substance of the testimony are prohibited. [p. 133]
80.	**NO**	Expressions of a lawyer's personal opinion on testimony by witnesses are improper. [p. 136]
81.	**YES**	Jurors are expected to decide the case as objective triers of fact, and appeals to personal feelings or sympathy are improper (but common). [p. 136]
82.	**DEPENDS**	Dan is obligated to follow ***local customs*** on extensions of time unless he notifies opposing counsel to the contrary. If oral agreements to extend time ***are accepted*** local practice, Dan could be sanctioned for attempting to take a default. In any case, Dan should abstain from offensive conduct, should treat opposing counsel with courtesy, and should comply with opposing counsel's reasonable requests. [p. 137]
83.	**NO**	A lawyer may properly challenge a court ruling by asking for reconsideration. While Smith's statement is strong, it is probably not disrespectful. [p. 137]
84.	**NO**	The restrictions on publicity regarding criminal proceedings do not preclude a defense lawyer from replying publicly to charges that may unduly prejudice the lawyer's client. [p. 143]
85.	**YES**	Each of these items of information is permitted under the ABA Code and Model Rules. [p. 142]
86.	**YES**	Where litigation is pending or contemplated, a lawyer may lend the client money for litigation expenses and may make the obligation to repay contingent on the outcome of the case, or may make no provision for repayment where the client is indigent. Thus, if Irving complies with the applicable provisions of the Model Rules, he may properly advance litigation costs to Clyde. [p. 30]

87. **PROBABLY NOT** — A lawyer may not handle litigation in which it is apparent that she may be called as a ***necessary witness*** during the proceedings. [p. 140]

88. **PROBABLY** — Since the matter for testimony appears to be an ***insubstantial*** one, and since there may be substantial ***hardship*** to the client in substituting new counsel at this juncture, Lawyer probably may remain as counsel. [p. 141]

89. **MAYBE** — It is ordinarily improper for B to communicate with the court ex parte on a pending matter without notifying opposing counsel so that she could be present. However, since this is a mere administrative matter not going to the merits, it may be allowed. [p. 138]

90. **NO** — Such out-of-court communications are ***not permitted,*** although Marvin might try to obtain such information by means of a proper investigation. (The question itself is a proper one for voir dire examination in open court.) [p. 138]

91. **PROBABLY** — Most courts would permit such communications (*e.g.*, as a means of improving the lawyer's advocacy skills), as long as there is no harassment of jurors. [p. 139]

92. **YES** — Government prosecutors are ***required*** to make timely disclosure to the defense of any available evidence that might negate guilt or otherwise mitigate the offense). [p. 144]

93. **NO** — A prosecutor ***must permit*** defense counsel to interview government witnesses and may not properly advise government witnesses not to talk to the defense. [p. 145]

94. **PROBABLY NOT** — This designation implies that Felix and Oscar are partners. Lawyers may not hold themselves out as partners unless they in fact are partners. [p. 151]

95. **FALSE** — Both sets of laws protect law firm associates. [p. 151]

96.a. **FALSE** — Nonprofit intermediaries were also prohibited from providing such services on the ground that the necessary relationship of trust and confidence between lawyer and client was lacking. [p. 156]

b. **FALSE** — "Closed panel" plans are constitutionally protected in at least some situations (*e.g.*, union retaining counsel for its members in workers' compensation disputes). And the ABA now imposes the same requirements on both open and closed panel plans. [p. 156]

c. **FALSE** — Such partnerships are prohibited where ***any*** of the activities include the practice of law. [p. 152]

d. **TRUE** — However, these situations are limited to profit-sharing retirement plans, payment of accrued fees to the estate of a deceased attorney, or sharing court-awarded fees with the nonprofit organization that hired the lawyer or recommended him as counsel in the matter. The general rule prohibits fee sharing with nonlawyers. [pp. 152–153]

97. **NO** Under the Model Rules, material of this kind may be published for the public generally, not simply lawyers. [p. 158]

98. **PROBABLY NOT** Under the Model Rules, Eager's conduct could be considered as prohibited direct contact with a potential client. However, with regard to class action litigation, the Supreme Court has held that it is improper for a court to set excessive limits on a lawyer's contact with prospective class members. Under this line of reasoning, it is not likely that Eager's conduct will be deemed to be prohibited solicitation. [p. 162]

99. **YES** Under the Model Rules, state-certified specialties may be noted on professional cards.

100. **PROBABLY** It has been held improper for former associates to ***encourage*** clients to follow them to their new firm. However, simple announcements merely ***informing*** former clients of the change of practice are proper. [p. 100]

101. **DEPENDS** Fee sharing among lawyers is permitted, but only if each lawyer assumes joint responsibility for the matter, the client knows and consents to the arrangement and the total fee is reasonable. If these conditions are met, the Nancy-Alice fee arrangement is permissible. [pp. 164–165]

102. **YES** At minimum, a lawyer is required to disclose any acts that violate professional standards and raise a substantial question about another lawyer's honesty. The fact that Smith and Jones are partners is no exception. [pp. 24–25]

103. **POSSIBLY** The factor of his child's illness probably warrants consideration on the issue of sanction, but not of guilt.

104. **YES** The normal exclusionary rules of criminal procedure (*e.g.*, as to illegal wiretaps) ***do not apply*** to disciplinary hearings. [p. 23]

105. **YES** The federal court is not bound by the state proceedings but will often follow a state's decision in such a case. [p. 26]

106. **DEPENDS** Luther owes Paolo a duty to exercise the ***skill and knowledge normally possessed*** by lawyers in the area. If Luther is a tax specialist, the duty is to exercise the care of other such specialists; if he is not, the duty is to associate such a specialist (with the client's consent), develop the necessary expertise, or decline the matter. If Luther has breached the applicable duty, he can be held liable for malpractice. [p. 28]

107. **DEPENDS** Smith owes a duty to discover recent developments in the law available through standard research techniques. Before civil malpractice can be proved, however, Jones must usually show that

summary judgment would have been avoided had Smith cited the case in question. [pp. 28–29]

108. **NO** A lawyer may not exculpate himself in advance from liability for malpractice. However, the Model Rules provide that the agreement could be made enforceable if Arthur were separately represented in making the agreement. [p. 32]

109. **NO** A judge may participate in community affairs but ***may not*** give the impression that persons are in a special position to ***influence*** her. [p. 169]

110. **NO** A judge may not contribute to a political organization, buy tickets to political dinners, and the like, unless she is subject to public election. Even when actually running for public election, a judge may publicly endorse or oppose only other candiddates for the same judicial office, not the party's candidates generally. [pp. 182–184]

Multiple Choice Exam Questions and Answers

QUESTION 1

A lawyer represented a company seeking to develop an online marketplace for marijuana products. Some state laws permit sales of such products by licensed dealers, but federal law still makes the sales a crime. The lawyer agreed to study whether the proposed company could operate legally. She wrote a report concluding that some of the company's activities might not violate the law but most likely would be considered crimes. Using a different law firm, the company began operations and was later found guilty of various crimes.

Is the lawyer subject to discipline for writing an opinion on the legality of the client's business?

A. No, because the lawyer is simply helping the client delineate the scope of the law.

B. No, because a lawyer may provide legal assistance on all client matters, even if they involve criminal behavior.

C. Yes, because the lawyer assisted the client to start a business that engaged in criminal conduct.

D. Yes, because the lawyer provided counsel to the client about how to operate its business on the edge between legal and illegal conduct.

QUESTION 2

A lawyer represented a plaintiff in a contract dispute. The defendant filed a motion for summary judgment and the lawyer filed a motion supporting the plaintiff's position. Two days after all filings were in, the judge granted the motion and dismissed the case. The plaintiff had 30 days in which to decide whether to appeal. The lawyer was busy on other matters and so shocked by the judge's decision that he failed to tell the client about the decision for two weeks.

Was the lawyer's delay in telling the client about the judge's decision proper under the Model Rules?

A. Yes, because the client still have two more weeks to decide whether or not to appeal.

B. Yes, because the lawyer was busy on other matters.

C. No, because the lawyer failed to keep the client reasonably informed about the status of the matter.

D. No, because the lawyer affirmatively misled the client by failing to inform the client about the judge's decision.

QUESTION 3

A lawyer represented a client who was charged with possession and distribution of cocaine. The client told his lawyer that he was in fact a cocaine dealer and the substance that had been seized was cocaine. Before the criminal trial, the cocaine seized by the authorities was lost by the police. The lawyer took the client's case to trial, the client pled not guilty, and the lawyer argued successfully that the government did not prove its case beyond a reasonable doubt.

Did the lawyer violate the Model Rules in his handling of this matter?

A. Yes, because the lawyer knew that his client committed the crime and entering a plea of not guilty was a materially false, in-court statement of law and fact.

B. Yes, because the lawyer relied on the government's failure to prove its case beyond a reasonable doubt rather than seeking a result consistent with the truth.

C. No, unless the lawyer presents a witness whom he knows will falsely claim that the client never distributed cocaine.

D. No, because lawyers who represent criminal defendants may require that the government prove every element of the case even when the client admits involvement in the crime to the lawyer.

QUESTION 4

A lawyer represented a computer manufacturer sued by a purchaser for failing to deliver computers under a long-term supply contract. In a response filed by the lawyer in the matter, the lawyer stated that the failure to deliver the computers resulted because of a shortage of memory parts. At the time, memory components were in short supply, but subsequently the president of the computer company informed the lawyer that company had stockpiled computer memory and that this defense was not true. The lawyer informed the president that he would need to correct his filing and the president ordered the lawyer to keep this information confidential. The president stated that they could correct the false statement later on, when it was no longer material. The lawyer disobeyed the president's order and informed the court that he had learned that the statement about the memory was not accurate.

Was the lawyer's disclosure to the court consistent with the Model Rules?

A. Yes, because the lawyer's earlier statement constituted a fraud on the tribunal.

B. Yes, because the lawyer made a false statement to the court and had a duty to correct it.

C. No, because the president disclosed the correct information to the lawyer in confidence and ordered the lawyer not to disclose the information to the court.

D. No, because the president informed the lawyer that the company would correct the false statement later on.

QUESTION 5

A lawyer represented a defendant sued by a plaintiff who fell while at the defendant's store. A jury found for the defendant and the plaintiff appealed. After the jury's verdict, the defendant's president informed the lawyer that he is grateful that the plaintiff never discovered that on the day of the accident, the store manager had an improper cleaning solution on the floor that made it slippery. The lawyer remembered that the plaintiff had questioned the manager about the products used on the floor and the answer was a bleach solution. The president admitted that the manager had lied on the stand to protect the company. The lawyer decided not to pursue this issue further because the trial was over and the issue was not raised on appeal.

Was the lawyer's decision not to inform the court consistent with the Model Rules?

A. No, because the case is still on appeal, and the lawyer has failed to take reasonable remedial measures to urge the client to disclose the false testimony.

B. No, because the lawyer before the trial had not inquired into the cleaning solutions used on the floor of the company store.

C. Yes, because the trial was over and the testimony of the manager had not been raised in the appeal.

D. Yes, because the manager's lie came out during cross examination by the plaintiff rather than direct examination by the defense.

QUESTION 6

A prisoner confessed to committing a crime for which another person was convicted and imprisoned. The prisoner informed the warden, who informed the prosecutor about the location of a weapon used in the crime. The prosecutor knew that the prisoner was not represented by counsel at the time of his discussions with the warden. The information was new, credible, and material because the prosecutor knew that the prisoner had information only someone close to the crime could have known. This information created a reasonable likelihood that the person convicted of the crime did not commit the offense. The conviction of the person had taken place in a neighboring jurisdiction, so the prosecutor informed the convicted person's lawyer about the new evidence, and assumed that would be sufficient to address the situation. The convicted person's lawyer was still representing the person in a collateral attack on the conviction.

Were the prosecutor's efforts to remedy the possible wrongful conviction consistent with the Model Rules?

A. Yes, because the prosecutor took steps to remedy the possible wrongful conviction by informing the person's lawyer.

B. Yes, because the possible wrongful conviction did not occur in the prosecutor's jurisdiction.

C. No, because the warden received the information from a prisoner who was not represented by counsel and the information could not be further disclosed until the prisoner gave informed consent.

D. No, because the prosecutor did not inform the court or other authority in the jurisdiction where the person was convicted.

QUESTION 7

An in-house lawyer for a developer personally approached a couple who owned 1,000 acres of land. The couple invited the lawyer to come into their home and told the lawyer that they had retained an attorney to represent them in all real estate transactions. The lawyer informed the couple that he could not speak to them without permission of the lawyer. The couple said, "We waive that requirement. Don't worry; if you give us a proposed contract, we will not sign it until our attorney to look at it." The lawyer accepted the couple's waiver and continued to negotiate a land transaction.

Was it proper for the in-house lawyer to communicate with the couple about a possible real estate transaction under the Model Rules?

A. Yes, because the couple waived the requirement that the developer's lawyer ask the couple's lawyer for permission to speak.

B. Yes, because the couple agreed that they would not sign the agreement without first showing it to their attorney.

C. No, because the in-house lawyer continued to speak to the couple after he discovered that they had already hired a lawyer to represent them in real estate transactions.

D. No, because the in-house lawyer is considered part of his client organization, so the discussion was one between principals and not treated as involving a lawyer at all.

QUESTION 8

A 200-person law firm, organized as a professional corporation, specialized in intellectual property law. It had many nonlawyer employees working in the firm who brought science expertise into the law practice. A majority of the law firm clients were involved in the technology industry. The firm shareholders elected a woman who had a PhD in Computer Science but not a law license to the law firm's board of directors. Such action was taken because the board of directors played an integral role in client development and needed the judgment of the computer scientist in that process. She will not give legal advice in her role as a director. No clients will be informed that the law firm includes a nonlawyer on the corporate board of directors.

Was it proper for the law firm lawyer shareholders to elevate the scientist to the law firm's board?

A. Yes, because this law firm specializes in intellectual property law and the special expertise of a scientist will be helpful for its effective operation.

B. Yes, because the computer scientist is a professional and will not be giving legal advice in her work as a director.

C. No, because the lawyers in the firm may not practice in the entity with a nonlawyer as a corporate director.

D. No, because the firm did not inform clients about its nonlawyer director.

QUESTION 9

A lawyer sought to comply with the Model Rules' pro bono provision, so she performed the following work without fee: (1) 15 hours at a meals on wheels project devoted to feeding the poor; (2) 20 hours providing religious education to children of persons of limited means; (3) 20 hours participating in a local judicial committee drafting new rules for electronic discovery; and (4) 25 hours representing an indigent criminal defendant on charges of assault and battery.

Did the lawyer satisfy the pro bono aspiration?

A. Yes, because the lawyer worked 80 hours without expectation of a fee.

B. Yes, because the lawyer's representation of the indigent defendant qualified as work for a person of limited means.

C. No, because the lawyer's work on the local judicial committee did not qualify as pro bono service.

D. No, because the lawyer's work for the food project and the religious education of children did not involve the provision of *legal* services.

QUESTION 10

A criminal defense lawyer operated a horse riding stable with his family on his personal time. The business rarely made any income, and the lawyer often deducted the losses on his income tax return even though the law was clear that this horse riding operation fell within a category of losses the Internal Revenue Service (IRS) calls nondeductible hobby losses. The IRS audited the lawyer's tax return and found that he had repeatedly deducted losses that were routinely disallowed in the past. The audit revealed that the deductions continued after the IRS had disallowed such losses taken by the lawyer and after the IRS had warned the lawyer to stop taking the losses. The IRS assessed civil fraud penalties against the lawyer and imposed a fine of $10,000. The lawyer refused to pay the penalties and unsuccessfully challenged them in an appeal. The IRS reported the lawyer to the state lawyer disciplinary authorities.

Is the lawyer subject to discipline?

A. Yes, because the lawyer engaged in conduct involving civil fraud.

B. Yes, because the lawyer did not accept his punishment; he challenged the penalties in an unsuccessful appeal.

C. No, because the lawyer's conduct did not violate any criminal law.

D. No, because the lawyer's conduct arose in the context of a personal business, not his law practice.

QUESTION 11

A real estate lawyer often sent clients to real estate brokers and the brokers often referred their customers to the lawyer for legal services. The lawyer regularized three of these arrangements so that clients who needed a broker would be given a list of the three brokers, told that the lawyer often uses them, and told that these brokers often refer their customers to the lawyer for legal work. No money is ever exchanged between the lawyer and the brokers, and these brokers include several other lawyers on the list provided to their customers.

Was it proper for the lawyer to refer clients to real estate brokers in this manner in exchange for their agreement to refer their customers to the lawyer for legal work?

A. Yes, because lawyers may refer clients to any outside service provider in exchange for an agreement that the provider refer customers to the lawyer.

B. Yes, because the lawyer's reciprocal referral agreement was with a licensed professional, was nonexclusive, and did not include the exchange of cash.

C. No, because this formal quid pro quo agreement threatens the independent judgment of the lawyer in advising real estate clients about brokers they might want to use.

D. No, because the lawyer is in essence paying the brokers to recommend him for legal work in the form of making real estate referral.

QUESTION 12

A lawyer discovered that the client she had started to represent in a divorce matter was one of several defendants in a long-standing case being handled for the plaintiff by another partner in her firm. The lawyer concluded that she thus had a conflict of interest that required her to withdraw from the divorce matter before it was filed in court. She informed her client, returned the unearned portion or her fee, and sent the client the names of three other experienced lawyers who could handle the case well if they were available. She took no other steps and treated the representation as at an end.

Is the lawyer subject to discipline for the manner in which she handled her withdrawal from the divorce representation?

A. Yes, because the lawyer's withdrawal from this case to allow her partner to pursue another case violated the "hot potato" rule.

B. Yes, because the lawyer failed to surrender relevant papers and give the client time to hire new counsel before treating the representation as ended.

C. No, because the lawyer was required by the Model Rules to withdraw as soon as she learned her firm had a conflict of interest.

D. No, because the lawyer took sufficient steps to assure that the client's case would not be prejudiced by her withdrawal as counsel.

Answers to Multiple Choice Questions

On the MPRE and most other multiple choice exams, you will be asked to pick the ***best*** answer among those shown. Focus on the legal point the question is testing and the factors that make up that standard.

1	A	This question tests the line between permitted analysis of the legality of a client's conduct and prohibited "counsel or assistance" to a client in committing a crime or fraud. In this case, the lawyer limited her work to analysis; another law firm did the prohibited work. Answer B is wrong because it seems to allow all counsel and assistance. Answer C is based on an inaccurate statement of what happened. Answer D is closer to accurate but not nearly as good an answer as A.
2	C	This tests the duty to keep a client reasonably informed about the status of a matter. The question is whether the lawyer told the client what he needed to know about the court's decision at a time that gave the client time to decide what to do next. Clearly, answers B & D are wrong. One could argue that two weeks is enough time to decide whether to appeal, but more time would have given the client more time to consult with others about what to do. Thus, while A is not a completely wrong answer, given the lawyer's lack of a good excuse for silence, the best answer is C and that is the one you should choose.
3	D	This is the classic question of whether a lawyer can let a guilty client go free, and the answer is that he can. Both answers A & B are wrong in saying that the Model Rules require a lawyer to have acted differently, and while answer C suggests something that a lawyer could not do, that did not happen here, and D correctly states the applicable rule.
4	B	Here the question asks when a lawyer's duty to correct an earlier unintended misrepresentation overcomes a client's desire not to disclose it. In this case, Rule 3.3 requires correction, so answers C & D are wrong. Answer A is too extreme; the lawyer made a mistake here rather than committed fraud. Answer B is correct.
5	A	The question here is how long the duty to correct continues. Rule 3.3 says it ends only after appeals are concluded or the time to appeal expires. In this case, the appeal is still pending, so as answer A says, the duty to correct is still applicable. The fact that the issue was not raised on appeal simply suggests that disclosure may be important.
6	D	Prosecutors have special duties to reopen cases when they believe an injustice may have been done. The question here is the nature of that duty, and answer D is the only one that correctly says the prosecutor must notify the court or other authority in the jurisdiction where the defendant was convicted. Answer A, notifying the person's former lawyer, is not sufficient; Answer B is irrelevant here; and Answer C about the prisoner's right to counsel is complete hot air.

7	C	In this question, the key point at issue is whether the represented parties may consent to talk to the in-house lawyer. The answer under Rule 4.2 is that they may not. Nor is showing the deal to their lawyer later sufficient. Thus, answers A & B are clearly wrong. Answer D is similarly wrong; an in-house lawyer is treated as a lawyer under Rule 4.2, not just another company employee. That makes C the only right answer.
8	C	Very little in this problem turns on the firm being a professional corporation; the answer would be the same in a partnership. Despite the persuasive claims in answers A & B, Rule 5.4(d) makes none of them relevant. Likewise, notice to clients has no effect on who may be a director. Instead, answer C correctly says the Model Rules have an absolute bar on making a nonlawyer a law firm director.
9	D	Pro bono service is only an aspiration under the Model Rules, but that doesn't keep Rule 6.1 from being picky. At the end of the day, the issue is not uncompensated service but legal service to the poor. Thus all kinds of good deeds do not qualify to be counted toward the 50 hour target. Answers A & B are correct, statements but neither gets the lawyer to 50. Answer C is accurate but incomplete; it ignores the fact that other things did not qualify as well. What makes D the best answer is that it says "No" and cites two things that keep the lawyer below the 50 hour mark.
10	A	This item tests the relevance of conduct not in the lawyer's professional role. This lawyer did not commit a crime, but Rule 8.4(c) also punishes a lawyer's fraud. Answer A is thus correct, and all the other answers are irrelevant and wrong.
11	B	In the world of attracting clients, there are many prohibitions, but use of reciprocal referral arrangements among professionals remain possible. Answer A is wrong; one can't have arrangements with just anyone, but Answer B correctly says that non-exclusive agreements with other professionals where no cash is involved are fine. Answers C & D are arguments against the practice, but they are not the law.
12	B	The lawyer may, indeed must, withdraw in this case because the other partner's action is already underway; it is not a hot potato situation and Answer A is wrong. Answers C & D may be persuasive, but Rule 1.16(d) is quite specific about what a lawyer must do in the process of withdrawal. She must give the client time to hire new counsel and surrender relevant papers, not simply return unearned fees. Thus Answer B is the best and only correct answer.

Essay Exam Questions and Answers

QUESTION I

Sarah Smart has just graduated from law school and wants to go into practice on her own.

1. Sarah's first potential client is an inventor who wants to issue stock in a company he has formed. Sarah talks to him for two hours and takes good notes, but she realizes she is not competent to handle a public issue of securities. She calls a friend in a well-regarded securities firm in the city and sends the client, plus a written summary of their discussion, to that firm. A week later, Sarah receives a check for $1,000 from the firm as "a down payment on your one-third of our fee in this matter." What should she do with the check? Discuss.
2. A local television station invites Sarah to appear on a talk show about "women's issues in the law." She expects to be asked questions by the host and telephone callers about child support, abortion, rape, etc. Do you have any advice as to the way she should respond to questions? May she offer to have viewers come to her office for further advice? Explain.

QUESTION II

Harry Johnson was an associate at Black & White in New York. He worked on prospectuses for securities issues, one of which was for G & E, a national manufacturer of electrical items. After three years in the firm, he took a position as Assistant U.S. Attorney for the Southern District of New York. One of his first assignments was to help prosecute G & E for tax fraud. In the middle of that case, he left the U.S. Attorney's office to become a partner in a Philadelphia firm. That firm was defending the G & E tax fraud case, but Harry was assigned to work on other cases exclusively.

Does anyone have a right to complain about Harry's career path? What relief could they obtain, if any? Explain.

QUESTION III

"Mister Tax" is the newest addition to the tax advisory firms springing up around the country. It has one difference—it purports to do tax planning as well as fill out tax returns. Mary Adams has been hired as general counsel and has been made a full partner in the firm. The other partners are accountants and financial analysts. Adams's job will be to write booklets explaining tax planning to clients. She will also give seminars for the CPAs who will actually fill in the blanks on the clients' preprinted wills. If Mister Tax can get itself named executor of clients' estates, Mary will act as counsel for the executor.

Mary describes this plan to you. After you recover your composure, what will you tell her about the propriety of the plan and her role in it? Explain.

QUESTION IV

Bob Brilliant became a busy barrister. He had plenty of time to talk to prospective clients and obtain retainers, but little time to follow up his cases. One day an inventor brought a great invention to Bob's office and asked him to apply for a patent. Bob did not know anything about patent law but accepted a $500 retainer and agreed to do the necessary work. He put the file in his "IN" basket, where it stayed until nine months later, when the inventor stormed into Bob's office. A competitor had applied for a patent on the same idea so that the inventor's claim was now worthless.

Does Bob have reason to be worried? What options does the inventor have? Explain.

QUESTION V

Jones and Yates have been partners for 12 years. They have a personal injury and probate practice, and each has worked on issues brought into the office by the other. Now they have decided to split up, although they will both remain in the same city. Each is concerned about keeping "his" cases.

1. Describe what they should tell their clients and in what way.
2. What are the rights and duties of each partner with respect to firm files?

QUESTION VI

Mary and Bill have come to you and say they want a divorce. They have two children but little money and want a "clean break." Neither one wants the children, but Mary says she will take them. Mary tells you privately that she will inherit a large sum of money soon. Publicly, Mary is asking for one-third of Bill's salary as alimony and another one-third as child support.

1. Can you take this case? After Mary has confided in you, are your obligations any different?
2. May you charge one month's child support as your fee in this case? Explain.

QUESTION VII

Mark Russell represented Pat Novak in a divorce. Pat was ordered to pay child support. He has fallen behind. Mark is subpoenaed and asked Pat's address. He refuses to give it, citing both the evidentiary privilege and his professional obligation. The court overrules both grounds and orders Mark to answer.

1. What should Mark do? How will the issue arise? Explain.
2. The court asks Mark, "Is Novak a drug addict?" Mark believes the answer is yes because, while handling Pat's case, Mark had overheard Pat and a friend discussing Pat's use of narcotics. What should Mark's answer be? Explain.

QUESTION VIII

Doris Dash represents Mavis Martin, a local building contractor. Mavis asserts that she has not been paid for materials used on a job she is doing for a larger firm. Doris has filed suit on Mavis's behalf. As Doris investigates, however, she hears that Mavis may actually have sold the materials to another contractor and may be trying to recover twice. She looks at Mavis's files more closely and sees a letter from the other contractor thanking Mavis for her help. Doris obliquely asks Mavis what is going on, and Mavis tells her to mind her own business.

What should Doris do? Explain.

QUESTION IX

Claudia Cams has finished law school and seeks admission to the bar. She had been a member of a radical environmental protection group in the 1980s. Arrested for 21 counts of arson at a manufacturing plant, she pleaded guilty to three counts of malicious damage to property and spent four months in jail. She was also charged with perjury for her testimony in a friend's trial on the same charges, but the perjury charges were later dropped in order to reduce the prosecutor's backlog of cases. She has refused "on principle" to fill out the required character and fitness committee form.

Will Claudia be denied admission to the bar for any of this? Explain.

QUESTION X

Former Governor Don Runner has filed a lawsuit accusing the current secretary of state of illegally overcharging for automobile license plates. Don called a press conference to charge the secretary with mismanagement and the present governor with lax supervision. Don issued a general call for citizens to send $10 and join his class action. During his press conference and later TV interviews, Don posed under a large sign reading "Don (The People's Lawyer) Runner: Law for the Little Guy."

Is there any basis for subjecting Don to professional discipline? Explain.

ANSWER TO QUESTION I

1. Sarah should hold on to the check until she informs the client of the fee division.

   Sarah has behaved properly in this case. She listened to the client's story, understood the limits of her own ability, and put the client in touch with a firm that would be able to serve his needs. She prepared a basic memorandum of the facts and is entitled to be paid for that effort.

   Under the Model Rules, if the client consents in writing to the terms of the fee division, and the total fee is reasonable, lawyers who assume joint responsibility for a matter may share the fee in whatever proportions they agree, regardless of how much work each did.

2. Sarah may appear on the program and provide general information about the law. However, she should not try to solve individual problems of viewers over the telephone, and she should not offer to have viewers come into her office for further advice.

   The public needs information about legal issues, and lawyers are often in the best position to provide that information. Sarah should certainly try to do a good job of communicating valuable information on the issues that viewers raise. However, each actual case is unique, and a lawyer should not try to solve an actual case without a detailed and careful understanding of the facts. This would violate the lawyer's duty of competence, and the public nature of a television talk show interferes with the confidentiality of the lawyer-client relationship, which is designed to give clients a chance to provide the facts candidly and fully. Thus, Sarah should refuse to give advice in specific cases.

   Sarah should not offer to have viewers come to her office. While a lawyer may advertise her services generally on television, under the Model Rules, all "in-person or live telephone contact" with potential clients whom the lawyer has not previously served is prohibited where a "significant motive" for the contact is the lawyer's personal gain. Sarah may (and sometimes should) recommend that callers seek advice of a lawyer, and if a viewer later turns up at her office seeking personal advice, Sarah is not forbidden to deal with the client's problem. She may not, however, solicit the person's business on the television show.

ANSWER TO QUESTION II

G & E can object to Harry's work while in government, and the Justice Department can complain about Harry's firm's participation in the tax fraud case.

The problem here is that of representation contrary to the interest of a former client. The first such problem arose when Harry went to work for the government and was assigned a case prosecuting a firm he had formerly represented. This was potentially a serious conflict of interest, and G & E could have filed a motion to have Harry reassigned. However, the kind of information Harry received in his work on the securities cases was probably not the kind of information involved in this alleged tax fraud; indeed, what he learned in the securities work may have been made public in the prospectuses anyway, so that G & E's interest in confidentiality would probably not have been great enough to cause Harry to be ineligible to prosecute the later tax case. Even if Harry were ineligible, however, other U.S. Attorneys could prosecute the case, as a court would be reluctant to attribute the knowledge of one Assistant U.S. Attorney to the whole office.

After Harry left government, he clearly could not defend the case he formerly prosecuted. That would run directly afoul of Model Rule 1.11(a), which prohibits a former government lawyer from representing a private client in a matter in which the lawyer participated personally and substantially while in government. However, Harry's assignment by his new firm to work exclusively on other cases would make it possible to effectively screen him from any participation in the tax fraud case. Under Model Rule 1.11(a)(1) and case law, a former government lawyer's firm is not necessarily disqualified if the lawyer is screened and he shares no fees earned from the case. Thus, it is probable that the government could not have Harry's firm disqualified as defense counsel for G & E.

ANSWER TO QUESTION III

Mary's new venture has a series of problems, the most basic of which is that she is practicing law with nonlawyers and helping persons engage in the unauthorized practice of law.

No problem is presented by Mary's writing booklets explaining tax planning to clients. Some activities of lay firms (*e.g.*, divorce clinics) have been held to be unauthorized practice, but the writing of booklets has generally been held not to constitute unauthorized practice, even booklets on subjects traditionally practiced by lawyers.

Giving seminars for CPAs is likewise not a problem, but having the CPAs fill in blanks on preprinted wills may constitute the unauthorized practice of law. There are cases holding that allowing real estate agents to fill in blanks for routine items on certain standard contracts is not unauthorized practice, but wills are sufficiently individualized so that it is unlikely that a CPA would be permitted to supply missing terms. Mary's assisting in this process would cause her to be in violation of Model Rule 5.5(b), which forbids aiding others in the unauthorized practice of law.

Furthermore, Model Rule 5.4(a) prohibits a lawyer from forming a partnership with nonlawyers where any of the activities involve the practice of law. Mary's involvement in the Mister Tax partnership would violate these rules. The nature of the tax planning activities is such that Mary, if not the entire company, would be deemed to be engaging in the practice of law, and thus Mary's role as a partner would be improper. Many sensible persons believe that this is an uncalled-for ethical prohibition because the work of firms such as this may well be of value to the public, but the Model Rules and the ABA Code clearly prohibit this type of arrangement.

Finally, Mary's acting as counsel when her company is named executor of clients' estates might also involve Mary in assisting improper solicitation. When a lawyer seeks to encourage a client to name her executor or counsel to the executor, there is a potential problem of overreaching, and Mister Tax is arguably heavily involved in that here.

ANSWER TO QUESTION IV

Neglect by busy lawyers is an all too common situation, and Bob should indeed be worried. The inventor may file a complaint with the state's discipline commission and almost certainly has a viable malpractice claim against Bob.

Although Bob was not familiar with patent law, it was not improper for him to take the inventor's case. However, upon doing so, Bob had an obligation to promptly become familiar with that area of law and to proceed to prosecute the patent claim. Alternatively, Bob had an obligation to involve a more experienced lawyer in the process and require him to get the patent on file. The failure to do either of these things constituted a lack of competent representation on Bob's part, and the inventor could file a complaint with the state's discipline commission.

To succeed in a malpractice claim against Bob, the inventor would have to demonstrate that Bob breached a duty to him and that he was harmed by the breach. Bob clearly breached his duty of care. If the inventor could show that he would have received the patent if Bob had proceeded expeditiously, he can successfully sue Bob. The damages might be the royalties the inventor would have received from the patent.

ANSWER TO QUESTION V

1. Each client should be sent a letter explaining that the firm is breaking up and informing the client that his file may be sent to the lawyer or law firm of the client's choice. Clients are not the property of either lawyer, and there is no proper way for Jones or Yates to compel or even properly encourage a client to remain with one of them.

2. Each partner may keep a copy of whatever material is necessary to protect that partner's interest. As indicated above, the clients are free to go with either partner or with another law firm, and their files must be sent to the selected lawyer or firm. However, if a client has not

paid his fees, the partners may have a lien for those fees that will allow them to retain some of the files. Likewise, either or both partners may be liable for malpractice with respect to any of the cases that they have been working on, and thus it may be in each partner's interest to retain copies of some or all of the files.

ANSWER TO QUESTION VI

1. Although the ABA does not specifically prohibit a lawyer's taking this kind of case, some state statutes do, and most lawyers would not try to represent both sides in a case like this.

   A lawyer may take a case involving conflicting interests where both parties understand the potential conflict and consent to the dual representation *and* the lawyer believes that she can adequately represent the interests of each client. Moreover, the lawyer may counsel Mary and Bill in an uncontested, nonlitigation situation, and it would be proper to draw up an agreement concerning child custody and property settlement. However, the lawyer can act for both clients only after full disclosure of the conflicting interests of Mary and Bill and with the express consent of both of them, confirmed in writing.

   Here, even if a lawyer believed at the outset that adequate representation of both Mary and Bill was possible, it would be hard to maintain that belief after Mary's confidence. Once the lawyer knows that Mary's needs are not likely to continue to be as they appear, the lawyer is forced to take a position that will in some sense constitute taking advantage of Bill. As Mary's private counsel, the lawyer probably could seek to get Mary a large alimony payment as long as no affirmative misrepresentations were made. However, as Bill's lawyer, she would presumably also be trying to make those payments as low as possible and would be obliged to use Mary's information on Bill's behalf. Absent Mary's consent, the lawyer cannot disclose confidential information elicited from Mary in preliminary discussions. The lawyer owes a professional duty under the Model Rules to preserve all client confidences. This obligation is not limited to legal proceedings but applies to any client confidence gained in the course of the lawyer-client relationship. Thus, the lawyer could not make a full disclosure to Bill and so is prohibited from representing him.

   Furthermore, a clear conflict of interests is apparent after Mary's disclosure, and Mary will certainly not let the lawyer reveal her secret as would be necessary to get Bill's informed consent. When a conflict of interest becomes apparent after employment, the lawyer must withdraw from representing one or both of the clients pursuant to Model Rule 1.7. At a minimum, the lawyer should suggest that Bill get other counsel. It may be that Bill's interest will not be prejudiced if the lawyer continues to represent Mary.

2. A fee based on the amount of child support awarded would not be proper. Under the Model Rules, a fee contingent on obtaining a divorce or on the amount of alimony or support would be prohibited. Particularly in a case in which the lawyer is representing both sides, such a fee might even encourage the lawyer to try to increase the amount of child support (to the disadvantage of one party) so as to increase her own fee.

ANSWER TO QUESTION VII

1. Mark should probably continue to refuse to answer, at least until the court's order is tested on appeal.

   Mark is probably correct in citing the evidentiary attorney-client privilege as a reason not to disclose Pat's address. A communication made in confidence by a client to his lawyer in obtaining legal assistance is generally protected under the privilege. Here, Pat himself "communicated" the address to Mark, and disclosure of the address would clearly not be in Pat's interest. Pat has not waived the privilege. Thus, Mark should not disclose the information.

Also, the information certainly qualifies as protected by the professional obligation of confidentiality. Thus, it is information Mark should not reveal.

If Mark refuses to disclose the information when the court orders him to answer, Mark will probably be sentenced for contempt of court. Mark will then be in a position to appeal the court's order to disclose, which is about the only way that he can get a judicial test of the privilege question. If the appellate court sustains the trial court, then presumably Mark has an obligation to disclose and should do so.

It should be noted that the Model Rules would ***permit*** Mark to reveal the client's secret when ordered to do so by the trial court, but he is ***not required*** to do so, and most lawyers believe their duty to their client is somewhat higher than the Model Rules standard.

2. Mark should attempt to avoid being ordered to tell the court what he heard. The information about Pat's drug habit is not protected by the attorney-client privilege since the information was not communicated to Mark by the client, but the information was something Mark heard in the course of representation that could be embarrassing or harmful to Pat. That puts the information again into the category of "confidential." A lawyer must reveal such information when ordered by the court to do so, but Mark should assert his professional obligation as a basis for trying to get the court not to issue such an order.

ANSWER TO QUESTION VIII

Doris should look into this situation more fully to assure herself that she is not perpetrating a fraud.

A lawyer is the client's representative, not her judge. However, the lawyer is neither required nor permitted to assist a client in perpetrating a fraud on someone else. In this situation, Doris has become aware of the possibility that her client may be making a false claim. Doris would not be required to go to the prosecutor and accuse her client of fraud or perjury, but she is under an obligation to try to prevent more damage from being done. Doris should not conduct a further search of Mavis's files; she is not permitted to use her role as a trusted advisor to become a self-appointed investigator. However, she should confront Mavis directly about the issue and try to get satisfactory answers. If she is not satisfied that Mavis's claim is legitimate, she should advise Mavis to drop the claim. If Mavis refuses, Doris must withdraw from the representation to avoid assisting in a crime or fraud.

ANSWER TO QUESTION IX

Claudia is likely to be denied admission to the bar.

Conviction of a crime such as arson is often sufficient to deny an applicant admission to the bar. The bar admissions committee is not limited by the label of an offense but may investigate all of the surrounding facts. A finding that Claudia consciously engaged in setting fires so as to do damage might be considered to make her a sufficiently "bad person" that admission would be denied, even if she were engaged in a form of political protest at the time.

The charge of perjury would be even more serious. Offenses involving deceit are thought to be particularly serious for potential lawyers. Although the charges were dropped, the bar admissions committee would again be entitled to look into the evidence that the prosecutor had and would not be bound by the fact that the charges were never brought to trial.

Finally, the refusal to fill out the required character and fitness form would probably itself cause denial of admission to the bar. The burden of supplying relevant information is on the applicant for admission. The Supreme Court has held that failure to supply information can be the basis for denial of admission. There may be substantive limits on the criteria that the bar admissions committee can consider in actually ruling on the applicant's case, but there is no excuse for not supplying relevant information.

Since all of Claudia's criminal behavior took place many years ago, it is possible that Claudia has been rehabilitated. However, since Claudia did not bother to fill out the form, she did not raise the rehabilitation argument, so it would probably not be considered by the committee.

ANSWER TO QUESTION X

Runner might be subject to discipline for improper pretrial publicity.

Lawsuits are to be tried in the courts and not in the media. The Model Rules and ABA Code allow a lawyer to reveal certain basic information about a case that has been filed, but they do not permit the lawyer to argue that case in the media. This problem presents a somewhat closer case because Don is obviously mixing politics with litigation. Some of his remarks are presumably partisan and possibly designed to aid a political comeback. The Model Rules and ABA Code do not prohibit political activity, but they may be read to require Don to do his politicking in some way other than by publicizing a litigated case.

Calling for citizens to join a class action and send in cash also might be prohibited. Soliciting clients for fee-generating work by an announcement on television could be considered improper solicitation, although Runner should be able to get court approval for his broadcasting notice to get more clients into his class action once the case is actually filed.

Advertising on television no longer necessarily violates professional standards and it is acceptable under Model Rules 7.1 and 7.2, but posing under a large sign extolling one's own talents might violate even the fairly narrow prohibition of false or misleading advertising.

Table of Cases

Citations to ABA Model Rules of Professional Conduct

Index